The Hidden Places of World War II

The Extraordinary Sites Where History Was
Made During the War That Saved Civilization

Jerome M. O'Connor

LYONS
PRESS

Guilford, Connecticut

An imprint of Globe Pequot, the trade division of
The Rowman & Littlefield Publishing Group, Inc.
4501 Forbes Blvd., Ste. 200
Lanham, MD 20706
www.rowman.com

Distributed by NATIONAL BOOK NETWORK

British Library Cataloguing in Publication Information available

Library of Congress Cataloging-in-Publication Data available

ISBN 978-1-4930-3038-5 (hardcover) | ISBN 978-1-4930-6548-6 (paperback) |
ISBN 978-1-4930-3039-2 (ebook)

♾™ The paper used in this publication meets the minimum requirements of American
National Standard for Information Sciences—Permanence of Paper for Printed Library
Materials, ANSI/NISO Z39.48-1992.

"More than anything, what would you like to do with the rest of your life?" she asked one fine day.

"I would like to return to journalism," said I.

With decades of experience writing features for print publications, it would be an easy return, so we left it there, but later she had a grander suggestion: "Why not expand your previous features about World War II into a book?"

The excuses were abundant, but the reasons were few. The seventy-fifth anniversary of the end of history's greatest war approached. If ever a time existed to further explore and discover even more of those history-making places—some of which I had a hand in revealing—the time was now. In writing a book I could tell new stories of heroism and sacrifice, enlarge the descriptions of failed plots and enormous misdeeds, and situate them in the actual places where they happened and which I would visit. Best of all, with the world preparing to observe the seventy-fifth anniversary of the end of the war that forever altered history, I could honor those still among us who saved civilization when it was most threatened. That became the principal motivation. So, Nancy with the smiling eyes, wife and partner, this is for you.

Contents

Preface

I have been writing this book since I was five years old, although it didn't seem so at the time. I still remember how empty it was in the neighborhood when the young men went to war. In our immigrant block in Chicago's South Side Englewood neighborhood and throughout Chicago, at least seven boys from every block also went to war. On our block and everywhere in America, there were banners in windows with blue stars or gold stars. The blue represented the sons, brothers, or fathers who had gone to war. The gold were for those who would never return. Blue flags were in many windows in my Paulina Street neighborhood, but there was also one gold star. I had so much sorrow, or perhaps it was fear, for what lay behind the lace curtain of the window with the gold star, that on the way to the corner candy store I crossed the street to avoid disturbing the grieving family inside. The other kids who played sewer-cover stickball or jumped rope were also silent near that bungalow. The thought of it never left me. Maybe the desire to someday tell the stories started then.

As a child I knew that something very big was happening, and, yes, it was a war, but I couldn't understand it for the history-changing epic it became. That took years more. But the need to learn about the war, and later to find and enter the same places where history was made, began on the streets of my multiethnic Chicago block.

What you will read is real, and, as with most true events, some of those who brought them about had feet of clay, while others rose to the challenge that would make them great or infamous. Every chapter describes a person or a place or actions that changed the history of our time. As one who has long sought out the places where epochal events happened, I have had a need if not a compulsion to give life to history by connecting from then to now the same places where the decisions were made. That helps otherwise dry history come alive.

Enter Churchill's Cabinet War Rooms as I saw them years before they were made known to the public. See where the Ultra secret—the breaking of the Enigma cipher—brought Nazi Germany to its knees and meet a "secret lady" who kept the secret of the century. Survey the same London mansion where fifty-nine Nazi generals were confined in surprisingly generous conditions, but with a reason. Experience the greatest collective ruins of the European war—the U-boat bases in France—and learn why relentless Allied attacks failed to destroy them. No need to imagine what it was like then as you walk with me now to view six square miles of monolithic Nazi structures and parade grounds in Nuremberg. Enter the mansion in Portsmouth, England, where General Eisenhower made the war's greatest decision—when to invade Europe—and made it under great stress. Every chapter has such discoveries.

It must be said that the war could not have been won without American participation, which includes millions on the home front who made the war goods that brought about the victory. Their story will also be told.

I especially enjoyed exploring the remains of some of the scores of former US Army Air Force bases in England and walking the same runways to view remains of control towers, barracks, and buildings. The Eighth Air Force had ten times the losses of US ground forces, as will be described in chapters that will take you on perilous missions that began from the same bases that time and tourism forgot. Over the years I interviewed participants in various battles, with their stories incorporated in the retelling.

I have attempted to dig deeply into the history of our time by connecting the past with the present from inside and near the same places where history happened. I hope I have succeeded.

—Jerome M. O'Connor, Elmhurst, IL

Introduction: The Last Days of Peace

Wir Werden weiter marschieren
Wenn alles in scherben falt
Denn heute gehort uns Deutschland
Und morgen die ganze welt.
We will march on
Even if everything breaks into pieces
Because today Germany belongs to us
And tomorrow the whole world.
—Hitler Youth marching song

Germany—Once Again Ready for War

Anticipating the beginning of the war in its immediacy if not on the actual day, at dawn on August 19, 1939, fourteen U-boats slipped their lines in Kiel and Wilhelmshaven for preassigned patrol sectors in the North Atlantic. The next day, U-30 and U-27 also left Wilhelmshaven for the soon-to-be-target-rich waters of the North Atlantic. The orders from Grand Admiral Erich Raeder, commander-in-chief of German naval forces, were to wait for his command to launch what Churchill called the Battle of the Atlantic.

Almost twenty-five years earlier on July 29, 1914, from the new Telefunken-operated 823-foot-high transmitter at Nauen, Germany, the Admiralty sent the same message to all German-flagged ships. "Come immediately to home or friendly ports." Intercepted by "Room 40" British intelligence wireless operators in London's Old Admiralty Building, and by Marconi Company operators on scores of ships at sea, the message received no immediate action. Three days later, on August 1, 1914, France ordered a general mobilization as the first German units crossed into Luxembourg and then neutral Belgium. On August 4, Great Britain declared war on Germany. That same day the United States promptly declared itself as neutral. A quarter-century later, history, as often happens, was about to repeat itself.

On the evening of August 21, 1939, the fifteen-thousand-ton "pocket battleship" *Admiral Graf Spee* sailed from Wilhelmshaven, where she was built, for the South Atlantic, followed by her sister, the heavy cruiser *Deutschland*, to lurk south of Greenland. The twenty-thousand-ton German fleet tanker, *Altmark*, had already departed Port Arthur, Texas, laden with diesel oil from neutral America to refuel the *Graf Spee*'s eight mammoth nine-cylinder MAN-built diesel engines. On August 27, five days before Germany invaded Poland to start the war, a signal sent to all German merchant ships worldwide ordered them home "within the next four days," or make for friendly or neutral ports. Germany had well prepared her naval *Kriegsmarine* for history's deadliest war that impended on the horizon. As would soon become unmistakable, her army had been equally well prepared.

GREAT BRITAIN—UNWILLING AND UNABLE

In London on August 30, at 11:30 a.m. at 10 Downing Street, eleven days after Germany's partial sea mobilization and two days before the start of World War II, Prime Minister Neville Chamberlain chaired a meeting of the twenty-one-member Cabinet. What the agenda called the "International Situation" in general and telegram #499 in particular were to be discussed first. The telegram had been sent on August 28 by Adolf Hitler through German foreign secretary Joachim von Ribbentrop to British foreign secretary Lord Halifax. Also up for discussion, "if time permitted," were the more sanguine matters of army recruiting practices and worker's unemployment insurance.

The foreign secretary informed the Cabinet of Hitler's requirement that "a Polish emissary with full power" be sent to Berlin on August 30, the same day as the now underway Cabinet meeting. Halifax earlier had replied by telegram that "we could give (it) careful consideration," but that not enough time remained to confirm arrangements with Warsaw's foreign ministry, and the meeting must be delayed. Halifax, an early and ardent advocate of the government's official appeasement policy, told the Cabinet that a Foreign Office telegram marked #330 had been sent to Warsaw stating that while the British government could not take responsibility for advising the Polish government to begin full mobilization, if they did it on their own, "we hoped their measures would receive as little publicity as possible." The British government desired that if Poland went to war it should do so decorously and without calling undue attention.

Interpreting conclusions from Hitler's telegram that events would soon disprove, Lord Halifax notified

Appointed chancellor in 1933, Hitler moved quickly to consolidate power.
LIBRARY OF CONGRESS

the Cabinet that "the terms of Herr Hitler's (August 28) reply were somewhat bombastic, but . . . when stripped of its verbiage, it revealed a man who was trying to extricate himself from a difficult position." Halifax proposed that Chamberlain send Hitler a personal telegram, confident in intelligence reports that gave Britain a negotiating advantage because of "anti-government demonstrations up and down Germany." Although the reports were untrue—the German people were firm if not devotional in their support of Hitler—Halifax suggested that the reply should be "at once firm yet unprovocative." (Another meeting unknown—Hitler already had postponed the invasion from August 25 to September 1.)

As described in the conference summary, Chamberlain then entered the conversation to grasp at Hitler's demand for an immediate meeting with a Polish emissary in Berlin as bargaining leverage, instead of understanding the telegram as an ultimatum. "This definitely represented part of the old technique . . . we were not going to yield on this point," Chamberlain said. At the eleventh hour for Great Britain, the prime minister concluded that Hitler was up to his old tricks and that stalling could buy more time.

Extensive discussion among the ministers then formed a decision to telegraph both the Polish prime minister and president to assert that while Britain had guaranteed Poland's independence, its policy "was to pin the Germans down to the good points . . . and to work for improvements on the points which were less satisfactory." The Cabinet agreed that their message to Warsaw should emphasize the conclusion "that the German government were prepared to negotiate." And wasn't Hitler at his core open to reason?

Chamberlain then proposed and the Cabinet agreed, that evacuating children from London should not be considered because of its harmful effects on the public morale, and that the "risks of air bombardment were not perhaps quite so imminent as . . . thought." He ended the "International Situation" part of the meeting with an illusory assessment: "There was reason to think that Herr Hitler would not start operations against us but would wait for us to attack him." With Hitler likely on the leash and with time remaining for discussion of other topics, the ministers agreed to Chamberlain's recommendation that "there would be no need for large numbers of recruits at the outbreak of war except for certain tradesmen." With the Cabinet concluding that war was not imminent, the meeting ended with the ministers returning to their offices and the normal business of state.

On August 29, the day before the Cabinet meeting, the *Telegraph* of London headlined an article by cub reporter Clare Hollingsworth, the newspaper's Warsaw correspondent: "1,000 Tanks Massed on Polish Frontiers." She had borrowed a car, crossed the Polish/German border, and saw large numbers of German troops, tanks, and military equipment gathered on roads adjacent to the border. If Chamberlain or his ministers read the article appearing in one of the country's most respected newspapers, no note was taken of its historic disclosure, the first report of the beginning of World War II.

While England slept in the fatal confidence that the Nazis would negotiate, that they were rational and reasonable, and that Germany would not be the first to attack, Hitler continued moving 250,000 troops in sixty divisions, nine of them armored, and sixteen hundred aircraft to bivouacs near the Polish frontier. An August 23 nonaggression pact and a secret protocol signed with the USSR would link the two dictatorships, at least temporarily, but after the war would enslave for decades Poland and other Eastern European countries.

At 4:45 a.m. on September 1, two days after the British Cabinet meeting, Germany formally began the Second World War by easily overcoming Polish forces, many equipped with more lancers on horses than modern arms. Of the more than 450,000 prisoners, many would never return to their homeland. (In the Katyn Forest and Smolensk the following spring, the Soviet NKVD, as ordered by Stalin, executed over forty-five hundred Polish officers and intellectuals, blamed it on the Nazis, and then concealed the crime for decades.) The war to decide the fate of western civilization was on.

THE PRICE OF APPEASEMENT

When Great Britain declared war on Germany on September 3, 1939, the roar of the once feared and respected British lion had been reduced to a whisper by government appeasement to an unopposed Hitler. Not benefiting citizen awareness of the imminent peril were the highly favorable editorial opinions of Hitler, regularly voiced by Britain's leading newspaper, the *Times* of London.

On the eve of war, the entire British army had only 487 light tanks and 167 vintage antitank guns. The one million members of the Home Guard trained with twenty thousand sporting guns, most without ammunition, many officers drilling without sidearms. With the Royal Navy lacking destroyers to escort shipping across the full breadth of the Atlantic, every month U-boats would sink 280,000 tons of Allied shipping. The Britannia that ruled the waves sailed a fleet of mostly ancient dreadnoughts, many soon to be on the ocean floor. Although rapidly expanding, the Royal Air Force (RAF) had fewer than one thousand trained pilots on September 1, 1939, while a depleted Bomber Command supplemented its ranks with thirty squadrons from the Royal Canadian Air Force.

Resulting from years of appeasing Nazi Germany, on the eve of war the army on the British homeland had only two divisions at full strength

By 1938 Germany had nearly fifty divisions under arms. NATIONAL ARCHIVES

and one at half strength. Their equipment, tactics, and most of the equally vintage military leadership dated from World War I.

Defeat then followed defeat. Beginning May 26, 1940, at Dunkirk, the entire 338,000 troops in the British Expeditionary Force evacuated the European continent. Poland surrendered in twenty-six days, Holland in twenty-four hours, then Norway, Belgium, Luxembourg, Denmark, and, shockingly, even mighty France, easily fell to the enemy. They surrendered to what Churchill called the "dulled, drilled, docile, brutish masses of Hun soldiery." Across the English Channel forty German divisions prepared for what all believed would be invasion and enslavement of the storied British race and its "sceptered isles."

THE UNITED STATES—AN UNCERTAIN ALLY

America, seemingly secure astride vast oceans but divided by rapidly increasing isolationism, had wide divisions in citizen support for the spreading European war. The United States fielded at best an underequipped territorial army and sailed an obsolete navy. As a further hindrance to rearmament, isolationists would soon form the America First Committee, quickly growing to eight hundred thousand dues-paying members in 450 chapters. Enlisting as their principal spokesperson an intolerant Charles Lindbergh, America's greatest hero of the era, and supported by powerful voices in Congress, America First demanded that the United States disengage from the world's challenges. They persuaded cheering throngs at massive rallies that the United States had no right to interfere in the affairs of other countries, no matter their peril. The new medium of radio became the platform for weekly anti-Semitic, pro-German commentaries by the Reverend Charles Coughlin, a Catholic priest with millions of devout listeners. Within the US government, faithless defeatism from Joseph P. Kennedy, ambassador to Britain, occupied newspaper front pages. And wasn't America safe behind its protecting seas?

Twenty million Americans each day read the twenty-eight Roosevelt-hating Hearst newspapers, while isolationist publishing czar Robert R. McCormick, a convinced America First member, crusaded against President Roosevelt from the pages of the *Chicago Tribune*. The president needed another way to lead his people and help Britain in its darkest hour. It had to be in secret.

FDR's SECRET INTELLIGENCE HELP

Knowing that an undefeated Great Britain would be America's first line of defense against German aggression, in June 1940 FDR approved an expanding intelligence-sharing network between the two countries, coordinated through a covert British facility in New York's Rockefeller Center. Publicly known as the British Passport Control Office, but operating as British Security Coordination (BSC), its director, Canadian-born William Stephenson, code-named "Intrepid," had a close friendship with Winston Churchill. The man called Intrepid asked Churchill to recommend to FDR the appointment of William J. "Wild Bill" Donovan to control intelligence activities between the two countries. This began America's prewar covert operations through the new Office of Strategic Services (OSS), the direct forerunner of the Central Intelligence Agency. On an ocean speck far from Manhattan, eleven hundred censors in Bermuda's Princess and Bermudiana Hotels became the conduit for a clandestine examination of all mail and telegraph activity between the United States and Britain.

Intelligence secrets now flowed in each direction. The United States gave Britain details of "Magic," the cryptanalysis project that broke the Japanese "purple" diplomatic cipher. "Purple" had been modified by the Japanese from Enigma machines that Germany sent to Japan. American technical experts led by William Friedman and Frank Rowlett reverse-engineered the Japanese Enigma devices to learn the "purple" key settings.

The celebrated fourteenth part of the Japanese diplomatic message decrypted at 1:00 p.m. Washington time on December 7, 1941, had been intercepted along with the other thirteen parts by the US Navy's OP-20-G intelligence unit at Fort Ward on Bainbridge Island, Washington. Although the message ended negotiations between the United States and Japan, its contents neither declared war nor announced the imminence of the war that had already started with the Pearl Harbor attack. Decades later, no credible evidence exists that President Roosevelt had advance knowledge of the surprise attack on Hawaii. Roosevelt preferred that Japan initiate the war he knew loitered somewhere in the vast Pacific.

Prologue: Nine Months Later—
The Hour of Destiny

This earth of majesty, this seat of Mars
This other Eden, demi-paradise
This fortress built by Nature for herself
This blessed plot, this earth, this realm, this England.
—*Richard II*, Act 2, Scene 1, *William Shakespeare*

The summons to Winston Churchill in the Admiralty came in the early evening on a dry and warm Friday, May 10, 1940. Come to the palace immediately. Only two days before, the House of Commons had returned a wavering vote of only faint confidence in Conservative prime minister Neville Chamberlain's conduct of the war. His eight months as premier following repeated attempts to appease Hitler had failed dramatically, ending with resignation in the presence of King George VI earlier that evening. In the early hours of that same despairing May 10, Germany massively invaded the Low Countries and France. An initial 75 divisions, growing to 141 divisions, supported by twenty-five hundred aircraft and sixteen thousand troops in gliders, were bombing airfields, seizing bridges and forts, and had invested the Dutch cities of Rotterdam, Leiden, and The Hague. A new type of warfare called *Blitzkrieg*, "lightning war," would soon cost retreating British forces dearly. The "phony war"—eight months of relative calm—exploded into all-out combat.

On September 1, 1939, as First Lord of the Admiralty, a post he held not altogether successfully during part of the Great War, Churchill had been Chamberlain's regular tormentor in opposing Britain's lack of fortitude in challenging Nazi Germany's belligerence. In criticizing the government's appeasement policy he wrote, "in having a choice between war and shame they chose shame and would later get war on less favorable terms."

Weighted with the solemnity of the occasion, Churchill exchanged no words with the driver or his bodyguard, Detective Inspector Walter H. Thompson, during the short drive from Admiralty House to Buckingham Palace. The king set him at ease: "I suppose you don't know why I have sent for you." Replying in kind Churchill said, "sir, I can't imagine why." Pointedly, the king said, "I want you to form a government." The hour was late for Britain and for democracy, and there was no time for an acceptance speech, cheering throngs, or an embracing benediction from the clergy. On the drive back, Churchill let slip to Thompson his deepest fear: "I hope that we're not too late."

At his quarters in Admiralty House Churchill delegated his aide Capt. Richard Pim and parliamentary private secretary and confidant Brenden Bracken to sort out the War Cabinet candidates into different parts in his private flat. Anthony Eden went to the drawing room; Lord Beaverbrook found himself in the dining room, with Archibald Sinclair, to be named Churchill's secretary of state for air, going to Churchill's bedroom. A. V. Alexander, soon to be Churchill's successor as First Lord, occupied the cloakroom.

The task ahead was formidable, maybe impossible. Since the Great War, the military had been bled white by successive budget cuts, leaving the RAF with fewer than seven hundred Spitfires and Hurricanes and even fewer fully trained pilots to fly them. He had until midnight to form a coalition government, knowing that many in Parliament preferred a negotiated peace with Hitler, never mind the consequences.

A final task awaited on that day of days, the inspection of an extensive but cheerless cellar in the sooty Office of Works building in Whitehall, across from St. James Park, and almost within view of his future Downing Street home. After settling the 1938 Munich crisis by allowing Hitler to keep already annexed parts of Czechoslovakia, as a temporary measure Whitehall approved development in London of a combined military and government headquarters, until a permanent central facility could be built underground outside London.

Churchill's darkest hours were lightened by secret aid from FDR. LIBRARY OF CONGRESS

In the expectation that Prime Minister Chamberlain's exultant promise after meeting with Hitler in Munich that "peace in our time" would endure, British officials nonetheless began planning for war. Needing immediate accessibility and communication, the central core of the British government's entire war effort became situated in one location in the heart of London. Ready only a week before the September 3, 1939 British and French declaration of war against Germany, it would expand into thirty thousand square feet to occupy the entire building.

Hastily converted from basement storage space, the four-story turn-of-the-century government building hulked in plain view at Clive Steps, directly across from St. James Park. As Britain prepared for assault by air and land, the central command and control nucleus for the entire war resided precariously a mere ten feet below the pavement, seconds from envelopment by German paratroopers dropping into the park.

Awaiting Churchill at the top of the steps were Gen. Hastings "Pug" Ismay, his chief of staff, and Maj. Leslie Hollis, assistant secretary to the new coalition War Cabinet. They descended a narrow staircase to view a dimly lit, concrete-floored corridor leading to a jumble of hastily built enclosures clawed from any available space, typists clattering at temporary desks in corridors, a weave of blue cigar and cigarette smoke above, everything pulsing with activity. Rows of flat multi-drawer cabinets held maps for every part of the world. Portions of the ceiling were crudely braced with thick diagonal wooden beams or red-painted horizontal steel girders, all imparting a sense of urgency rather than order.

The new prime minister entered a room with a green steel door marked "Cabinet." The largest in the enclave, it had unobstructed space for a hollow square of tables covered with the same cloth used for policeman's uniforms. Metal chairs with armrests were set for eighteen ministers and military aides. Another table inside the enclosure had three chairs for the chiefs of staff who directly faced Churchill from mere feet away. A battered red wooden dispatch case contained messages for delivery to the king. Occupied only by Churchill, a curved wood chair with spindles and upholstered leather seat occupied the top of the square in front of an eight-foot-high, wall-mounted Rand McNally world map. Both arms of the Windsor chair would become pitted with dents from his signet ring and grooved with finger-nail scratches. He approvingly took in the room arrangement, turned to Ismay, and said, "this is the room from where I will direct the war." Although the first Churchill-chaired War Cabinet meeting in the bunker basement was two months distant, it would be the location for 115 wartime meetings.

Returning to the Admiralty in the big Humber Pullman for a sleep that wouldn't come until 3:00 a.m., he had time to reflect on the ordeal ahead and the potential it held to complete the purpose for which he had prepared all

King George VI. WIKIMEDIA COMMONS

his sixty-five years. He later wrote: "I felt as if I were walking with destiny, and that all my past life had been but a preparation for this hour and for this trial . . . I was sure that I should not fail."

As Churchill assumed office on that bleak May day, an American journalist summarized its importance for the ages. CBS correspondent Edward R. Murrow would soon broadcast live descriptions of the Battle of Britain as it reached its full fury with nightly attacks on London. About Churchill he said: "Now the hour had come for him to mobilize the English language and send it into battle, a spearhead of hope for Britain and the world."

CHAPTER ONE

The Fall of France: "Blood, Toil, Tears, And Sweat"

Once more unto the breach, dear friends, once more;
Or close the wall up with our English dead.
In peace there's nothing so becomes a man
as modest stillness and humility.
But when the blast of war blows in our ears,
Then imitate the action of the tiger;
Stiffen the sinews, summon up the blood . . .
  —*HENRY V*, ACT 3, SCENE 1, WILLIAM SHAKESPEARE

IN HIS FIRST ADDRESS TO A SOMBER HOUSE OF COMMONS ON MAY 13, Churchill began the language's mobilization with a five-minute speech of poignant eloquence and immediate peril. The country faced "an ordeal of the most grievous kind." The British people and the commonwealth must now prepare "to wage war against a monstrous tyranny, never surpassed in the dark, lamentable catalogue of human crime." His three-day old government had an undeviating policy: "victory, victory at all costs, victory despite all terror . . . for without victory there is no survival. Let that be realized, no survival . . . for the urge and impulse of the ages, that mankind will move forward toward its goal." For the British people listening over the BBC and for all mankind including the United States twenty-seven months before its own date with destiny, Churchill had a

solemn promise: "I have nothing to offer but blood, toil, tears, and sweat."
All would be needed soon enough.

A Cascade of Defeats

On May 15, only forty-eight hours after addressing the House of Commons, Churchill awakened at 7:30 a.m. in his Admiralty flat. Paul Reynaud, appointed only two months before as the French prime minister, waited on the telephone. Speaking in English, his voice under strain, he said "we have been defeated." Still not fully awake, Churchill said nothing. The premier repeated: "We are beaten; we have lost the battle." The German invasion had begun only five days before and already the French were finished? He thought in astonishment.

Dumbfounded, Churchill said, "surely it can't have happened so soon." Referring to the French Second Army in headlong retreat, Reynaud said, "the front is broken near Sedan." As he spoke, the lead elements of Gen. Gerd von Rundstedt's Army Group A with forty-six *Wehrmacht* divisions, seven Panzer divisions, hundreds of motorized infantry regiments, thousands of trucks, motorcycles, communications vehicles, and half-tracks, were rapidly exploiting a fifty-mile bulge past the remnants of two French armies.

Now fully alert and out of bed, Churchill asked Reynaud to repeat the apocalyptic statement. With knowledge that Churchill didn't have, Reynaud knew that three other French armies were soon to follow the Second Army in retreat. Again he said, "we are beaten . . . the front is broken near Sedan."

A keen observer of French history, Churchill knew that in 1870 Sedan surrendered to Prussian troops resulting in the abdication of Napoleon III, the collapse of the Second Empire, and the 1871 Paris Commune. In World War I, Sedan had again been invaded and occupied by Germany for four years. Three times in seventy years Sedan has been easily overwhelmed by Germany, he thought; have they learned nothing from their history?

Unwilling to accept the catastrophic news and seeking even a flicker of hope, Churchill said that one of the lessons from the Great War was that an offensive must stop after five or six days, otherwise it would out-

September 1, 1939. Appeasement fails. AUTHOR

run its train of supplies. That would be the time for a counteroffensive. "I learned this from the lips of Marshal Foch himself," Churchill said to Reynaud in near anguish.

As if bewitched, Reynaud again returned to the same dazed statement that began the call to say with finality: "We are defeated, we have lost the battle." In addition to his Second Army at Sedan, the lines of his Ninth, First, and Seventh Armies would also be deeply pierced, and soon. No one, and Churchill suddenly knew it, no one had any preparation for this new type of lightning war. To find a stop-gap, anything to slow the German advance, he must meet urgently and immediately with the French premier and his general staff.

At 3:00 p.m. the same day, along with Gen. Sir John Dill, chief of the Imperial General Staff (CIGS), Air Marshal Joubert de la Ferte, and Col. Hastings Ismay, his chief military assistant, the delegation flew from Hendon Aerodrome in North London for the one-hour flight to Le Bourget Field in Paris in a new De Haviland DH95 fourteen-passenger military transport escorted by twelve Hurricane fighters. It would be the ninth conference of the Anglo-French Supreme War Council. Hopes were low; none of the previous meetings had achieved an agreeable plan to thwart Nazi intentions. The entourage first went to the British Embassy on the Rue Faubourg St. Honore, for a desultory briefing by the British ambassador Sir Ronald Hugh Campbell. Through empty Parisian streets they arrived at the Quai d'Orsay, the Ministry of Foreign Affairs on the banks of the Seine overlooking the Alexander III bridge. The 5:30 p.m. meeting would decide the fate and future of France and the entire British Expeditionary Force, if not all of Western Europe.

The British delegation entered a gilded receiving room in the 1855 Second Empire mansion to face a haggard Prime Minister Paul Reynaud. Also at the meeting were Edouard Daladier and Gen. Maurice Gamelin, in command of the French army. He didn't know it, but his command would end in three days. As the previous French prime minister, Daladier, along with Neville Chamberlain, had signed the fatal 1938 Munich accord with Adolf Hitler, both expecting "peace in our time."

Churchill noticed that no one had taken a seat or would sit for the entire meeting. An anxiety of desolation pervaded the proceedings, to include his view of smoke rising like a pall from the garden below, where black-suited ministry staff were pushing rows of wheelbarrows heaped with government records into bonfires. He thought in astonishment: "the fight is being gallantly waged, and Paris is already becoming abandoned." The War Council gathered around a small map on an easel with dotted lines showing the rapidly changing front, an ominous bulge like a boil showing at the breakthrough near Sedan. The surging panzer divisions had wheeled toward the coast heading to Abbeville, Dunkirk, and the Channel, and for the moment were avoiding Paris.

General Gamelin then spoke without pause for five minutes. Every word describing the unfolding calamity appalled and stunned the British delegation. When Gamelin finished, the room again fell into a despair of silence. Churchill later said that never in his life had he been so shocked. He then pointedly addressed General Gamelin in English: "Where is the strategic reserve?" He said it again more vigorously in French: *Ou est la masse de manoeuvre?* Gamelin replied in French, the answer barely perceptible: "*Aucun.*" None. There were no reserves. With 117 divisions, Europe's largest army already neared defeat and they had no reserves. Didn't the General Staff know that this new modern war would be one of maneuver and would outflank the fixed defenses of the Maginot Line? The French had prepared for the wrong war!

With the Allied armies in hurried retreat, Holland surrendered on May 15, followed by Belgium on May 28, then Norway on June 10, the same day that Mussolini's Italy, looking for plunder, declared war on Britain and France. When told about Italy's deceit, President Roosevelt was preparing to deliver a commencement address at the University of Virginia at Charlottesville. He famously penciled in a statement to label Mussolini's treachery. "The hand that held the dagger plunged it into the back of its neighbor."

EVACUATION AND DESPAIR

On May 26, the quiet French port of Dunkirk became the scene of frantic activity as nearly one thousand vessels from small sailboats to destroyers raced from British ports to rescue 338,000 men of the British Expeditionary Force (BEF). Comprising elements from Britain, Canada, France, Belgium, the Netherlands, and Poland, most would fight another day, but one in seven were left behind as prisoners or casualties. Most of the forty thousand French and another forty thousand British troops who surrendered were mistreated and abused, with many summarily executed by the SS Totenkopf Division on the same day they surrendered. The others, with only the clothes on their backs, abandoned 880 field guns, seven hundred tanks, and forty thousand vehicles, to wade out neck-high to rescuing vessels and flight. Nine of forty-one assisting destroyers—six British and three French—were sunk, with another nineteen damaged.

London's June 5, 1940 *Daily Mirror* headline called it "Bloody Marvelous," and Churchill gamely called it a "miracle of deliverance." He also told the House of Commons that "wars are not won by evacuation," and there would be more defeats before deliverance. Two days later in the North Sea, the German battlecruisers *Gneiseneau* and *Scharnhorst* sank the twenty-five-thousand-ton aircraft carrier, *HMS Glorious*, and her two escorting Royal Navy destroyers, a combined loss of over fifteen hundred sailors with only forty survivors.

On June 1, 1940, near the beginning of a stream of 950 prewar and wartime cables to President Franklin D. Roosevelt, Churchill asked FDR to replenish the armaments lost in the Dunkirk debacle. The cables, all marked "top-secret," with many stamped "Triple Priority," were channeled through the coding facilities of the US Embassy in Grosvenor Square. Joseph P. Kennedy, America's ambassador to the Court of St. James and no friend to Great Britain, had little faith that England could survive the Nazi juggernaut. In a telegram to the president he scorned Britain's war preparations as "pitiful." In June 1940, Kennedy cabled Secretary of State Cordell Hull, stridently objecting to American arms shipments to Britain, leaving no doubt that he expected a British defeat and soon. "I am of the opinion that outside of some air defense the real defense of England will be with courage and not with arms."

Ambassador Joseph Kennedy, no friend of Britain. LIBRARY OF CONGRESS

Knowing the inevitability of the rescue of the old world by the new, FDR believed otherwise; keeping England afloat until his countrymen could be rallied to the cause of freedom dominated his European foreign policy initiatives and decisions. He could only hope that Europe's liberation wouldn't begin from ports on the East Coast of the United States, and that the first invasion wouldn't be to tear away what remained of England from Hitler's grip. With Congress and the American people almost evenly divided in supporting the war, FDR's secret support had to avoid discovery by Congress, with Churchill's urgent appeals fulfilled in secret. It wouldn't be the first time that FDR evaded Congress or turned away from popular opinion.

Gen. George C. Marshall—Chief of Staff 1939–1945. NATIONAL ARCHIVES

In a sequence of moves to be envied in the next century for their alacrity in fulfillment, on the same day that he received Churchill's plea, FDR ordered US Army chief of staff Gen. George Marshall to urgently inventory all US Army depots for arms being stored as surplus from America's eighteen-month involvement in the first great war. Within forty-eight hours, a growing list already had a half million .30-caliber rifles, each with 250 cartridges, all packed in grease and ready for shipment. Also catalogued were nine hundred field guns with a million rounds of ammunition. Eighty thousand never-used machine guns were found in their original packing, along with other arms and munitions, all quickly made ready for transport. Railroad companies were asked for an immediate release of six hundred rail cars for routing to the Army depots. Before the end of the week and to avoid congressional consequences from the isolationist neutrality acts, the entire inventory had been sold to the British government through a third party for $37 million. The subterfuge prevented tracing the arms transfer to Washington or FDR. From the depots, the munitions were dispatched to US Army docks at Gravesend, New Jersey. By June 11, only ten days after Churchill's appeal to FDR, twelve British merchant ships were dockside, loading the arms for transit across the Atlantic to beleaguered Britain.

After the war, Churchill wrote a testimony of thanks to the country that would eventually awaken and lead the world to salvation: "a supreme act of faith and leadership for the United States to deprive itself of this very considerable mass of arms for the sale to a country which many deemed already beaten. They never had need to repent of it." The arms and FDR's secret support, an impeachable offense if discovered, arrived, as did much of British fortunes early in the war, just in time.

After Dunkirk, the Nazi noose drawing tighter, and an onslaught soon to descend from the skies, the entire army in England maneuvered with a mere 487 light tanks, of which only fifty were ready for immediate service to repel the invasion all thought to be imminent. Even worse, in the entire country there were only five hundred howitzer artillery pieces. Churchill later wrote: "Never had a great nation been so naked before her foes." The fortunes of war then turned even more decisively against Great Britain and her beleaguered allies.

On June 5, the Nazi hordes turned south, easily breaching the new French line on the Somme and Aisne, to aim directly for the Seine. On June 14, with Paris declared an "open city," legions of German troops entered Paris, to march around the Arc de Triomphe and down the wide Champs d'Élysées to the Place de la Concorde. The humiliating surrender documents dividing the country in two were signed in the same railway car in the forest of Compiègne where France accepted Germany's surrender in November 1918. Almost two million French troops became prisoners of war. By June 20, major elements of what would become a German invasion force of 3.35 million, with 5,638 aircraft, 2,445 tanks, and uncounted thousands of horses, pushed the remaining Allied armies nearly into the English Channel. Churchill made three more increasingly bleak trips to France, the last as Paris fell, the little delegation diverting to Tours, with Churchill's De Haviland landing amid a cratered runway. It was for naught; France was finished. In Paris on June 22, now in possession of nearly all of Western Europe, Hitler posed for photos like a tourist, with the Eiffel Tower as the backdrop. In only six weeks, the Nazi rabble-rouser had become a conqueror, with most of Western Europe at his feet. Next it would be England's turn.

CHAPTER TWO

Wednesday, September 4, 1940, A Cabinet Meeting in the Bunker

I lived through the whole war,
Being of an age to comprehend events
and giving my attention to them
in order to know the exact truth about them.
—THUCYDIDES, *HISTORY OF THE PELOPONNESIAN WAR*

WHEN THE PRIME MINISTER REMOVED HIS EYESHADES AROUND 8:30 a.m. in the second-floor flat he now occupied with his wife Clemmie at 10 Downing Street, the Battle of Britain had been underway for two months. With London already under relentless attack, the battle's outcome, he knew, would determine the existence of the island kingdom. In beginning the Blitz in three days, *Reichmarschall* Hermann Göring would send 950 bombers against London in the heaviest daylight raid of the war. He would then shift the Me-109 and Me-110 fighters and bombers to night terror air raids against London for fifty-six of fifty-seven nights, destroying sixteen Christopher Wren churches, thirty-one of thirty-four ancient guildhalls, and setting alight five million books in Paternoster Row, London's publishing center. In the first thirty nights, thirty thousand bombs dropped into the heart of the two-thousand-year-old city.

The fearless prime minister often watched the progression of the attacks from the roof of the building housing the War Rooms, but as the attacks edged ever closer to Whitehall it was time to move more of the War Cabinet meetings from the highly vulnerable 10 Downing Street to the hardly more secure Cabinet War Rooms (CWR) a few hundred yards away.

He could have walked in two minutes from Downing Street to the Cabinet War Rooms, cigar clenched in his jaws and black homburg securely on his head, but it wasn't Winston's way. Instead, he had the driver go around nearly the entire block, first to Parliament Street, past the shrapnel-scarred Cenotaph, to St. George Street, then right on Horse Guards Road to deposit him at the steps of what the three hundred military and civilian analysts and operators who worked there in great secrecy called either George Street or "the hole."

As he entered the building late on the evening of September 4, a single Royal Marine sentry came to attention, the thudding sound of his boots deadened by a specially made coconut and rubber mat. The prime minister had acute sensitivity to any sound, except the sound of his own voice, with special contempt for anyone whistling. As he entered the enclave, a rising hum of activity became separated into voices, typewriters, teletype machines, telephones, the hiss of the American Frigidaire air-conditioning, and whistles and pings from canisters in overhead pneumatic tubes carrying messages to different stations. Col. William J. (Wild Bill) Donovan, in charge of the OSS, a frequent visitor to the War Rooms, likened the activity to stepping into a Shakespearean play, with stage directions such as "army heard in distance, sound of trumpets."

Although Churchill regularly called for the War Cabinet to assemble well after midnight (attendees called them the "Midnight Follies"), tonight's meeting began at 10:20 p.m., accompanied by background explosions and the drone of aircraft engines above. As with every Cabinet meeting in those uncertain times, almost every item on the agenda needed urgent attention or "action this day." The purpose of the meeting, the second of the day, would consider reasons for or against allowing workers to leave their places during the "red" immediate attack siren wail, or to stay in place until the attack appeared directly overhead. Staying at their benches could cost them their lives but leaving critical war work undone would result in a loss of production. As often happened within a temporary coalition government, the discussions became heated, but as

St. James Park entrance to CWR. AUTHOR

summarized in the typed meeting minutes distributed the next morning, the prime minister had the final word: "Everyone should be urged to sleep by day or by night in some place where he could stay put during air raid warnings." Although War Cabinet meetings continued to take place at 10 Downing Street or the Admiralty, as the war and the Battle of Britain intensified, many more meetings would take place underground.

The prime minister entered the Cabinet Room first, to sit at the top of the table, followed by the War Cabinet ministers. They were Clement Attlee, lord privy seal (to replace Churchill as prime minister in 1945), Lord Beaverbrook, minister of aircraft production, and Sir John Anderson, holding the joint portfolio of home secretary and minister of home security (the ubiquitous corrugated metal family bomb shelters were named after him). Arthur Greenwood, officially titled minister without portfolio, had no special duties but if needed could be relied upon to break a tie in Churchill's favor. Sir Kingsley Wood, chancellor of the exchequer, would be joined by Ernest Bevin, in a dual cabinet position

St Paul's Cathedral, London, after incendiary attack December 29, 1940. NATIONAL ARCHIVES

of minister of labour and minister of national service. Depending on the need, War Cabinet meetings also included the first sea lord, the chief of Navy Staff, the chief of the Imperial General Staff, and Churchill's personal chief of staff, Gen. Hastings Ismay.

Reports from ministers early in the war were uniformly dire. At one meeting the first sea lord described the precarious state of the vital convoys. "The situation in regards to shipping losses is very serious," he reported. With U-boats sinking merchant ships faster than they could be built, the first sea lord had an immediate need for the prime minister to ask President Roosevelt if "the United States government could go back on the undertaking which they had made only to bring goods to this county in American bottoms." Britain needed a constant stream of ships to deliver munitions, spare parts, and food or they would lose the war. Everyone in the room knew it. Churchill informed the Cabinet that any change to the American non-intervention policy required the consent of Congress. With ample reason, the epic battle at sea, Great Britain then on the losing side, had prominence then and at most War Cabinet meetings.

In only the first six months of 1940, U-boats sank 232 ships, with 563 going down for the entire year. The ponderously progressing vessels swayed like elephants on parade, many in unescorted convoys, most sailing between North America and Britain. With an average of one-and-a-half ships sunk every day, a U-boat captain could have been focusing his periscope on a slow merchantman at the very hour of the Cabinet meeting. What the War Cabinet and Churchill didn't know was that another 501 ships would be torpedoed in 1941, with an unsustainable 1,322 ships sunk in 1942, far exceeding what British or American shipyards could replace.

Voiced at the September 4, 1940 meeting and at most meetings that year were conclusions that major assistance could not be expected from the United States. Its munitions industry had "little to contribute," its army ineffectual, the navy obsolete, and the American public unwilling to express solidarity in the epic struggle being waged by Britain alone, a battle that so far was being lost. Churchill then informed the War Cabinet of the severity of air raids the last two nights, that rail lines were disrupted, and that "the main force of the German night attacks will be directed against London."

In a memoir about his relationship with Churchill as private secretary, John Colville summed up the general feeling of the War Cabinet in 1940: "America is sitting on the fence as usual . . . the Americans still do not realize that their own fate, as that of civilization, hangs on the result of that battle" (the Battle of Britain).

CHURCHILL'S HEADQUARTERS DEFENSELESS AGAINST ATTACK

Although the squat Portland stone building that became Churchill's central command had communication links to other individual commands and with every war theatre in the world, it was already obsolete when the war began. Making matters worse, it stood out like a jack-o'-lantern in a snowbank.

Even with barrage balloons in the parks and the Home Guard on constant patrol, elite commandos could easily be integrated within the hundreds of bombers in the nightly air raids, to descend from parachutes or land in gliders with orders to kill the prime minister at the sacrifice of their own lives. Everyone in the country and the US government expected imminent invasion. Planners knew that the greatly deficient coastal defenses, even with their miles of redoubts and tunnels, could easily be overcome by the invaders.

An attempt to kill Churchill was well within German capabilities. In September 1943, Hitler handpicked SS captain Otto Skorozeny and 108 Waffen SS commandos, to snatch Italian dictator Benito Mussolini from captivity at a ski resort high in the Italian Apennine mountains. A dozen DFS 230 gliders silently landed near the Campo Imperatore Hotel, with Mussolini in the custody of two hundred heavily armed Carabinieri police guards. Without a shot being fired "Il Duce" was rescued and flown to Vienna to stay overnight at the Imperial Hotel, then to Berlin and a hero's welcome. Even Churchill admired the bold rescue, calling it "one of great daring."

In anticipation of such an attempt against the prime minister's life, modest security enhancements were added during the cellar's conversion into the Cabinet War Rooms. They included interconnected escape tunnels and the billeting of a small detachment of Royal Marines in the sub-basement. Yet, only a push-button alarm that operated like a door-bell by the single sentry at the door stood between the building's entry and envelopment by the enemy. Modest later enhancements included an interior overhead concrete slab, an exterior four-foot-high blast wall at the foundation level, and a sand-bagged pillbox as a façade of protection to the occupants. They were the only visible exterior signs of the epic developments taking place inside.

LIFE IN THE WAR ROOMS

Entry into the low-ceilinged rooms began through a long corridor fitted with negligible defenses against attack, including valves for gas filters and racks with rifles as a last line of defense. A mounted wooden board listed various warning signals. For "GROUND ATTACK from OUTSIDE or INSIDE the BUILDING," the signal was "KLAXON—*continuous sounding for two minutes' duration.*" For a gas alarm, rattles would be heard, with hand bells signaling all clear. Every-one had a gas mask at the ready, although gas was never used in the war.

Chief of Staff's Conference Room with updated maps of all war theatres. AUTHOR

For "FIRE IN C.W.R." occupants would hear "AUDIBLE BLASTS of WHISTLE." Another notice posted outside Churchill's bedroom had a more specific caution: "THERE IS TO BE NO WHISTLING OR UNNECESSARY NOISE IN THIS PASSAGE." Because most of the self-described "moles" were unlikely to be outside for hours or days on end, another sign with interchangeable slots summarized the weather above as COLD, SUNNY, WINDY, or FINE. The "windy" referred to air raids underway, with the enclave's wishful believers decreeing that there should be no sign for rain.

When Churchill was in London, he continued to meet and sleep at 10 Downing Street until it was damaged in an air raid on October 14, 1940 while he was dining. He and Mrs. Churchill then relocated to a suite above the War Rooms called "Number 10 Annexe." When the attacks were especially relentless, he reluctantly went to the War Rooms in the cellar below to fitfully sleep in a narrow bed inside an austere eighteen-by-twenty-foot cell, the door marked "The Prime Minister."

The CWR Cabinet Room, where the War Cabinet met 155 times. AUTHOR

Mrs. Churchill had an equally stark room adjacent to his, although enlivened with family photos.

The prime minister's bedroom also had a desk with a green-glass lamp, two telephones, one with a green handset used for voice scrambling, and two BBC microphones from where he made four radio addresses to the world. To introduce Churchill in the confined space, the announcer had to balance himself on the concrete floor with one hand, while holding the microphone in the other, and then quickly set it down in front of Churchill in time for the BBC chimes and start of the live broadcasts. In the rare event that he faltered for descriptive words, a 1940 pocket-sized edition of *Dod's Parliamentary Companion* awaited his perusal on the desk. It also held an upright leather writing box with paper, envelopes, and a candle. An antiaircraft shell base collected his numerous cigar ends.

Unknown to almost everyone in the most secret bastion in Britain, behind Churchill's bed, covering an entire wall, protected by a drape that was always closed, and forbidden to all eyes except his, a floor to ceiling color-coded map of the British Isles revealed the expected invasion beaches. Even Churchill feared the worst.

Nerve Center—The Map Room

Staffed twenty-four hours daily from when the war started until it ended, the Map Room's singular purpose made it one of the CWR's two most essential rooms. Duty officers in constant motion answered nine scrambled multicolored telephones with blinking lights, known as the "beauty chorus," or were in switchboard contact with other commands. If they were outside, calling in was as easy as ringing Whitehall 5422.

Other staffers darted to or from maps or charts fastened to every available space to pin underway convoy and battle movements. The floor to ceiling maps were punctured with thousands of pinholes that wove like a web, as they depicted the perilous course of convoys or the last known U-boat positions. Even locations of the *Queen Mary* and *Queen Elizabeth*, converted into fifteen-thousand-passenger troopships, were displayed. After America's entry, General Eisenhower and officers of the new Supreme Headquarters Allied Expeditionary Force (SHAEF) headquarters, first in Grosvenor Square and then at Bushy Park near

Staff from each service branch were connected by multicolored telephones with internal messages sent by pneumatic tube. AUTHOR

London, were regular visitors. Occupying Room 59, a shadowy figure in charge of SIS, the secret intelligence service, and known only as "C," made periodic presentations. He would later appear fictionally in novels by John Le Carre.

SIGSALY AND SECRET CONVERSATIONS
IN CHURCHILL'S LAVATORY

In mid-1943 American engineers from Bell Laboratories and the US Army's 805th Signal Services Company installed the first hotline, a direct telephone connection between Churchill and Roosevelt. The product of research by Bell Telephone Laboratories that began in 1936, the system that bore the cover name of SIGSALY became the first synthesis of analog voice to digital signals and then back to voice again. The system employed a twelve-channel, seventy-two radio-frequency array patented by Bell Labs and manufactured by Western Electric. The multistep process needed for each conversation required error-free operation from forty seven-foot-high relay racks producing 30 kilowatts of electrical output. Installed into the racks were four-inch-diameter, fourteen-inch-high mercury-vapor rectifier vacuum tubes or valves, ninety-six different step-circuits, multiple relays, two turntables, synchronous motors, and other electromechanical equipment, all cooled by refrigerated air-conditioning. At fifty-five tons, the apparatus needed a location other than the CRW. One mile away, a 200-foot-deep sub-basement in an annex of Selfridges' Department Store on Oxford Street held the apparatus in one large and well-ventilated room. Across the Atlantic, the new Pentagon installed an identical system, with hotline calls between Washington and London timed to start precisely together. SIGSALY went into wide use in war theatres worldwide, continuing into the Cold War, and remaining top-secret until 1972.

Churchill made or received hotline calls from FDR inside a narrow former broom closet, behind a door tagged with a red "engaged" dial that everyone thought was a lavatory. If correct, it would have been the only proper toilet in the entire facility. In true Churchillian fashion, he wouldn't accept a call until notified that FDR was already waiting. FDR's irritation at being called by Churchill at various times day or night had an easy solution by painting a red indicator on the wall clock displaying both London and Washington times.

CHURCHILL AT WORK

From his bed or desk the prime minister dictated early morning correspondence to a rotating team of secretaries, often changing a word, a sentence, or an entire paragraph in mid-dictation as his thoughts were clarified or new information became available. His private secretary, Jock Colville, recalled that Churchill chewed on a cigar, usually a

Havana-made *Romeo et Julieta*, and "fidgeted his toes beneath the bed-clothes and muttered under his breath what he contemplated saying." The completed dictation then went by hand to typists in nearby cubicles or in the "dock," the humid, hot, and poorly ventilated sub-basement below the War Rooms. Lacking toilet or bathing facilities and accessed only by a narrow trap door and a steep wooden ladder, the gloomy quarters, once part of a wine cellar, had concrete ceilings only four feet high, to be used as a dormitory for Churchill's butler, valet, clerks, administrators, and the Royal Marine guards.

After typing, correspondence went back to Churchill for approval or changes. "Gimme," he growled. After acceptance, the documents were retyped, then initialed or signed, machine duplicated or printed over-night, and individually numbered for placement by Marine orderlies on desk blotters next to each minister's place in the Cabinet Room. Each page bore the inscription: "This document is the property of His Britannic Majesty's Government." The first page had the stamp, "To Be Kept Under Lock and Key," with a further admonition to the government's top officials: "It is requested that special care may be taken to ensure the secrecy of this document." Each agenda also had a rubber-stamped designation in blue ink, either "Top Secret" or "Secret."

AFTERMATH

The day after the war ended, the CWR lights were turned off for the first time. The watch officers, civilians, and Marines who staffed the installation every day and night for almost six years returned to their duties elsewhere or were discharged. The war-winning work and its decisions, the lives saved or lost, all slid into obscurity, to be overlooked by history for decades.

In 1977 the author learned of the intact existence of the rooms from a British friend, a former RAF pilot who knew the curator and could obtain special entry. Room after room had the appearance of being suddenly abandoned at the end of the war, with the occupants leaving everything in place and departing forever. Heaped throughout were files, documents, notices, maps and charts, furniture, and fixtures.

While perusing files in the Map Room—so complete that it seemed as if its occupants had left for a pint at the local—a file folder bumped off a table. Hand-lettered in red on the yellowing cover were the words, "Operation Overlord, Top-Secret." The file had part of the plan for D-Day, the June 6, 1944 invasion of Europe.

The decision made in conditions of a national emergency to place Churchill's war center in an undefended office building and not in a stronghold outside London could have changed history if suspected by Hitler, his own heavily fortified headquarters also in the center of his nation's capital. During only the nine months of the Blitz and against only London, the *Luftwaffe* launched seventy-one raids with thousands of sorties. If only one sortie with one armor-piercing one-thousand-pound bomb hit the CWR building, it could have collapsed the entire structure onto the basement War Rooms, resulting in forever stilling the rolling resonance of the lion who gave wartime Britain its roar.

VISITING THE WAR ROOMS

As the most complete depiction anywhere of a government in its darkest hour, CWR is in its original location, with its original furnishings. Except for the clear plastic viewing partitions, the bunker basement is unchanged from when Churchill said, "this is where I will conduct the war." Admission charge. Open daily except Christmas. Westminster Underground. In 2017, the CWR had 634,000 visitors.

CHAPTER THREE

Secret Services: Liverpool and the Western Approaches Command Center

Eternal Father, strong to save,
Whose arm hath bound the restless wave,
Who bidd'st the mighty ocean keep,
Oh hear us when we cry to Thee,
For those in peril on the sea.
—WILLIAM WHITING

INTRODUCTION: LIFELINE OF THE ATLANTIC

CHURCHILL AND ROOSEVELT KNEW THAT WINNING THE WAR DEPENDED on a continuous supply of materiel from merchant ships navigating sea highways in convoys connecting North America and the British Isles. As an island nation, Britain's very survival depended on imports, its sixty-seven hundred ships outranking the United States merchant fleet, its nearest rival, two to one. Hitler equally knew the importance of the convoy lifeline; it had to be cut or Nazi Germany would lose the war.

On any day, at least twenty-five hundred British registered ships were at sea somewhere in the world, with multiple convoys of ten to over one hundred ships in movement between North America and Britain. Old or new, coal or oil-fired, large or small, fast or slow, they were loaded to the gunwales with everything from locomotives and landing craft to tinned meat and instant coffee. Oil, the most important resource of all, needed daily delivery by at least four tankers. After emptying their cargo and in ballast, the ships again sailed outbound in convoy for the next consignment. No captain wanted the label of a straggler unable to maintain position or straying from the zig-zag sequences. Every captain feared the sudden appearance of bad-stoking—the view of black smoke belching from a stack revealing the convoy to prowling U-boats or searching enemy aircraft. The worst possible outcome, and it happened regularly, came with the sudden appearance of a U-boat inside the convoy box.

No one better knew the perils of being a wartime mariner than the unheralded merchant seamen of the many nationalities billeted in harsh working conditions, given only two days off for each month at sea, who repeatedly voyaged the 2,872 nautical miles between New York and Liverpool. Slighted by history, 33,962 British merchant seamen on 2,603 steamers went to the bottom. The US Merchant Marine lost 1,554 ships and 9,521 men, including 537 along the US East Coast and the North and Northeast Atlantic. But when dawn broke on D-Day, 2,770 merchant ships were part of the Normandy armada.

Center of Gravity for the Convoys

Of all the ports landing supplies for the European war, none had greater importance than Liverpool, the center of gravity and the eastern terminus of a movement that began in Halifax, New York, or in numerous other American ports. The convoy train ended at the Western Approaches, the funnel leading from the Atlantic to the port of Liverpool. Before the war it managed 40 percent of the world's sea commerce, embarking millions of immigrants for a new life in Canada and America. During the war, it landed over 1.5 million American troops, some being the same immigrants who had returned to rescue the world they left. The former home port for the *Titanic* and *Lusitania*, Liverpool administered 90 percent of all wartime shipping within the world's largest interconnected and enclosed port system. On average, one convoy a day entered the seven-and-a-half miles of Mersey River ports to berth at docks named Albert, Birkenhead, Brunswick, Canada, Canning, Coburg, Gladstone, Salthouse, Prince's, Queen's, or Wapping.

Through signals intercepts, spies, transmitter triangulations, and insights from the *Abwehr*, the Nazis' intelligence-gathering agency,

Germany knew that Liverpool had to be destroyed to meet its war aims. It became a target second only to London, itself having lost 75 percent of its port capacity early in the war. In eighty air raids, the Luftwaffe destroyed 80 percent of Liverpool's waterfront, killing twenty-five hundred Merseysiders.

The essential importance of keeping open the Liverpool convoy conduit became the basis for construction of a two-level, seventy-foot-deep underground convoy control headquarters beneath an existing seven-story office building in the city center. Compared to the feebly fortified cellar sheltering the CWR, Western Approaches Command (WAC) had been built as a citadel, with a seven-foot-thick concrete roof over the original building, three-foot-thick poured concrete walls, and one hundred rooms within fifty thousand square feet. For the sake of convenience but without regard for its own possible destruction, the underground convoy control center nearly viewed the same docks where the convoys berthed.

THE "DUNGEON"—INSIDE WESTERN APPROACHES COMMAND

As a potential target for German raiders the 1931-built Derby House, to later house the WAC, had the doubtful distinction of being clad with a glaring white slate façade, and within walking minutes of a trio of splendid and highly visible waterfront buildings that locals called the "Three Graces." As proud symbols of Liverpool's mercantile success, they became tempting targets and aiming points for German bombers. The extravagant Cunard–White Star headquarters, the 322-foot-tall Royal Liver Assurance Building with its two gleaming towers, and the 220-foot-tall lavishly decorated Port of Liverpool Building, dominated the midpoint of the extending docks, where prewar transatlantic passenger liners embarked or disembarked passengers.

On the morning before sailing, the commodores, captains, and radiomen of the 1,285 Liverpool war convoys met at Derby House with Royal Navy escort officers, and, after America's entry, with US Navy commanding officers. After entering from the street through unmarked black doors they registered with staff, were given badges, and went down steep concrete steps to one of two windowless, high-ceilinged bunkers,

Entrance to Derby House, Liverpool, Headquarters Western Approaches. AUTHOR

one above the other. Constantly active were one thousand Royal Navy and RAF officers, telephone, teletype, and radio operators, technicians, women naval WRNS (Wrens), and air force WAFs, all transported by bus from separate dormitories. The self-named "cave dwellers" worked twelve-hour days seven days a week, enveloped by thick humidity, thin lighting, telephone and teletype discord, cigar and cigarette smoke, and the burden of executing sudden changes to convoy operational orders. With containment of the growing U-boat threat the sea war's main emphasis through 1943, the expanding WAC later appropriated two hundred thousand additional square feet and the trading floor in the adjoining Cotton Exchange Building.

All concerned had ample reason for anxiety over the survival of the ships and men in the convoys. In 1941, U-boats and enemy actions in North Atlantic waters sent 568 ships to the bottom. Rapidly increasing from fifty-seven on September 1, 1939, by January 1941 at least ninety

U-boats were in commission, with fourteen patrolling at any one time. A year later over 250 were at sea, further growing to four hundred by the end of 1942. The newest U-boats were equipped with radar and improved torpedoes, and all had the vital Enigma cipher device. In 1942, they sank 1,160 Allied ships, 507 flying the stars and stripes. So far, U-boats were winning the war at sea.

WHERE THE ATLANTIC CHARTER STARTED

In mid-March 1941, nine months before the United States entered the war and immediately after passage of the Lend-Lease Act, US Navy captain Louis E. Denfeld, chief of staff to the commander-in-chief Atlantic (CINCLANT), Adm. Ernest J. King, flew to Liverpool for meetings in the newly opened WAC. As a link to FDR's secret collaboration with the British war effort, the joint US/UK strategy talks in the underground enclave implemented Roosevelt's vow to give Britain "all aid short of war." The talks ended with agreement that defeating the Atlantic U-boats would be the principal objective. The decisions made at the meetings evolved into the August 14, 1941 Atlantic Charter, to be declared by Roosevelt and Churchill in Placentia Bay, Newfoundland.

With America in the war four months later, the convoys greatly increased in type and number. As developed in the WAC's "dungeon," their routings were planned with the precision of a train timetable, with a convoy scheduled to arrive in port near the time when another departed. As the war progressed arrivals and departures became fully linked, with eastbound convoys leaving on a day coinciding with a westbound departure. This avoided overloading a port or sending ships to a vulnerable stand-off

Adm. Max Horton changed a failed doctrine to help win the Battle of the Atlantic. LIBRARY OF CONGRESS

Admiral Horton's office overlooking two-story Operations Room. AUTHOR

anchor. So rigorous were the system's efficiencies that they even allowed convoy entry by late "joiners" into the underway flow.

THE US NAVY IN LIVERPOOL

After America's entry into the war, three former transatlantic passenger liners, all with the speed to outrun any U-boat, became regular visitors to Liverpool. The twenty-four-thousand-ton USS *Mount Vernon*, converted from the liner SS *Washington*; USS *Wakefield*, the former SS *Manhattan*; and the largest and fastest of all, the thirty-five-thousand-ton USS *West Point*, the former SS *America*, were requisitioned from United States Lines. Never losing a ship or a man, they carried scores of thousands of troops across the Atlantic. Steaming alone and without escort, the large tonnage "lone wolves" benefited from a fifteen-hundred-foot floating jetty at the Prince's and George's docks. The landing stage tamed the notorious four-time daily twenty-nine-foot tidal changes, its rising and falling relieving crews from constant line corrections.

A FATAL FLAW—U-BOAT RADIO REPORTS TO HEADQUARTERS

Deep inside the WAC's concrete cavern, scores of radio operators listened for reports of U-boat communication as intercepted by thirty-nine "Y" or listening stations, widely and diversely placed in stately homes such as Kedelston Hall in Derbyshire, at RAF bases, or in beachside huts. Knowing that the British were listening, U-boats transmitted on the surface nearly every night in quick coded bursts to their commander, Adm. Karl Doenitz, in his own underground headquarters near Lorient, France. Y station listeners had direction-finding equipment to fix a U-boat's location for attack by surface or air assets coordinated by WAC. A network that included Bletchley Park, RAF air bases, the Admiralty in London, SHAEF, and the Cabinet War Rooms richly exploited and eventually ended the advantage U-boats had in the Atlantic.

Playing Games in the Western Approaches

On large tables and on concrete floors in two well-lighted rooms deep within WAC, simulations set two teams of twelve players against each other. One team represented the commanders of Allied convoys, while the opposing side imitated U-boat commanders and their likely tactics. Pushing long wooden rods like pool cues, the gamers moved varicolored

Simulations with commanders. Move a ship the wrong way and fail the exercise.
AUTHOR

paper symbols across a gridded chart resembling the North Atlantic. One of the players portrayed U-boat commander Adm. Karl Doenitz and his likely tactics, as players on both sides either moved ships in convoys or positioned U-boats in wolf packs. Over six thousand convoy commanders and officers attended the six-day training course. Those who failed the final simulation test were handed a printed card by a smiling WREN officer. It said, "your ship has just been sunk; you have no further part in this exercise."

Joint Forces Operations Center

Every component and activity centered on the two-level combined forces Operations Room, jointly controlled by the British army and Royal Navy—the principal reason for WAC's existence. Neatly arranged desks held metal-clipboard reports designated by type and time. Wrens wheeled telescoping ladders along an eighty-foot-long, thirty-foot-high, black-painted plywood chart separated into grids. Occupying an entire two-story wall from floor to ceiling, it continued along another high wall to blackboards displaying chalked summaries and updates. Color-coded paper designated target types, the Wrens balancing high on ladders to twist color-coded elastic string around pushpins, extending the string to other pins to illustrate inbound convoys. Officers viewing the activity had continuous telephone, teletype, and motorcycle messenger contact with coastal airfields, ships, the Admiralty, CWR, Bletchley Park, and other locations. Real-time results allowed immediate adjustments to underway actions.

Adding to the communication layers, an underground canal connected WAC to the nearby Mersey River and a waiting submarine. For a time 4,719 boxes containing 280 tons of Britain's gold reserve sent on three trains from London to Lime Street station on May 22, 1940, resided in the basement bullion room in the adjacent Martin's Bank. After the invasion that nearly everyone expected, boats on the canal would transport both WAC's ciphers and the bank's bullion to the submarine and Canada. (Between June and August 1940, the bank's gold and securities went to the Bank of Canada in Halifax and to the Sun Life Building in Montreal.)

The Operations Room charted all convoys directly into the Western Approaches.
AUTHOR

Another room with an armed guard outside contained a single teletype machine and one operator with only one duty—wait for "flash priority" transmissions from Bletchley Park (BP), where the Enigma device had been unraveled. Encrypted messages received from BP were printed on narrow, spooled, punched-paper strips. An operator decoded the message, then passed it through a tiny rectangular window to a messenger in the main teletype room for delivery to the duty officer. The teletype room housed ten model M15 machines, known for their recurring "chunk chunk" sound, manufactured by the Teletype Corporation in Skokie, Illinois, a Chicago suburb.

An Eccentric Commander

From an office with an oversize plate-glass window overlooking the Operations Room below, Adm. Max Horton, one of three WAC commanders, displayed rather odd behaviors in the performance of his duties in the underground enclave. From a colleague's war diary: "He had some maddening habits. He played golf all afternoon, then returned (to WAC), played a rubber or two of bridge, and came down to his office and started sending for his staff." As with Churchill, the admiral functioned best at night—late night—suddenly appearing "in worn and split pajamas, hair hirsute fore and aft." To ensure that no one violated his duty hours, the admiral issued a memo: "My routine is golf every day from two to six, and I usually finish my work at 1.0 am. I hope you will arrange your routine to suit." The staff gave the salty admiral sea room aplenty, knowing that his war-fighting abilities far exceeded the unconventional behavior. Admiral Horton had the rare ability to discern wolf-pack strategy, resulting in the transformation of a failed doctrine and upending of the prior use of convoy escorts. Instead of relying on a conventional perimeter escort defense, he added separate support warships inside convoys, with open orders to stay on target as long as necessary. With the changed strategy, escorts no longer dropped depth charges followed by an immediate return to convoy duties. They now lurked inside the convoy. As a result, U-boat losses dramatically increased from thirty-five in 1941 to eighty-seven in 1942, and to a crushing 244 in 1943. In May 1943 alone, forty-one were sunk. Coinciding with Horton's revised anti-submarine warfare tactics came improved sonar, expanded use of air assets, and a major increase in escorts, all resulting in a dramatic end to the North Atlantic U-boat threat. On D-Day, with over five thousand vessels crossing the English Channel, not one was lost to U-boats.

Aftermath

By the end of the war WAC had become a gigantic enterprise. The one-thousand-member staff had expanded into 121,500 personnel, with another eighteen thousand Wrens and WAFs quartered in separate buildings or bases. In recognition of his war-winning leadership Gen. George C. Marshall awarded the Legion of Honor to Admiral Horton. The overlooked Western Approaches Command, with many of its original fittings, including Admiral Horton's unchanged office overlooking the floor below, and the same mammoth wall chart is open six days each week. Numerous daily trains connect London and Liverpool.

CHAPTER FOUR

FDR's Undeclared War

Whoever dwells in the shelter of the Most High
will rest in the shadow of the Almighty.
I will say of the Lord, He is my refuge and my fortress,
My God in whom I trust . . .

—PSALM 91

INTRODUCTION: A CALL TO ARMS

IN THE WHITE HOUSE DIPLOMATIC RECEPTION ROOM AT 9:30 P.M. ON December 29, 1940, an audience of twenty sits expectantly on wobbly, gilt wooden chairs before a desk drilled with holes for the wires of seven microphones. On the desk are two sharpened pencils, a blank notepad, two glasses of water, and an open pack of Camels. Among the invited guests are matinee idol Clark Gable with his wife, blonde Carole Lombard. Cordell Hull, the sixty-nine-year-old secretary of state, nervously fingers his pince-nez ribbon. Print and radio reporters casually smoke. In the first row, dressed in a gray-blue evening gown, Sara Roosevelt awaits her son, Franklin D. Roosevelt, thirty-second President of the United States. Throughout the country almost everyone with a radio gathers around Philco, Emerson, or RCA sets for the sixteenth of thirty radio addresses that FDR calls "fireside chats."

"Never before . . . has our American civilization been in such danger as now," he says in the familiar baritone his 132 million fellow countrymen have come to trust. "By an agreement signed in Berlin, three powerful nations, two in Europe and one in Asia, joined themselves together

. . . that if the United States of America interfered with or blocked the expansion program of these three nations—a program aimed at world control—they would unite in ultimate action against the United States."

"And why," he asks like a schoolteacher, "does the European war concern the United States?" He answers his own question: "If Great Britain goes down, all of us in the Americas would be living at the point of a gun. There are those who say that the Axis powers have no desire to attack the Western Hemisphere. That is the same sort of wishful thinking which has destroyed the powers of resistance of so many conquered peoples . . . the vast resources and wealth of this American Hemisphere constitute the most tempting loot in all of the world."

Wiping his broad forehead with a handkerchief, the fire crackling in the white marble fireplace in front to his right, Roosevelt finishes the thirty-seven-minute talk with a ringing plea to arm faster, to build more airplanes and ships . . . "we must be the great arsenal of democracy." Almost a year before Pearl Harbor, FDR's call to arms has committed the United States to save Britain, even to enter the war if necessary, no matter the cost, no matter the burden. It would take decades after the war for the public to learn the extent to which FDR secretly committed the United States to Britain's survival, a risk taken at the potential cost of his presidency through impeachment by an isolationist Congress.

FEBRUARY 1, 1941 THE US NAVY TO NAZI GERMANY— "DON'T TREAD ON ME"

Little more than a month after the fireside speech, the Atlantic Squadron, the US Navy's neutrality patrol, received a new name, the Atlantic Fleet, and a daring new offensive mission intended to further lower the threshold for all-out war at sea with Nazi Germany. Appointed by President Roosevelt to command the fleet, sixty-three-year-old Adm. Ernest J. King, the Navy's premier strategist, would soon wage a little-known undeclared war on the high seas.

In addition to being openly Anglophobic, the hard-driving, hot-tempered admiral also had an aversion to the November 1940 Roosevelt/ Churchill "Germany first" decision confirming Nazi Germany as the principal opposition in the coming war. Blends of rumor and fact clung

FDR fireside chat: "We shall do everything possible to crush Hitler and his Nazi forces." FDR PRESIDENTIAL LIBRARY

to the new commander-in-chief, Atlantic Fleet (CINCLANT) like wet snow to a windshield. Profane, arrogant, humorless—no one remembered him ever smiling—and reputedly a womanizer and known hard drinker, his own daughter said, "he's the most even-tempered man in the Navy; he's always in a rage."

In liberty bars from Norfolk's East Main Street to drafty cabins in barren Newfoundland, fleet sailors spun legends that increased with each shot thrown back. With as much awe as hyperbole, they avowed that the admiral didn't think that he was God, but that God thought he was Admiral King. An admiring FDR said, "he shaves with a blowtorch." On learning of his appointment, King characteristically had the last word about himself: "When they get into trouble they send for the sons of bitches."

On March 11, 1941, Congress ended the fiction of US neutrality by passing the Lend-Lease Act. It became the principal means of supplying arms without payment to Britain or to any nation, "whose defense the

President deems vital to the defense of the United States." Isolationist Ohio Senator Robert Taft condemned the act. It would give, he said, "the President power to carry-on a kind of undeclared war all over the world, in which America would do everything except actually put soldiers in the front-line trenches where the fighting is." Neither Taft nor the US Congress knew it, but the "undeclared war" he feared was about to begin.

Implementing FDR's assurance to Churchill to give "all aid short of war," on April 18, 1941, Admiral King issued Operation Plan 3-41. It declared that the US Navy would promptly take offensive action if the warships of any belligerent—except for nations having West Indian possessions—came within twenty-five miles of a vastly expanded Western Hemisphere. The ocean meridians now covered greatly expanded areas, extending west to the International Date Line beyond Iceland, including Greenland, the Azores, the Gulf of St. Lawrence, and all the Caribbean Sea and Gulf of Mexico.

Inspired by Churchill's Cabinet War Rooms, FDR's small White House basement map room. FDR PRESIDENTIAL LIBRARY

Stamped "SECRET" until April 2003, OPPLAN 3-41 had precise orders for the commanding officers of US Navy warships in the new Atlantic Fleet: "Entrance into the Western Hemisphere by naval ships or aircraft of belligerents . . . is to be viewed as possibly actuated by an unfriendly interest toward shipping or territory in the Western Hemisphere." The already defeated French navy and Dutch and British warships were allowed unimpeded passage to their possessions or even to US ports for replenishment, but not the Axis powers. Their intrusion into the Western Hemisphere would designate them as trespassers to be dealt with as pirates. By warning the Axis that incursions into Allied waters represented an act of war, OPPLAN 3-41 placed the expanding Atlantic Fleet directly into the path of opportunistic German and Italian surface raiders and U-boats.

FDR Calls Germany "An International Outlaw"

To ensure no misreading of orders originating with Admiral King's commander-in-chief, Franklin D. Roosevelt, King's OPPLAN 3-41 then underlined its two operative words: "If any such naval vessels or aircraft are encountered within twenty-five miles of Western Hemisphere territory, except the Azores, warn them to move twenty-five miles from such territory and, in case of failure to heed such warning, attack them."

Now on a collision course with Germany and with a much-reduced provocation as cause for America's entry into a war already underway for eighteen months, what would it take to provoke the US Navy into direct action, and, more importantly, where would it happen? It came less than a month later.

On May 21, in the second week of a patrol in the South Atlantic, U-69 encountered the five-thousand-ton American freighter SS *Robin Moor* sailing alone 750 miles off Freetown, Sierra Leone. Prominently painted in white on the ship's port and starboard sides were the letters USA. The U-boat surfaced to inform the thirty-three-member crew and four passengers that they had thirty minutes to abandon ship, and then torpedoed the neutral American-flagged ship. Given tins of black bread and butter, the lifeboats drifted for eighteen days before rescue, but without loss of life.

The president branded Germany as an "international outlaw," and closed all German consulates in the United States, allowing only the German embassy in Washington to remain open. Senator Gerald Nye (R-ND), one of the America First Committee founders, immediately blamed Britain for the sinking. "I would be very much surprised if a German submarine had done it because it would be to their disadvantage." (Nye later issued a retraction through America First.) Roosevelt, always the sagacious politician, knew that incurring the wrath of its influential membership, and powerful press barons such as William Randolph Hearst and Robert R. McCormick, risked getting too far

Adm. Ernest J King: FDR said, "He shaves with a blowtorch."
NAVAL HISTORY AND HERITAGE COMMAND

ahead of the mood of the people. If taking a major risk to avoid a British defeat became necessary, FDR had no regrets, but with no loss of life in the sinking of *Robin Moor*, he lacked a *casus belli* for all-out war at sea with Nazi Germany. Instead, FDR had a better way of avoiding the isolationist press to directly reach the public. Once again it was through radio.

ROOSEVELT: "THE WAR IS APPROACHING . . . VERY CLOSE TO HOME"

On Tuesday, May 27, 1941, at 9:30 p.m. Eastern time, less than a week after the sinking of the *Robin Moor*, the president spoke to the country from the East Room of the White House. In his seventeenth "fireside chat" he declared "an unlimited national emergency," validating what the country increasingly knew, that "what started as a European war has developed as the Nazis always intended it should develop, into a world war for world domination." He left no doubt that the United States would decisively act if its national interests were threatened. "I call upon all loyal citizens to place the nation's needs first in mind and in action to the end that we may mobilize and have ready for instant defensive use all of the physical powers, all of the moral strength and all of the material resources of this nation . . . the war is approaching the brink of the Western Hemisphere. It is approaching very close to home."

In a swipe at the America First Committee and Charles Lindbergh, he said: "Some people seem to think that we are not attacked until bombs actually drop on the streets of New York, or San Francisco, or New Orleans, or Chicago. But they are simply shutting their eyes to the lesson that we must learn from the fate of every nation that the Nazis have conquered. . . . Nobody can foretell tonight just when the acts of the dictators will ripen into attack on this hemisphere and us. But we know enough by now to realize that it would be suicide to wait until they are in our front yard."

The president ended the twenty-five-minute address with a series of pledges that would change the life of every American. "We are placing our armed forces in strategic military positions, (and) as the president of a united and determined people, I say solemnly: We reassert the ancient American doctrine of freedom of the seas."

A RAPID MOVE TO WAR

On June 14, in solidarity with the now defeated peoples of Western Europe, Roosevelt issued an executive order freezing the bank assets of Germans and Italians living in the United States.

On July 24, 1941, on the other side of the world, an expanding Japanese empire seized French Indochina and occupied Saigon. Two days later, President Roosevelt released another executive order freezing Japanese assets in the United States, and separately embargoed the export of oil from the United States to Japan. Japanese militarism now edged ever closer to the Philippines, then governed by the United States, where America had bases and troops being rearmed under the command of recently reactivated Gen. Douglas MacArthur.

But in mid-1941, although willing and eager, the United States was anything but ready to enter history's greatest war. The mightiest fleet the world had yet to see navigated mostly design offices and shipyards.

The Bureau of Ships overflowed with plans on paper for new types of auxiliary ships, submarines, destroyers, cruisers, aircraft carriers, and battleships. But the battle-line to be could not change the melancholy fact that on September 1, 1939, the day World War II began, the entire US Navy had in commission, in addition to its mostly obsolete warships, only two ammunition ships and two troop transports. Most of America's battleships—then the principal means of projecting power at sea—dated from the Wilson and Harding administrations.

Yet, needing only targets to come within Navy gunsights, America's entry into World War II could have started as much by intention in the Atlantic as by surprise eight months later in the Pacific. As confirmed by the author from declassified operational orders at the Naval Historical Center and the National Archives in College Park, Maryland, months before Pearl Harbor, the US Navy prepared for all-out war at sea with Nazi Germany. As the United States rearmed and the Navy rebuilt its fleet, in mid-1941 the Atlantic Fleet went on a war footing. Ships' flammables were removed, ammunition lockers topped off, and the fleet received full wartime crew complements. One of them, the president's middle son, Ens. Franklin D. Roosevelt Jr., went to the destroyer *Mayrant* (DD-402). The Naval Academy graduated its 1941 class in January instead of June. With the first peacetime draft underway since September 1940, thousands of naval recruits swarmed boot camps in Newport, Rhode Island, Bainbridge, Maryland, Great Lakes, Illinois, and San Diego, California. By early summer 1941, German and American naval forces were poised like title contenders jabbing in the middle rounds. In each corner, basing their moves on the other's assumed intentions, the opposing fighters received cautious orders. Test, irritate, provoke, thrust here and there, even deliver a few uppercuts if opportunity presents. But no knockout punch—not yet.

FDR TO NAVY: "ELIMINATE THE THREAT OF ATTACK"

In early July 1941, six months after his "arsenal of democracy" speech and five months before the Japanese attack on Pearl Harbor, the president wrote to Chief of Naval Operations (CNO) Adm. H. R. Stark. (On April 4, the CNO had informed FDR that "the situation is obviously critical in the Atlantic . . . it is hopeless unless we take strong measures to save it.") The president intended to take the recommended "strong measures" by greatly expanding the basis for war at sea with Germany.

"It is necessary under the conditions of modern warfare to recognize that the words "threat of attack" may extend reasonably long distances away from a convoyed ship or ships," the president wrote. "It thus seems clear that the very presence of a German submarine or raider on or near the line of communications constitutes "threat of attack." Therefore, the presence of any German submarine or raider should be dealt with by action looking to the elimination of such 'threat of attack' on the lines of communication, or close to it."

CNO Adm. H. R. Stark eager for combat four months before Pearl Harbor.
NAVAL HISTORY AND HERITAGE COMMAND

The president's syntax may have been inexact but not his intent. On September 1, 1941, Admiral King interpreted the presidential directive as sufficient reason to place the Atlantic Fleet into potential conflict with the German *Kriegsmarine*. Set in uppercase and underlined "SECRET," a revised nine-page Operation Plan 7-41 described four scenarios that conformed with FDR's reassessment of a "threat of attack." The order went to Navy task forces and patrols—Northern, Gulf, Caribbean, and Panama.

MY INTERPRETATION OF THREAT TO UNITED STATES OR ICELAND FLAG SHIPPING WHETHER ESCORTED OR NOT, IS THAT THREAT EXISTS WHEN: 1) POTENTIALLY HOSTILE VESSELS ARE ACTUALLY WITHIN SIGHT OR SOUND CONTACT OF SUCH SHIPPING OR ITS ESCORT. 2) POTENTIALLY HOSTILE SURFACE RAIDERS OR SUBMARINES EITHER APPROACH WITHIN 100

*MILES OF SUCH SHIPPING, ALONG THE SEA LANES
BETWEEN NORTH AMERICA AND ICELAND. 3) POTEN-
TIALLY HOSTILE SURFACE RAIDERS OR SUBMARINES
EITHER APPROACH WITHIN 100 MILES OF SUCH SHIP-
PING, OR TRAVERSE ROUTES DEFINED IN PARAGRAPH
3 (W) (5) BELOW OR ENTER THE PROCLAIMED NEU-
TRALITY ZONE. 4) ANY POTENTIALLY HOSTILE FORCES
APPROACH TO WITHIN FIFTY MILES OF ICELAND.*

It ended with an order, also in uppercase, that left no doubt as to its meaning: "DESTROY HOSTILE FORCES THAT THREATEN SHIPPING NAMED IN (B) (2) AND (C) (3) ABOVE."

Only four days later on September 5 came the "incident" sought by the president and the US Navy. Two hundred miles southwest of Reykjavik, the old four-piper destroyer *Greer* barely evaded a torpedo fired from U-boat U-552, and then unsuccessfully attacked the U-boat with depth charges. The next evening an enraged president went on the radio and spoke directly to Nazi Germany: "You shall go no further. . . . If German or Italian vessels of war enter the waters . . . necessary for American defense, they do so at their own peril." The New York *Daily News* said it with a bold headline: "Shoot, FDR Tells Navy."

ADM. H. R. STARK: "WHETHER THE COUNTRY KNOWS IT OR NOT, WE ARE AT WAR"

Events in the North Atlantic continued to rapidly advance. On September 10, 1941, Admiral King ordered the Atlantic Fleet to escort convoys originating in Halifax, Nova Scotia, all the way to England. For the first time in the secret and undeclared war, the US Navy now had the entire North Atlantic for its expanded offensive operations. An overly ambitious Chief of Naval Operations, Adm. H. R. "Betty" Stark wrote to FDR: "Whatever we do, I am anxious that our first real shooting contact with the enemy be successful. Particularly would I like to get *Tirpitz* if opportunity comes our way. Early victory would breed confidence and be a wonderful stimulant."

On September 22, further adding to the flash-point for all-out war at sea with Germany, Admiral King revised OPPLAN 7-41 with

The 52,600-ton battleship *Tirpitz* moored in a Norwegian fjord circa 1943. NAVAL HISTORY AND HERITAGE COMMAND

an annex, OPPLAN 7B-41. The words almost leapt from the page: "MEETING WITH A GERMAN OR ITALIAN VESSEL. The vessel may not be stopped and boarded. If there is conclusive evidence that she is a combatant naval vessel, she shall be destroyed. Operate as under war conditions, including complete darkening of ships when at sea East of longitude 60 degrees West."

On October 15, the new $5 million destroyer *Kearney* took two torpedoes from U-56, limping into port in Iceland with eleven dead, the first US casualties of World War II. "Whether the country knows it or not," Admiral Stark said, "we are at war." The country was beginning to know it; a Gallup poll registered 65 percent approval for US intervention. FDR finally had the firm support of the American people. His side-stepping of the Neutrality Act succeeded. The United States continued to frantically rearm, while secretly expanding operations to prevent a British collapse across the three-thousand-mile Atlantic sea highway.

Aftermath

For the eager prewar US Navy and an equally determined president, there were no fleet actions against Axis ships in the Atlantic before (or during) World War II. In 1939 Germany had no viable navy, with only three battleships, eight cruisers, seventeen destroyers, and fifty-seven U-boats. Only the U-boat forces made it a real battle. But Admiral Stark's prospect of "getting" the technically advanced *Tirpitz*, the largest and last battleship Germany ever built, could have resulted in humiliating defeat for the US Navy if one of the three 1917-commissioned battleships on Atlantic neutrality patrol had encountered the Nazi super-ship. Commissioned in February 1941, the 52,600-ton, 30-knot titan's main battery of eight Krupp-designed fifteen-inch guns had an over the horizon range of thirty-four miles. As for the three US capital ships then in the Atlantic, they first saw water only fourteen years after the Wright Brothers first flew. The *New Mexico*, *Mississippi*, and *Idaho* could muster only a dignified 21 knots flank speed going downhill and with a following wind.

Conspiracy theorists may sense opportunity by linking the US Navy's aggressive prewar posture with long-running revisionist intrigues connecting President Roosevelt with advance knowledge of the Pearl Harbor attack. In 1941, Great Britain hovered over the abyss of defeat. If it required active US Navy belligerence to prevent Britain's surrender FDR's commitment was complete. Yet, the former assistant secretary of the navy preferred provocation to conflict and had no intention of sacrificing his beloved fleet on the high altar of war expedience. Instead, it was the US Navy that may have been ahead of the president's commitment. But try as it did repeatedly, the Navy could neither manufacture a pretext nor discover an opportunity to "eliminate the threat of attack" in the Atlantic, thus averting that date with infamy in the Pacific.

Chapter Five

Secret Mission to Singapore

Introduction: A Friend in Need

In midsummer 1941, with the new world war almost two years old, Britain had yet to win any significant victories on land or at sea, faring even worse in the fight against U-boats. Wall graphs in the Cabinet War Rooms and the Admiralty spiked like fever charts, telling of ships sent to the bottom loaded with trucks, lubricants, fighter planes, and precious aviation fuel. In June, July, and August, 119 merchant ships were sunk in the North Atlantic, heading to 501 ships for the year. That would be almost a victory when compared to the unsustainable losses in 1942 when 1,322 ships never reached their destinations. Without oil and arms Britain's survival would be measured in months. Churchill followed the dreary daily reports of ship losses like a doctor monitoring a terminally ill patient. Twenty-five percent of the entire British merchant fleet already lay on the ocean floor. The First Sea Lord, Adm. Sir Dudley Pound, said it bleakly: "If we lose the war at sea we lose the war."

In that despairing summer the prime minister yearned for another type of aid as precious as the arms and aircraft in convoys crisscrossing the Atlantic. He urgently needed troop transports. The new Eighth Army neared a desert confrontation with Gen. Erwin Rommel's panzers. Planning a campaign to merge over 220,000 troops from throughout the empire required the movement of entire divisions at one time from British ports to Suez and the Persian Gulf. Britain lacked the large ship capacity to transport troops over vast distances. Only the officially neutral United States had the ability. The butter was being spread very thin; it was time to parley with the president.

Crews of both nations with President Roosevelt and Prime Minister Churchill for services aboard HMS *Prince of Wales*, Atlantic Conference, August 10, 1941. *Prince of Wales* and *Repulse* were sunk four months later. NATIONAL ARCHIVES

THE ATLANTIC CONFERENCE

On Sunday August 3, 1941, the *New York Times* reported FDR's departure aboard the presidential yacht USS *Potomac* for "a week's vacation in New England waters." Instead, unknown to all but a few, the 165-foot-long, 370-ton vessel he regularly utilized for relaxation and fishing became a decoy for transfer to the heavy cruiser *Augusta*, and departure for a secret meeting with Winston Churchill in Newfoundland. The meeting's outcome, to become known as the Atlantic Charter, not only set the course of the war but became the postwar underpinning for the incipient United Nations. It declared the beginning of a new world order to follow the war. The first of twelve wartime meetings between the two patricians and cultural cousins also included a recitation of needs and wants one from the other, but mostly by Churchill from FDR.

Also in secret on the same day that FDR departed on the *Augusta*, Churchill and an entourage of twenty left London on a private train for the seven-hundred-mile trip to Scapa Flow, Scotland, to board the new but already bloodied HMS *Prince of Wales* for the much-anticipated first meeting with the American president. The 43,786-ton battleship had acquitted herself well in the May 24, 1941 tactical victory over battleship *Bismarck* in the Battle of the Denmark Strait. But as the great ship, her 1,521 sailors, and the government delegation threaded around the Orkney Islands into the broad Atlantic, no one envisioned that she had only four months of life remaining. Only three days after the Pearl Harbor attack, not only *Prince of Wales* but the thirty-two-thousand-ton battlecruiser *Repulse* and 840 men from both ships went to the bottom of the South China Sea. The unequal contest, the first between airpower and ship defenses, sealed the fate of the battleship era. Land-based Japanese bombers and torpedo bombers easily destroyed the colossal warships at the loss of only three Japanese aircraft and eighteen lives.

As FDR and his fifteen strategists awaited the arrival of Churchill and *Prince of Wales* in Placentia Bay, the knowledge of Britain's plight must

The Atlantic Conference, the first of twelve meetings between FDR and Churchill, aboard the ill-fated HMS *Prince of Wales*, August 10, 1941. NATIONAL ARCHIVES

have vexed the president like a constant migraine. The war had reached the eleventh-hour for Britain's very survival, its strategic position so dire that the Atlantic Conference could well decide Britain's fate. And how much more time can we buy, the president thought, before it becomes our turn?

The success of the four-day meeting began a mutual respect and friendship between the two leaders that never wavered, although it was regularly tested. After the conference, Roosevelt cabled Churchill: "It is fun to be in the same decade as you." Churchill later wrote about FDR: "I felt that I was in contact with a very great man who was also a warm-hearted friend and the foremost champion of the high causes which we served."

Not on the official conference agenda were other needs regularly intimated by Churchill and the British mission that loitered at the edges of the talks like an unwelcome guest. It was hinted that American troop transports crewed by American sailors were needed, and soon. There could be only one purpose; they were needed to take British troops to war. To the president's relief, at least Churchill didn't openly appeal for American troops to fight alongside the British. Not yet.

The previous year, on May 15, 1940, only five days after becoming prime minister, Churchill already knew his American counterpart well enough to send a telegram listing Britain's "immediate needs." He catalogued necessities that stretched like washing on a line: older destroyers, newer aircraft, steel, antiaircraft guns, ammunition, even a US Navy port call in Ireland, as an unsubtle message to keep the Irish neutral. As fair exchange for the assistance, he offered FDR use by the US Navy of Britain's near-impregnable Singapore naval base "in any way convenient," hoping in so doing to "keep that Japanese dog quiet." Neither leader knew then how soon Singapore would become entangled with the fates of both nations.

A Desperate Message

Two weeks after the Atlantic meeting, Churchill said—referring to the United States—"that those who hitherto had been half blind were now half ready," and sent Roosevelt the first in a series of "Triple Priority" telegrams. Troops were urgently needed to maintain Britain's tenuous position in the Middle East: "Would it be possible for you to lend us twelve United States liners and twenty US cargo ships manned by American crews from early October until February? I know from our talks that it will be difficult to do, but there is a great need for more British troops in the Middle East." The message ended pleadingly: "It is quite true that the loan of these liners would hamper any large dispatch of US troops to Europe or Africa, but as you know I have never asked for this in any period we can reasonably foresee in the near future."

With Churchill's plea to FDR for American ships crewed by American sailors to carry British troops into harm's way, he handed the president a Hobson's choice. If a transparent violation of the Neutrality Act became known by Congress, his presidency would be in peril, but its rejection had equally dire consequences. Britain could lose both Suez and the war, and it would be the United States that history would blame. Yet, helping Britain avert defeat with ships was preferable to giving Churchill American troops, and it would give the United States more time to rearm. In approving the loan of the ships, FDR had a clear conscience, but it had to be done in utmost secrecy.

On September 5, the president replied by telegram. "I am sure we can help you with your project to reinforce the Middle-East army . . . we can provide transport for 20,000 men. These ships will be United States Navy transports manned by Navy crews. Our Neutrality Act permits ships of the Navy to go to any port . . . I am loaning to you our best transport ships." In referring to the Neutrality Act's approvals, the president was being too clever by half. Subsequent legislation allowed the arming of US merchant ships, but neither the original act nor its revision authorized the transport of a belligerent's troops in US ships. The law had to be evaded.

Concocting a diminutive fig leaf to elude the Neutrality Act's remaining provisions, FDR proposed to route the 18th Infantry Division via Halifax instead of from a US port as Churchill preferred, thus avoiding transferring the troops of a belligerent in the port of a neutral country. Churchill replied on October 9: "If you agree, our experts can make a firm programme whereby nine British liners arrive at Halifax with 20,800 men comprising the 18th Division and start trans-shipment to your transports."

Five weeks before Pearl Harbor a top-secret order would send American warships and passenger liners deep into a war zone. The resulting saga would bring the converted liners to within inches of destruction, not by Nazi Germany in the Middle East before Pearl Harbor, but by Imperial Japan in the Singapore harbor *after* Pearl Harbor. The events would develop in the final days of the British empire's last stand in the Far East. Decades later, the eventual eighteen-thousand-mile globe-circling voyage continues as the least known in US Navy annals.

THE GHOST SHIPS OF TASK FORCE 14

On September 26, 1941, Chief of Naval Operations (CNO), Adm. Harold R. Stark sent a message marked "Secret Serial Letter 077388" to the commanding officers of eighteen US Navy ships. "Pursuant to a revised agreement with the British government, Task Force 14 will proceed on or about 3 November 1941 from the United States for the Middle East, via Halifax, Trinidad and Cape Town South Africa, and return to the United States. From Halifax to the Middle East, Task Force 14 will transport one division of British Troops consisting of approximately 20,000 officers and men. While no commitment has yet been made, it is possible that a second trip from Halifax to the Middle East may be authorized." The CNO ended the order with a caution: "Attention is invited to the highly secret nature of the movements and plans of this expedition. Information pertaining thereto is not to be disclosed to other than those immediately concerned with its accomplishment."

At a meeting point in the Atlantic at 0700 on October 30, 1941, British soldiers of the 18th Infantry Division at the rails of nine westbound transports in convoy WS12X watched as the foretops of numerous warships gradually appeared on the horizon. The masts were on American warships, part of Task Force (TF) 14.3, detached from Task Force 14. The task group included the battleship *New Mexico*, aircraft carrier *Yorktown*, and light cruisers *Savannah* and *Philadelphia*, screened by nine ships in destroyer squadron (DESRON) 2. Their orders were to escort the troops to Halifax for immediate boarding on six US Navy transports, three of them hastily converted from ocean liners. With the Pearl Harbor disaster five weeks in the future, TF 14.3 would bring 20,800 troops on a multi-week, seven-thousand-mile voyage to the Middle East and the war. Or so it was intended.

Showing US neutrality, SS *Manhattan* before conversion into troopship USS *Wakefield*. NAVSOURCE

Decades later in London, one of the surviving soldiers of the ill-omened 18th Division related his experience to the author. Snowden "Snowy" Fiskin was one of 5,342 troops assigned to the USS *West Point* (SS *America*), with the remainder of the division billeted on five other transports. A former butcher's apprentice from Watford near London, he and the division expected to fight Germans in the desert. "We trained two years to fight Rommel, and only a madman would have predicted that we would end up in Singapore with little more than our uniform kit." He was part of the 5th "Beds and Herts," the Bedfordshire and Herefordshire regiment, one of six units hastily assembled into the second-line 18th Infantry Division, part of the Territorial Army, corresponding to the US National Guard. "I never saw a bigger or more beautiful ship," he said about the *West Point*. Of the six US transports, *West Point*, *Oriziba*, and *Mount Vernon* were crewed by US Navy sailors. US Coast Guardsmen manned *Wakefield*, *Dickman*, and *Leonard Wood*. A sixty-man Marine detachment guarded each ship.

A LOAN OF AMERICA'S BIGGEST AND BEST OCEAN LINERS

FDR's intent to loan the "best transport ships" became evident in the first sight of the now camouflaged *Wakefield*, *Mount Vernon*, and *West Point*, the three principal ships of United States Lines, with a combined $90 million investment. In prewar commercial service to Britain and the continent, *Wakefield* and *Mount Vernon*, the former SS *Manhattan* and *Washington*, offered transatlantic voyagers moderately priced "cabin-liner" service. Launched in 1931 and 1932 by the New York Shipbuilding Company in Camden, New Jersey, the 24,289-ton identical twins featured steam turbines geared to twin screws, producing an acceptable 20 knots. In promoting the ships, brochures breathlessly advertised: "The maximum in ocean travel comfort. Your stateroom is more than just a cabin—it is a real living room with paneled walls, carpeted floors, and easy-chairs. A scientific ventilating system (you can regulate it yourself) keeps your stateroom at just the right temperature."

The third transport, the 22-knot, 33,961-ton *West Point*, the former ocean liner SS *America*, reigned as the queen of America's seaborne passenger fleet, and the pride of the small company. In commercial service less than a year, at 723 feet long with a ninety-four-foot beam, she carried 1,046 passengers plus crew. Until converted by the US Navy she sailed from Manhattan's Pier 86 to Southampton and Le Havre.

At 0800 on November 10, 1941, TF14 stood fair in the Halifax channel in two task groups (TG), fast and slow. In front, TG 14.1 averaged 21 knots. The slower TG 14.2 trudged ever further in the rear at an average 15 knots, later to dearly cost the unlucky 18th Division. The US aircraft carrier *Ranger* took the lead station followed by heavy cruisers *Quincy* and *Vincennes*. On the flanks, six screening destroyers activated their sonars. The six transports bulged from the convoy's center. *Mount*

Advertisement for America's three most prestigious passenger ships. AUTHOR

53

Vernon's commanding officer, Capt. Donald B. Beary, a 1906 Naval Academy graduate, also had the honorary role of convoy commodore.

Interviewed by the author, John H. Horrigan, then a seventeen-year-old Navy seaman from Weymouth, Massachusetts, manned one of *Mount Vernon*'s newly installed five-inch guns. "During Philadelphia and Boston refits in mid-1941," he said, "they installed a main battery of four five-inch and four three-inch dual-purpose guns, and a secondary battery of 30 and 20mm cannons. Then the British brought four Bofors 40mm antiaircraft guns. We constantly drilled on the guns and felt good about our ability to fight off any attacks."

Underway, the British troops and the US Navy sailors swapped sea stories over smokes on fantails, the vibration of the screws underfoot, foaming wakes trailing behind. They took pride and comfort in the view of the protecting American warships, the stars and stripes extending from the mainmasts, their crews at the ready. But less than one month later there would be no American escorts.

A camouflaged USS *West Point* entering port in New York. NAVAL HISTORY AND HERITAGE COMMAND

At a November 18 Trinidad refueling, *Ranger* and two destroyers departed the convoy as fleet oiler USS *Cimarron* and the British heavy cruiser *Dorsetshire* joined as escorts for the longest part of the voyage, the six-thousand-mile South Atlantic crossing to the Middle East. Aboard *Mount Vernon*, Maj. M. T. L. Wilkinson, commanding officer of the 287th Field Artillery, Royal Engineers, made laconic entries in the regiment's war diary: "15 November—pay parade (they were paid in US currency), lecture by OC (officer in command) on sunburn. Six plumbers extended the salt-water showers and regulated the drinking fountains. 23 November: 'Crossing the Line' ceremony this afternoon. Two British officers were at the initiation. Weapons training on Tommy Guns and discussion of independent Brigade group operations in Libya. Good weather."

On December 1, warned by Ultra intercepts that four U-boats were expected to attack near the island of St. Helena, HMS *Dorsetshire* set off in pursuit, making contact 260 miles southwest of the convoy, dodged two torpedoes, failed to locate the wolf pack, but sank their supply ship, *Python*. The near-contact reminded the convoy of its fate if attacked by U-boats.

The convoy with the British 18th Division and three American converted troopships initially included carrier US *Ranger* and heavy cruiser USS *Quincy*. NATIONAL ARCHIVES

CHAPTER SIX

Fall of the "Gibraltar of the East"

"Now Thank We All Our God"

Now thank we all our God,
with heart and hands and voices,
who wonderous things has done,
in whom this world rejoices;
who from our mother's arms
has blessed us on our way
with countless gifts of love,
and still is ours today
—TEXT, MARTIN RINKART, MUSIC NUN DANKET

INTRODUCTION: THE PEARL HARBOR ATTACK ANNOUNCED

AT 2000 HOURS ON DECEMBER 7, 1941, NEWS OF THE PEARL HARBOR attack pulsed through the task force like heat lightning. Jack Horrigan recalled that the *Mount Vernon News* printed an extra edition of *The Traveler*, the ship's daily newspaper. "FLASH FLASH FLASH—at least two Japanese bombers, their wings bearing the insignia of the rising sun, appeared over Honolulu about 735am Honolulu time. Unverified reports said a foreign ship appeared off Pearl Harbor and began firing at defenses." The war had finally although suddenly arrived. Now the increasingly exposed convoy faced peril from both Germany and Japan.

With war declared, the US Navy escorts were ordered back to the United States or to new escorting duties. The six transports continued

A SB2-U scout bomber over the convoy as it changes from column to line-abreast formation. The two-stack ships in front row are the *West Point, Mount Vernon,* and *Wakefield.* NAVAL HISTORY AND HERITAGE COMMAND

to Capetown on December 13, then to Bombay where *Orizaba, Leonard Wood,* and *Dickman* disembarked their troops for additional training and then returned home. *West Point* and *Wakefield* awaited the reboarding of their troops for what they still thought would be Basra in Iraq, to ready for battle with Rommel's forces in North Africa.

Churchill reacted to the dramatic events that brought America into the war in one of a series of telegrams to Roosevelt: "We feel it necessary to divert 18th Division round Cape in your transports to Bombay to reinforce army we are forming against Jap invasion of Burma and Malaya." FDR penciled a staff note on the margin: "I think OK. Check Army and Navy. Expedite." From the original eighteen-ship convoy now near Cape Horn and the legendary Drake Passage, this left only the three exposed American ocean liners with their troops and no escorting warships, to arrive in Mombasa on Christmas Day, 1941.

ARRIVAL AT THE FICTITIOUS FORTRESS

With the syrupy Kenyan air thick with rumor, the British and Canadian soldiers who embarked in Halifax and the US Navy crewmen traded scuttlebutt about the next port for the now isolated transports. Would it be the Middle East as originally intended, or Australia for more training, or even, some extravagantly daydreamed, back to England? For those who followed the ominous shortwave radio reports, a clearer vision emerged. The three US transports and Maj. Gen. Merton B. Beckwith-Smith's desert-trained and desert-equipped troops were destined instead for Singapore and its equatorial heat, enveloping mangrove jungle, and fetid swamps. Churchill had failed to learn from the sudden loss in the same waters of *Prince of Wales* and *Repulse* on December 10. Believing the island to be a genuine fortress, he concluded that the battle of Singapore could be won.

At 1300 hours on December 29, USS *Mount Vernon*, with the same 5,342 troops who sailed so expectantly from Liverpool and Grennock, Scotland, exactly two months and eleven thousand miles earlier, now voyaged another forty-five hundred miles from Mombasa to Singapore, this time as a hastily assembled, mixed nationality escort with no US Navy warship presence. Lacking confirmation of their final destination, the troops on *Wakefield* and *West Point* were temporarily sent to Bombay. Although soft from inactivity and trained for the wrong war in the wrong place at the wrong time, the 18th Division had confidence in themselves; they could defeat the Japanese and do it quickly. But one in three would never again see England's green hills.

Aboard *Mount Vernon* on Sunday, January 11, 1942, British and Canadian soldiers and American sailors joined at Divine Service to share the spiritual bonds of the old comforting hymn, "Now Thank We All Our God." Unknown to anyone on the Allied ships, at that moment in Singapore eighty-five thousand British, Australian, Indian, and locally enlisted mercenaries were being funneled like water down a spout toward the narrow causeway connecting the Malaysian mainland to Singapore island. As the embattled island drew nearer, the seas calm, the sky a cobalt blue, the convoy passed volcanic Krakatoa Island in the Sunda Strait, crossing from the Indian Ocean to the Java Sea.

Steaming at 15 knots in a single column, at 0630 the next morning the escorting British, Australian, and Dutch destroyers set Condition One full air defense watches and then went to General Quarters. Fort Canning military headquarters radioed at 0907 that ninety Japanese bombers and fighters were over the city headed southward toward the convoy. At 1000, a sudden obscuring squall enveloped the ships in lashing tropical rain. Fifteen minutes later, topside sailors heard the uneven drone of numerous aircraft passing unseen directly overhead. The danger passed without a shot being fired.

Late the next morning, January 13, 1942, *Mount Vernon's* lookouts sighted the 277-square-mile island dead ahead. The convoy's guns saluted the forts, to enter the uncertain embrace of what everyone except the oncoming Japanese knew to be an unassailable bastion, the very symbol of the British Empire and its might.

Mount Vernon's log recorded her arrival in Singapore's Keppel Harbor on Tuesday, January 13: "1214; slowed to one-third speed approaching Singapore dock yard. 1303; landed on pier. 1315; moored port side to dock at Navy Yard, Singapore, Malay Peninsula, with lines 1–8 singled. 1342; secured main engines on 12 hours' notice." Sixty-three days and eleven thousand miles after TF14 and Convoy WS12X departed Halifax, the convoy's first section arrived at Singapore's heavily fortified front door, as the rapidly advancing Japanese troops were preparing to assault its undefended back door.

MYTH OF THE "IMPREGNABLE FORTRESS"

The island bastion celebrated by the British press had been in the bull's eye only minutes after the Pacific war began one hour and twenty minutes before the Pearl Harbor attack, with the Japanese invading by land at Kota Bharu. In repeated prior assessments of Singapore's defenses, military authorities expected invasion from the sea, allowing for only modest land defenses. Instead, it came by land from the northwest. As the French had prepared for the wrong war, so too had the British prepared for the wrong invasion.

The nine- and fifteen-inch guns in the three forts and twenty-seven batteries had the ability to traverse 180 degrees, but were of World War

I vintage, and were allotted only thirty armor-piercing shells each. The celebrated defenses intended to repel a naval assault were ineffectual against invasion by land. If Singapore held out for 180 days, each gun could fire only one shell every six days. For all the defense they offered, the casemates could have been fortified instead with telephone poles. The "impregnable fortress" became the great myth.

As the 18th Division prepared to disembark, the mostly unopposed invaders were averaging nine miles for every day of the campaign, existing on bags of rice, living off the land, pedaling bicycles through the rubber plantations, and had already claimed half the peninsula. That same day, Japanese troops approached ever closer to the new $100 million naval base, the largest in the British Empire, with twenty-two square miles of deep-sea anchorage, dockside cranes able to lift a gun turret, and a floating dry-dock towed from England that could enclose the largest warships. The immense dry-dock could contain the *Queen Mary*—and did twice—in February and March 1941, to install guns on the sun deck and for engine maintenance. British newspapers boasted that the dry-dock could hold sixty thousand people, and that oil in the base's storage tanks could refuel the entire Royal Navy in one operation. Along with its European and Asian professional staff, the twelve thousand employees made the base Singapore's largest employer. The enemy would soon enter underground stores crammed with munitions, take for themselves food set aside for three months of siege, operate the precision tools, enter barracks built for thousands of troops, and casually walk into churches, cinemas, shops, and seventeen football fields.

The island city of one million reeled from daily, nearly unopposed air attacks. Rubber, sugar, and timber godowns (warehouses) dissolved into smoldering heaps. Shattered oil and gasoline dumps blew dense smoke sky-high, becoming beacons for waves of Japanese bombers. Destroyed water mains allowed fires to spread throughout the city center, the panicked residents rushing to the Empire Docks for what they prayed would be deliverance. The disembarking 18th Division would enter a disorder swiftly plunging into outright chaos.

As a Territorial Army, the ranks of the 18th contained storied units representing British regions and towns, such as the Sherwood Foresters, Royal Norfolk, Royal Suffolk, Bedfordshire Yeomanry, and Royal Northumberland Fusiliers, many in existence for hundreds of years. But Snowy Fiskin remembered decades later that as a forward-deployed desert division in the tropics with few supplies and equipment, they entered battle with little-more "than the shirts on our backs."

As slender opposition to the invasion faded, the disembarking troops saw dogfights overhead, perhaps a hopeful sign. But a ragbag remnant of obsolete Australian and British Brewster Buffalos, a few Lockheed Hudsons, three lumbering Consolidated Catalinas and open-cockpit Vickers Wildebeest biplanes, were no match for 459 Japanese first-line fighters and bombers. The proud RAF, so stalwart at home, were *hors de combat* in Singapore. A stingy prewar Whitehall government had cut back to the basics and now paid the piper. "I never saw a British plane the entire time I was there," Snowy Fiskin said. Yet, there were airfields aplenty; twenty-three in all, although fifteen of them had grass runways that became muddy messes in the tropical climate. It didn't matter; there were so few aircraft to occupy the airfields, the runways could have been used to grow vegetables. The few antiaircraft batteries were carelessly sited in places where they had the least effect and had limited ammunition. Futile ground to air, air to air, and ground to ground communication became the failed outcomes of rivalries between the military branches. And there were no tanks to block the final sixteen miles between Johore and Singapore. As if it mattered.

To patrol the vulnerable harbor and shoreline, the Royal Navy could muster only six mechanically unsound wooden boats. The sixty-foot craft lacked any armament, slow-walked at 4.5 knots, and had a turning radius of 150 yards, more akin to a warship than harbor craft. Each three-man crew—a coxswain and two mechanics—had never even glimpsed a marine engine. And the Royal Navy liaison officer assigned to the 18th Division couldn't read nautical charts; he wore the insignia of an army ordnance officer.

By 1400 on January 13, as *Mount Vernon* urgently refueled and reprovisioned, the 53rd Infantry Brigade and 287th Field Company Royal Engineers departed the ship into the teeth of a driving tropical rain, marching to the abandoned position of an artillery battery. Finding the battery deserted, they continued in the general direction of the front, wherever it was. They were the only British troops to reach the Malayan mainland.

As the 155th Field Regiment left the ship at 1600, *Mount Vernon*'s luck almost ended. Decades later, George Ramos, a US Navy seaman from Imperial Beach, California, a telephone talker on the bridge, recalled the terror of watching forty Japanese warplanes come directly at his ship. "We actually counted each plane and watched the leader drop his bombs," he said. "All the others followed suit. Six bombs exploded only 100 yards away in a pattern the exact length of the ship." After the near-miss, the 5th Battalion, Royal Norfolk Regiment had the doubtful distinction of being the last to leave, accompanied by shouts of "good luck," "good hunting," and back slaps from the US Navy crew they would never see again.

With troops leaving the ships and evacuees waiting to board, *Wakefield*'s blessings ended. Lookouts spotted two bomber groups with twenty-seven aircraft in each formation, each group unimpeded by either antiaircraft fire or British fighter planes. A rain of bombs shrouded the waterfront as a single 250-pound bomb struck *Wakefield* abreast the number two hatch, penetrating three decks to sickbay.

Seaman 1st Class John J. Jordan, twenty-one, a Coast Guardsman on *Wakefield*, made a later diary entry: "An awful mess. Medicines spilled over, strong smell of chemicals; bunks twisted and torn, bedding and furniture blazing; bulkheads were blown wide open and others bulged like sails in the wind. Water up to our knees. I saw the bodies when they found them. I felt sick and wanted to cry at the same time but couldn't do either."

Interviewed by the author, 97 years old in 2018, the former US Navy Pharmacists Mate Second Class and USS *Wakefield* survivor, Marshall Doak, had clear memories of the attack. At General Quarters on the ship's fo'c'sle and knocked unconscious from the explosion, his best friend was among five killed. "I could see them heading directly for us, about twenty-seven in two groups. I went to the battle-dressing station and helped with giving morphine syrettes to the most seriously

Shrapnel kept by Marshall Doak from the Japanese attack on USS *Wakefield*. AUTHOR

burned, but I can still hear their voices." (Doak placed a fist-sized piece of shrapnel from the bomb in the bottom of his seabag, to present it seven decades later at his home in St. Joseph, Michigan, as a mournful memory of the attack.)

With the Japanese in sight of the causeway leading to the island, they could almost see the stacks on the two giant American ships, perhaps anticipating the immense propaganda value of their capture or sinking. But as the invaders crossed to the island the next day, *Wakefield*, able to jury-rig repairs, let go all lines, cleared the submarine net, rang the engine rooms for full speed ahead, to arrive in Colombo, Ceylon (Sri Lanka) on February 6, 1942, then to anchor at Suez on February 7.

Good fortune also stayed with *West Point*, the US Navy's largest and most active troop transport. Replenished with 362,970 gallons of bunker oil and 350 tons of fresh water, at 1511 on January 15 she cleared the Changi buoy, to disappear into the enfolding smoke and haze. Unluckily for the throngs on the dock yearning to escape aboard one of the American liners, the Singapore authorities allowed only 1,946 officials and refugees to leave the dying city on *West Point*, a ship with more than three times greater passenger capacity. Although the three American transports made good their escapes from Singapore, for the despairing thousands remaining on the pier or in the city, forty-three months of cruel captivity or death awaited.

USS *West Point*. (SS *America*) safely carried over 350,000 troops in every war theatre. NAVAL HISTORY AND HERITAGE COMMAND

SUNK WITHIN VIEW OF THE DOCKS

A final desperate effort to avert defeat in Singapore began from Bombay on January 23, with the dispatch of thirty-eight hundred British soldiers on four ancient steamers with a six-warship escort. They expected to reinforce the island's besieged troops and yet win the battle of Malaya, insurmountable odds to the contrary. Reaching Singapore on February 5, their arrival only further added to the reign of terror soon to engulf everyone; the surging Japanese 25th Army were now less than twenty-five miles from occupying the island.

One of the ships in the rag-tag relief convoy, the converted liner *Empress of Asia*, the most essential vessel in the convoy, had been chasing the 18th Division for almost fourteen weeks. She carried a critical consignment—almost all the 18th Division's supplies that should have arrived three weeks earlier.

On the steamy morning of February 5, convoy BM 12 entered the Banka Strait at the Sultan Shoals Lighthouse near the harbor entrance, the Keppel docks invitingly near. Nine Japanese dive-bombers suddenly appeared, aiming for the luckless *Empress of Asia* that had fallen behind other convoy members. Her long voyage began in Liverpool on October 28, 1941. Launched in 1913, at seventeen thousand tons, the Canadian-Pacific steamer had supplies stacked to the gunwales. Targeted by nine Japanese dive-bombers, the weary *Empress* went to the bottom with all the kit intended for the 18th, but with the loss of only sixteen of 1,808 soldiers. The rescued troops would soon face another unexpected threat.

On January 30, the 2nd Battalion of the decimated Argyll and Sutherland Highlanders, one of the few British units trained in jungle warfare, had retreated four hundred miles to the island's single entry and exit, the causeway connection with the mainland. The Argylls lost eight hundred soldiers in the fighting withdrawal. Their commanding officer, Lt. Col. Ian Stewart, and the regimental pipers were the last British troops to cross to the island. A final, sad bagpipe skirl carried across the jungle murk as sappers blew a sixty-eight-foot gap in the eleven-hundred-yard-long causeway, destroying railroad tracks, a lift bridge, and a pipeline carrying water to the island. To slow the Japanese but with little result, as they retreated Royal Engineers dynamited over one hundred bridges. The naval base and the city became as impotent as the fable spun in Whitehall about the "Gibraltar of the East." Another myth ended that day: the invincibility of European soldiers over the "little men" of the Far East.

On February 10, Prime Minister Churchill, still believing that Singapore's defenders were greater in numbers and better equipped than the Japanese, sent a final critical cable to Field Marshal Archibald Wavell, commanding Allied forces in Southeast Asia. "There must at this stage be no thought of sparing the troops or saving the population. The battle must be fought to the end at all costs. The 18th Division has a chance to make its name in history. Commanders and senior officers should die with their troops. The honour of the British Empire and of the British Army is at stake. I rely on you to show no mercy to weakness in any form."

Churchill had it half-right. Lt. Gen. Arthur Percival's eighty-five thousand British, Australian, Indian, and Malayan volunteers numerically did surpass Gen. Tomoyuki Yamashita's thirty thousand soldiers, overlooking that the Japanese general's troops were battle-hardened from four years fighting the Chinese. They were also better equipped, easily adapted to jungle warfare, and had the advantage of maneuver, speed, and surprise. Most importantly, they had close air superiority. The minimum six months expected for Singapore to resist invasion before relief arrived lasted only seventy days.

The Japanese troops had another advantage unknown to Western thought; they lived by the code of Bushido, "the way of the warrior." First came duty, honor, sacrifice, the emperor being accorded the devotion of a god, with honorable death to be desired. The Western armies were degenerate and materialistic. In their long and mostly isolated history, Japan had never lost a war. Not yet.

SURRENDER, STARVATION, AND DEATH

On February 14, having repaired the causeway and well advanced on the island, Japanese troops were seen moving up from Ayer Rajah Road near Alexandra Hospital, the main British military hospital. Marked with red crosses and with no armed defenses, it was deemed a safe space. A British officer approached carrying a white flag of truce, to be immediately bayoneted to death. The soldiers swept through the hospital bayoneting anyone in view, including fifty doctors, nurses, even patients on operating tables. Another group of 150 staff separately surrendered, to be marched along a railway track into three small buildings. The prisoners' hands were tied, with windows and doors barricaded and nailed. Pressed tightly against each other, unable to sit or breathe, many died overnight from exhaustion or asphyxiation. The next morning Japanese troops opened the doors, allowed the survivors to exit, then bayoneted them to death. A shell struck one end of a building allowing a fortunate few to escape and later attest to the massacre at Alexandra hospital.

At 0930 on February 15, General Percival met with his officers at Fort Canning to discuss whether to surrender or continue the fight. Little food or ammunition remained. Rioting and fires were rampant in the city center. Desertions buckled the increasingly panicked Allied ranks. Heated debate concluded with a decision to surrender. A British deputation displaying a white flag and the Union Jack went by car toward the enemy lines. The Japanese demanded that General Percival personally surrender the garrison.

Around 5:00 p.m. that evening, General Percival and three aides, one carrying a white flag, another holding the Union Jack, entered the new Ford factory to sit at a conference table in the boardroom. General Yamashita and his staff arrived in a black sedan thinly camouflaged with palm fronds across the roof. Japanese cameramen filmed the surrender. Speaking through an interpreter, Yamashita forcefully demanded: "Will you surrender unconditionally?" Percival began conferring with his staff. Yamashita interrupted, pounding his fist on the table: "Will you surrender unconditionally, yes or no?" Softly, General Percival said a simple, "yes."

AFTERMATH

For the Japanese, a daring land campaign that extended over 650 miles of mostly dense jungle from Singora, Thailand, to Singapore, became one of the war's major victories and the greatest loss in history for British arms. Only three understrength divisions defeated the world's greatest empire. Most of the Allied troops, including the 18th Division, never fired a single bullet. Nissan Motor Co. converted the Ford factory to manufacture military vehicles. The battle cost the Japanese only thirty-five hundred killed. Churchill never overcame the loss. When told about the surrender he later wrote, "I had to put the phone down and was glad to be alone."

In a campaign that was all defeat for the Singapore defenders, the British, Australian, Indian, and Malayan forces lost seventy-five hundred killed, ten thousand wounded, with 130,000 taken prisoner including eighty thousand British and Australians. On February 28, 1942, after the sinking of the USS *Houston* and HMAS *Perth* in the Battle of Sunda Strait, 368 American and an additional 307 Australian survivors joined the other captives.

Building the 258-mile Burma-Siam "death railway" and its 688 bridges took the lives of 6,904 British, 2,802 Australians, and 133 Americans. Another twenty thousand died in "hell ships," the Japanese transports that brought prisoners to Japan as slave laborers in mines, railways, and shipyards. Allowed neither food nor water, the prisoners were crammed into sunless and airless holds, unable to sit or breathe. None of the transports were marked with red crosses, although other Japanese transports carrying war supplies were deceptively painted with red crosses and allowed to proceed by the Allies. Unaware of the priceless human cargo in the transports, American submarines torpedoed and sank many of the "hell ships."

After the war it was estimated that four of every ten prisoners in Singapore and the Philippines died from torture, malnutrition, dengue, beri-beri, malaria, tropical ulcers, pellagra, diphtheria, scurvy, dysentery, cholera, starvation, and exhaustion. For uncounted thousands, only death liberated them from the unending deprivations and atrocities. In comparison, Allied forces taken prisoner by Germany died at a rate one-seventh of the Japanese toll.

General Yamashita fought again, this time against the Americans in battles to retake the Philippines, to survive the war but much longer than that. Before the December 7, 1945 pronouncement of death by an American tribunal, he wrote an extraordinary admission: "My attack at Singapore was a bluff—a bluff that worked. I had 30,000 men and was outnumbered more than three to one. I knew that if I had to fight longer I would be beaten. That is why surrender had to be at once. I was very frightened all the time that the British would discover our numerical weakness and lack of supplies and force me into disastrous street fighting." Yamashita's small army had outrun its supplies and had only two days of food and ammunition remaining when Singapore surrendered. Not knowing Yamashita's bluff cost the British the battle, the island, and the empire. But the Japanese tide of victory had already reached its high-water mark.

Sixteen weeks after the fall of Singapore, in the Battle of Midway on June 4, 1942, one thousand miles northwest of Honolulu, the US Navy sank four Japanese aircraft carriers and one cruiser. Sunk were the same aircraft carriers that began the Pacific war on that day of infamy, December 7, 1941. The US Navy lost the carrier *Yorktown* and destroyer *Hammann*. The epic battle stopped the Japanese advance across the Pacific. Before Midway it was all loss; after Midway it was all victory.

REMAINS OF THE BATTLE

Fort Siloso on Sentosa Island, operates as a museum open to the public, with the only remaining coastal gun battery, ammunition bunkers, barracks, and tunnels. The separate Fort Canning "battlebox" has the same twenty-six-room underground command center never used in combat. Alexandra Hospital is part of the National University of Singapore Medical School. Changi was both a prison and a place where most of the British and Australian POWs were confined, until moved to other locations later in the war. Changi was demolished in 2000, but the original entry gates and one wall through which POWs entered were made part of a new prison.

In 1947 the Ford factory, the first such facility in Southeast Asia, resumed the assembly of vehicles, until closing in 1980. Much of the interior was later demolished for condominiums, leaving the original façade and part of the remaining interior as a war museum and exhibition gallery. The surrender table in the intact former boardroom is in the Australian War Memorial in Canberra. Seven of the room's teak chairs are in the Fort Siloso museum.

Portions of the Thailand/Burma "death railway" can be seen on tours from Bangkok. "Hellfire Pass," the twenty-four-foot-long, fifty-six-foot-high solid rock, which the POWs cut through by hand for the rail tracks, is a highlight.

During prewar preparations, the Imperial Japanese Army staff told General Yamashita that he could have only five divisions for the assault on Singapore. "No, four will be enough," he said. He did it with three.

THE BRIDGE ON THE RIVER KWAI AND WAR CRIMES

No bridge passed over the Kwai river at the location depicted in the award-winning film, *Bridge on the River Kwai*; however, two bridges, one made of wood, known as Bridge 277, and the other of steel and concrete were built by POWs over the Mae Klong River. Allied bombing destroyed both bridges in two attacks, with the steel and concrete bridge rebuilt by the POW's. The same bridge continues in use with train tours from Bangkok, and with visits to other sites associated with the notorious railroad, including the infamous Hellfire Pass rail cutting. The nearby

Kanchanaburi War Cemetery has the graves of 6,982 British, Australian, and Dutch POW's. The remains of 133 Americans who died at the hands of the Japanese from the 368 who survived the sinking of USS *Houston*, were repatriated to the United States.

The POWs who died in building the Burma/Siam "death railway" were buried where they died, with the prisoners documenting their names and death locations. After the war, all but fifty-two grave sites were found.

Australian war crimes tribunals indicted 924 Japanese, with 644 convicted and imprisoned, and 148 sentenced to death. On February 23, 1946, a still defiant General Yamashita, his clemency appeal rejected by the US Supreme Court, walked up thirteen steps to the gallows and death by hanging at the former Los Banos prison camp.

Chapter Seven

From Sea to Shining Sea— The Unknown Odyssey of the SS *America* / USS *West Point*

On a bright Thursday morning in late August 1939, First Lady Eleanor Roosevelt and a small entourage entered the Presidential Suite at Washington, DC's ornate Union Station. The private waiting room, designed to resemble her husband's Oval Office in the White House, had regular use by the president before his departure on numerous rail trips. On this day, it gave seclusion to Mrs. Roosevelt before she boarded the Chesapeake and Ohio's *George Washington* for the four-hour trip to Newport News, Virginia.

In anticipation of the event that would finally give the United States an ocean liner to compete with the finest in the world, the dense crowds awaiting her arrival at the ferry terminal station stretched to the extending 550-acre Newport News Shipbuilding and Drydock Company. In an era when only ships connected to the world beyond the seas, major and minor countries built their own "ships of state"—luxurious floating representations of a nation's pride in its accomplishments. The United States would finally have its own symbol of greatness, the SS *America*, and it would be built in an American shipyard.

Among the world's celebrated prewar passenger liners, Cunard White Star Line's eighty-two-thousand-ton *Queen Mary* had its maiden voyage May 27, 1936, the same day that the company approved construction of the *Queen Elizabeth*, to first sail in 1940 as a troopship. Voyaging between Le Havre and New York, French Lines had the art deco *Ile de France*, and the most elegant of all, its flagship *Normandie*, rated as the most refined way to cross the Atlantic. In 1938, Holland America Line's *Nieuw Amsterdam*, "the ship of tomorrow," featured Murano glass fixtures, ivory walls, columns covered in gold leaf, highly polished satinwood furniture, two swimming pools—inside and out—and the unusual feature of a private bath in every first-class cabin, but not in the other classes. The fifty-five-thousand-ton German twins, *Bremen* and *Europa*, efficient products of North German Lloyd, received the Blue Riband trophy for the fastest speed afloat, needing only five days between Hamburg and New York.

On this day the new ship's namesake nation would launch its own ocean-going symbol of influence and majesty, proudly displaying a red, white, and blue livery on rakish twin funnels. (The designer of America's largest merchant ship to date, noted naval architect William Francis Gibbs, would plan hundreds of warships during the war.) In a first for any shipping company, *America*'s twenty-three public rooms and 395 staterooms in three classes were designed by women, the New York firm of Smyth, Urquhart, and Marckwald.

As described in the sales brochure, designers emphasized a more refined décor, deliberately ignoring the opulence of her more famous competitors. Wall murals in the first-class dining room displayed the skylines of New York, London, Paris, and San Francisco. "In this beautiful air-conditioned dining room," enthused the sales brochure, "you will satisfy the hearty appetite that brisk sea air and your daily activities will stimulate." The two-deck high dining room featured "a series of unique carved lacquer murals representing the scenery—flora and fauna—of geographic regions of the United States." In another departure from tradition, colors in public areas and cabins were a light "streamlined modern," with indirect lighting replacing the chandeliers common in other ocean liners. A two-deck-high first class main lounge had "two tones of beige in the thick pile carpet, pale creamy beige in the lacquered walls, bronze in the metal leaf ceilings and light brown in the natural walnut of the furniture. This room is also used for the showing of pre-release motion pictures, horse racing, and bingo games. Chairs are of a highly polished ebonized wood," the brochure enthused, "and are covered with plain beige pile fabric. A dark brown floor is inlaid with a large design of squares in beige." The new Lucite and aluminum accented cabins in all classes. A reviewer rhapsodized that the furnishings "shared a similarity with the slick stage sets of a Ginger Rogers, Fred Astaire film."

As the time for *America*'s launch arrived, Eleanor Roosevelt, surrounded by flower bouquets, filmed by newsreel photographers, and broadcast live by radio stations WGH and WRVA, energetically swung the tethered and wrapped champagne bottle to burst white foam against the black hull, the crowds cheering as the band played. As the last supporting timbers were knocked away from the hull, the 35,440-ton liner slid down the ways for final dockside fittings. The next day everything changed forever. At 2:50 a.m., September 1, a transatlantic telephone call awakened the president. The call from William Bullitt, ambassador to France, said that Hitler had attacked Poland. World War II had begun.

Although behind all major and most minor military powers in overall war readiness, as a seafaring power the United States had not neglected its maritime capabilities. In 1936, FDR established the US Maritime Commission as an auxiliary naval force to requisition merchant ships in a time of national emergency. SS *America* became the first of a nearly unimaginable 5,777 ships of every type in World War II to be chartered, requisitioned, or built by the commission. The government subsidy came with a provision that fittings, such as self-contained compartments, separated engine rooms, and magnetically operated fire doors, would be part of the construction, allowing for faster conversion into a troopship. Two years before he became ambassador to Great Britain, Roosevelt appointed Joseph P. Kennedy to be the Maritime Commission's first chairman.

As Europe slid into all-out war while the United States grappled with neutrality and isolationism, *America*'s expected itinerary also changed. The now hazardous circuit of New York, Southampton, Le Havre, and back to Manhattan's Pier 86 instead became sedate cruises to Bermuda and the Caribbean. The $30 million ship's peacetime Atlantic crossings wouldn't begin for another six years. Yet, there were risks in the Caribbean, although not as intense as in the Atlantic. U-boats regularly sank crude oil tankers and shelled oil refineries on the Dutch island of Aruba. To deter opportunistic U-boat attacks, large American flags and the name *United States Lines* were painted on the port and starboard hull. For good measure, her sides were brightly illuminated at night. *America* had no incidents during her time cruising the Caribbean, but no one could have foreseen how often she would confront impending catastrophe in each of the war years ahead.

On June 1, 1941, the US Maritime Commission made good on its subsidy requirement by appropriating *America* for the US Navy and changing her name to USS *West Point* (AP 23). Six months before the nation went to war, the sophisticated ocean liner returned to the Newport News shipyard to exchange red, white, and blue livery for camouflage gray and conversion into a troopship. Most of the staterooms were removed, fittings stored, and the comfortable 1,843 peacetime capacity expanded

Before sailing to glory as USS *West Point*, SS *America* was the country's premier ocean liner. NAVAL HISTORY AND HERITAGE COMMAND

to 7,678 troops and their equipment crammed into every possible space. Windows and portholes were painted over, with rafts fixed to the sides as a replacement for lifeboats in davits on the boat deck. Gunners mates trained on newly installed five-inch antiaircraft, four-inch naval, and eight .50-caliber machine guns. A degaussing strip to repel magnetic mines girdled the hull below the surface. Because of her prewar fittings, the conversion took place in only eleven days.

Life Aboard a Troopship

The well-being of the country's most important war asset, her fighting men, had top priority aboard ship. For *West Point*'s many overseas deployments to every war theatre, troop organization and control began at the gangway. Struggling up the narrow walkway, soldiers followed one behind the other, balancing one-hundred-pound duffle bags, rifles, packs with bed rolls, steel helmets and other gear, then threaded through passageways, hatches, and up or down narrow ladders to a preassigned berthing area. Assisted by signs and guided by ship's personnel, a card given to each soldier had directions to a sleeping location and assigned sleep time. All had been issued lifejackets and told that abandon-ship drills would be frequent. Hundreds of troops were billeted in the former ballroom and mezzanine, some with "standee" bunks, others on canvas-backed, five-high, aluminum-tubed "hot bunks," each rack separated by a mere sixteen inches. Large commercial galleys and new meal areas replaced the passenger kitchens. Over twelve hundred men per hour had assigned meal times on a specific chow line, with two hot meals daily. With few seats or tables on the mess deck, troops usually ate standing, as they steadily moved along a chest-high table, cleaning their empty mess kits at the opposite end.

Navy chow may have been indifferently accepted, but it was plentiful. Bakers removed twenty-five hundred loaves of bread from the new commercial ovens every twenty-four hours. What the sailors called "gedunks" or shipboard canteens sold the troops "pogey bait," candy, gum, and cigarettes for fifty cents per carton, limit two. Red Cross personnel aboard often distributed free cigarettes. Cokes were inexpensively available. *West Point* and other troopships, especially the converted ocean liners, even had ice cream machines, although available only at special times. With weeks at sea ahead and knowing little about their destination until later in the crossing, the troops constantly drilled and exercised on the weather decks, but also had time to watch boxing matches, or even jitterbug with each other to the sounds of swing from musical ensembles within their own ranks. They played craps, acey-deucy, blackjack, and poker, and being healthy young men, they consumed forty thousand pounds of food daily. Recently released 16mm movies were shown on large screens mounted on the fantail, and then swapped with other ships after docking. Several troopships, including *West Point*, had rotating USO groups, even movie stars such as Red Skelton as entertainers. The men kept current both about the war and the home front from the mimeographed news posted daily. Despite these distractions, boredom also shipped out with the troops on the long voyages over unchanging slate gray or sapphire blue seas. The troops were also absorbed in what warriors have done throughout history—they griped about everything, including the rock-hard soap, saltwater showers, and Navy chow. They laughed when "Axis Sally," the German propaganda voice who was actually an American, claimed once again that *West Point* had been sunk. All would change soon enough. One day someone would shout, "land ahead."

After their escape from Japanese bombs during Singapore's dying days, *West Point* and *Wakefield* brought their refugees to another uncertain fate in Batavia (Jakarta) in the Dutch East Indies, itself under punishing Japanese attack and soon to surrender. Unable to land their human cargo, *West Point* instead embarked more escapees and headed for what they hoped was a safe port in Colombo, Ceylon (Sri Lanka). A priority message caused another change of plans. Two Japanese submarines were active along the charted course and had sunk six mixed nationality ships in the past forty-eight hours. That meant a two-hundred-mile course change through the narrow Sunda Straits. Then everyone grinned when word was passed about another passenger added to the manifest—a newborn baby boy.

In 1942 *West Point* steamed back to Australia, then to Christchurch, New Zealand, New York, Halifax and Liverpool, then back to New York. She then cast-off for Rio de Janeiro, Bombay, and Melbourne, then back to Melbourne with 7,478 Marines to end the year. That year, she steamed

Laden with nine thousand victorious troops, USS *West Point* docks in New York.
NAVAL HISTORY AND HERITAGE COMMAND

99,830 nautical miles with 113,786 GIs. In 1943 she transported 113,786 troops across 216,000 total miles. In 1944, with 117,300 troops staging for the invasion of Europe, she repeatedly crossed the Atlantic from Boston, New York, and Newport News to Liverpool, or Greenock and Gourock in Scotland.

When *West Point* or any troopship docked at a British port, at least twenty trains waited under steam to transport the GIs to towns near hundreds of US bases sprawling over the British countryside. It seemed that almost the entirety of England had been converted into a series of vast bases, with masses of troops already in place and thousands more arriving daily. If America had lacked the advantage of Great Britain being converted into the equivalent of an enormous fixed-in-place aircraft carrier, the rescue of the old world by the new world might have begun on American shores. If Germany had defeated Great Britain, America would first have liberated a devastated Britain before invading

Europe. The war would have extended into 1947 and beyond. Britain's survival changed the strategic conduct of the European war.

Beginning with the first meeting and transfer of British troops in Halifax on October 30, 1941, to the Japanese surrender on September 2, 1945, *West Point* participated in every theatre and major campaign in the war. From March 12 to 25, 1942, she carried 5,364 Marines from Suez to Freemantle and Adelaide in Australia, to begin the long way back from the defeats that began the Pacific war. This led to August 7, 1942, when the First Marine Division went ashore on the four islands that were part of the land, sea, and air Battle of Guadalcanal. The six-month campaign caused sixty-eight hundred Marine and twenty-four thousand Japanese casualties. In a series of associated sea battles, the Japanese lost two battleships, four cruisers, one aircraft carrier, six submarines, and eleven destroyers, at a US Navy loss of eight cruisers, two aircraft carriers, and fourteen destroyers.

From the same Newport News docks where SS *America* was built, on January 3, 1945, *West Point* embarked the 85th and 87th regiments of the 10th Mountain Division, the famed "soldiers on skis," arriving in Naples on January 13. One month later in Italy's Apennine Mountains, the thirteen-thousand-man division began a night assault on Riva Ridge, climbing two-thousand-foot vertical cliffs with ropes and pitons. A second night assault fought entrenched Germans with bayonets on Mount Belvedere, the highest peak in the mountain range. After winning both battles, the division remained in combat for 110 days until the end of the European war, at a cost of 992 killed and 4,154 wounded, a casualty rate of 40 percent of the entire division.

LAND OF THE FREE

In one 1944 crossing, constantly changing course and almost always traveling alone, *West Point* carried a record 9,305 troops. In 1945, with over twenty round-trip crossings, she surpassed all previous records with 184,097 passengers, including sixteen thousand GI patients returning for care in US hospitals. After bringing US troops over, she brought back scores of thousands of German POWs, thanking providence for the rest of their lives that Americans captured them and not the Red Army.

In fifty-five months of service to her country *West Point* never needed major repairs and never lost a single soldier or sailor. As the largest of 358 US troopships, she carried the most troops and passengers (505,020), sailed the most miles (436,144), to make 151 voyages between 1941 and 1946. She became the only ship of any type in the war to serve in every war theatre—South Pacific, Asiatic, African, Middle East, and European.

On January 15, 1946, her final cruise as a US Navy ship brought *West Point* from Boston back to the South Pacific, from where she had narrowly escaped four years and hundreds of thousands of miles earlier. From Manila, she transported 7,737 souls, many of them recovering POWs, beginning a nine-thousand-mile journey back to New York and the world they left, a world many thought they would never live to see again. Disease and deprivations took the lives of one in three American prisoners in the Pacific Theatre. Many of the British had been captive up to two years longer than the Americans and were at the start of their return.

Home of the Brave
From her beacon-hand

> *Glows world-wide welcome; her mild eyes command*
> *The air-bridged harbor that twin-cities frame*
> *"Keep ancient lands, your storied pomp," cries she*
> *With silent lips. Give me your tired, your poor,*
> *Your huddled masses yearning to breathe free,*
> *The wretched refuse of your teeming shore.*
> *Send these, the homeless, tempest—tost to me*
> *I lift my lamp beside the golden door.*
> —EMMA LAZARUS, *THE NEW COLOSSUS*

On the evening of February 2, 1946, the last night at sea, the men said their farewells, made promises to stay in contact, packed what little they had, and went to sleep earlier than usual. The next morning, just after sunrise—and they had been talking about it for days—there would be a view and a memory to be treasured for the rest of their lives.

Around 7:30 a.m. on Sunday, February 3, they crowded the bow and every open deck space. The excited talk dropped to near-silence as the ship passed the glinting red Ambrose Lightship, turning for the Lower Bay and the Narrows into the Upper Bay and the Hudson River docks. They weren't looking for the docks.

Someone saw it first on the port side. Appearing out of the mist and then enlarging and taking shape and form and meaning, it was suddenly there and real. What it meant is what they had fought for, and even the strongest who survived against all the odds and adversities in history's greatest war gripped each other, wept, and didn't even push away the streaming tears. They were home.

The SS *America*'s first class gala banquet menu cover on her final voyage as a US flag carrier. AUTHOR

AFTERMATH

Nearly a generation later aboard the *America* it was another 7:30 a.m., this time in late September, 1964, and another sailing past Lady Liberty into New York harbor. The farewells had been said at the gala banquet the evening before, and almost everyone pressed to the portside for the same views that the "huddled masses" and the GIs and refugees had seen. It was also the last day the great ship would sail under the banner of United States Lines. Her larger and faster big sister, SS *United States*, continued the tradition of Atlantic crossings in the struggling final days before jet travel condensed into five hours what steamships accomplished in five days.

The author and his wife were among those searching for the first view of the colossal copper work, having vainly sought shipboard reminders in recall of *America's* earlier fame as the heroic troopship that overcame the dangers of war. As the great statue came into view, the author's hand gripped a mahogany handrail on the boat deck. Preserved along the railing were the names, initials, dates, and pen-knife carved hearts of those who had arrived before: the GIs and refugees, orphans and immigrants, silent witnesses all to valor, sacrifice, and salvation.

CHAPTER EIGHT

Bletchley Park: The Secret War

In wartime, truth is so precious that she should always be accompanied by a bodyguard of lies.

— WINSTON CHURCHILL

INTRODUCTION: THE BEGINNING OF MODERN COMPUTING

IN HIS SIX-VOLUME MAGNUM OPUS, *THE SECOND WORLD WAR*, CHURchill gave no hint as to the existence of the historic discovery. In fear of a lengthy prison sentence under the Official Secrets Act, or because of patriotism, the twelve-thousand-member Bletchley Park staff who revealed the secret remained silent for decades. In thousands of books written about the war, nothing was said about the unceasing exploitation of Nazi Germany's primary means of secret communication. Until the British government permitted its disclosure in 1974, few knew the significance of what took place at "Station X," the code-name for Bletchley Park (BP). Only at the very summit of wartime British and American leadership were commanders told the secret and then given only partial access to its revelations. Even within the hurried activity of Bletchley itself, only four on the staff had full details of top-secret Ultra, the breaking of the Enigma cipher. Until Churchill's higher designation of "Ultra" to identify the breaking of Enigma, previous high-grade intelligence had the label of "most secret." Along with the development of the atomic bomb, unraveling the Enigma device became the greatest secret of World War II, although the Ultra secret continued to be unknown for three decades after the end of the war.

Bletchley Park, where twelve thousand codebreakers revealed the secret of the century. AUTHOR

Until the 1970s, those passing near the run-down scatter of crude "huts" that began only steps from the Bletchley Park rail station saw only another of many temporary wartime bases awaiting demolition. They didn't know that what happened inside won the war in 1945 instead of 1947.

BEGINNINGS

In 1918, German electrical engineer Arthur Scherbius began development of an electro-mechanical "cyphering typewriter" for coded transactions between financial institutions, confidential uses by business and industry, and for secret government correspondence. The first model, an improvement of a 1917 product by American Edward Hebern, resembled a clumsy cash register including a handle, and had four rotors driven by four geared wheels. Pressing any key on a standard German typewriter keyboard moved a disk or rotor that partially turned a wheel, in turn, advancing the wheel to a different position to show a different result with each movement. Press the letter A and L resulted. Press A again and T displayed. The keys were arranged in three rows to total twenty-six characters, comparable to present-day keyboards. Each wheel had gaps in its teeth at different positions. By pressing any key, the four drive wheels moved each of the rotating disks into a different position. As one of many internal complications, each rotor paused when encountering a gap in a wheel and could be set at a different position for each action by the operator. Later battery-operated models had built-in electrical circuitry that returned or "reflected" back the entry along a different pathway, thus further scrambling the original entry.

An input operator arranged the settings order from a frequently changed code table to enter a message in the original German. Enter "ZWEI" (two) and the cipher text might display DWNM, or anything. The enciphered message then became part of a telegram, later a radio transmission, in standard Morse code sent to a receiving operator. The operator first input the prearranged settings order, then entered the received cipher text to view the recovered plain text. Although complex, so far its functions were sufficiently rational to expect that with trial and error enciphered messages could be broken. But its intricacies were only beginning.

Although logical in its input and outcome function, for codebreakers seeking insights into its ways, Enigma became an infernal and demonic device in its internal operation. Because the rotor of an entered key wouldn't return to its original position for thousands of entries, each entry therefore would not be repeated for thousands of additional attempts. With the addition of a plugboard—a mini switchboard—on the device, the progressions only increased the repetition of key entries into the scores of millions, greatly growing the number of unrepeated changes. As would confound the BP codebreakers, to understand the Enigma variations one had to know that what happened internally between the input and the output is what mattered, and it would either produce a solution or it wouldn't.

Even with three US patents, Scherbius had only modest success with the first three models, the first weighing a portly 110 pounds, but he had sufficient confidence in its eventual acceptance to exhibit an improved Model C at the 1923 Congress of the International Postal Union in Bern, Switzerland. After many variants, the size and weight of later models took on the appearance of an oversized portable typewriter, with an illuminated panel instead of paper displaying results. Set within a lacquered wooden box with a hinged lid, the name "ENIGMA" proudly embossed into the cover, Model D became the most successful of the commercial models. After further transformations, it became the first of many military versions.

To promote the device, Scherbius printed a two-page flyer, with orders taken at his office, Shiffriermaschinen Aktiengesellshaft (Cypher Machine, Inc), at Steglitzer Strasse 2 in central Berlin. Advertising assured the buyer of a machine "unassailable in its cypher security . . . every attempt at a solution wastes time . . . cannot be operated if improperly used . . . can be used after only 30 minutes' instruction . . . any one of the 227,304,461,200 (sequences) can be input in half a minute." And it now weighed only twenty-six pounds.

Enigma's early success received acclaim from at least one foreign army to become a future adversary. Captain Henri Koot, a Dutch army cryptologist expert wrote: "I dare say that it satisfies all requirements, be they ever so high, even in the possession of an equal machine with the same electrical connection . . . it will not enable an unauthorized person to find out its solution." A German military that had earlier rejected Enigma as having no widespread use now intended it to be the principal means of secret communication within the rapidly expanding Luftwaffe, Wehrmacht, and Kriegsmarine. Enigma's most successful uses were just ahead.

THE GIFT THAT KEPT GIVING

For examination in early 1928, the Warsaw customs office impounded a shipment from Germany labeled as containing radio parts. Fearing discovery, the German firm's Warsaw representative repeatedly demanded its immediate return to Germany without a customs inspection. This caused speculation as to its contents, and an examination by twenty-seven-year old Polish mathematician and cryptologist, Marian Rejewski. Before returning it to Germany, his detailed notes and diagrams yielded nothing less than the internal wiring of the Enigma device. Rejewski,

Entrance to the mansion's converted ballroom where the BP hierarchy, including Alan Turing, had meals. AUTHOR

a civilian employee of the Polish General Staff Cypher Bureau, began examining Enigma's inner workings in 1932, and by 1939 had six working copies of a separate deciphering machine, called for mysterious reasons a "bomba." It produced limited solutions to Enigma messages on perforated paper known as "Zygalski sheets." With war near and lacking further scientific and technical resources, after seven years of keeping the secret to themselves the Polish General Staff decided to share the high-value data with their British allies.

On July 25, 1939, two intelligence officers and cryptanalysts, Alastair Denniston and Alfred Dillwyn "Dilly" Knox, alighted from a train in Warsaw's Central Station for a crucial meeting with French and Polish cipher experts. The meeting at the cipher bureau would be the only time that Polish, French, and British cryptology experts met before or during the war that began five weeks later. The British already knew the meeting's potential but couldn't know that what they were given would mean victory instead of defeat in the looming war.

Both Denniston and Knox were veterans of London's secret intelligence group known as Room 40, located in the Old Admiralty Building on Horse Guards Parade. From World War I signals interception experience, they knew how to gather and use enemy intelligence. Denniston had been the first head of the Government Code and Cypher School (GC&CS), to later evolve into the Government Communications Headquarters (GCHQ). The Polish passing of Enigma's complex circuitry schematic, along with details about the "bomba" deciphering machine, saved months of false starts and dead-ends for the BP codebreakers. With plans in hand, the British would have the same knowledge that the Poles had taken years to acquire. They would comprehensively inspect the inner workings of the mysterious machine inside the lacquered wooden box, and in time all would be known.

———

PART ONE

THE SECRET OF THE CENTURY

My geese that lay the golden eggs but never cackle.
—Winston Churchill (Referring to Ultra)

In 1997, the author traveled from London's Euston Station past Harrow, Apsley, and Cheddington to a deserted station at a quiet rail junction forty-seven miles northwest of the city. Directly across the street and almost buried under untrimmed vines, a narrow lane outlines rusty barbed wire tacked on tilting concrete posts leading to a barrier with a rusting sign and the warning: "Government Property. Unauthorised Entry Prohibited." Two hundred yards past the fence, a large, spreading, red brick mansion hulks in late Victorian vulgarity.

Beyond and around the house, in various shapes, sizes, and degrees of deterioration, gradually appear the nondescript, flat-roofed buildings that their long-gone occupants called "huts." The temporary structures had been scattered without plan, but with immense and immediate purpose, across fifty acres of the estate's once refined lawns. Some huts had portions of exterior blast walls; others had long strips of peeling paint on warped surfaces. Most were built with pine or raw brick, some more complete than others, the windows covered with boards, the roofs with asphalt sheets, the interiors stripped of furnishings, everything hollow with neglect.

Known as Station X, hiding in plain sight during the war and for decades after, it became the least known but most vital location in Britain, and for a time the sole sentinel between victory or defeat. Within its thin walls, the presumed to be impenetrable Enigma device eventually surrendered all its secrets.

The odd-bodies and boffins summoned to Bletchley to penetrate Enigma's mechanical and electronic armor were a curious lot, even by the droll British standards of the time. There were mathematicians, musicians, language teachers, and German language speakers, tweedy dons from Oxford and Cambridge, linguists, and pedagogues from newspapers, publishing houses, museums, and rare bookstores. Crossword-puzzle experts, hieroglyphics translators, philosophers, and chess-masters completed an eccentric aggregation.

Originally part of a three-hundred-acre purchase by London financier Herbert Leon, sixty acres were set aside as a country estate, with an approximately thirty-thousand-square-foot two-story mansion built in 1883. Passing through different owners added a servants' wing, stables, ice house, a new entrance hall, library, ballroom, and more bedrooms. Midway between Oxford and Cambridge, fertile ground for codebreaker recruitment, the location made it ideal for future clandestine use. Across the road, the mainline Midland & Scottish Railway connected Bletchley to the entire rail network, with the nearby A5 highway as another essential transportation link for what would soon begin. After government purchase of the estate in 1938, an inspection group in the guise of "Captain Ridley's Shooting Party" pronounced the house and location as ideal for the headquarters of Station X, with every corner and crevasse soon pressed into urgent use.

The quickly built huts varied in appearance and purpose. AUTHOR

Charles Langbridge Morgan, an early cryptanalyst, later wrote: "Like many other recruits I heard of the job through a personal introduction—advertisements of posts were at that time unthinkable . . . I took an entrance exam which had been devised by Oliver Strachey, a former member of MI 1B, and included a number of puzzles, such as filling-in missing numbers in a mutilated newspaper article and simple mathematical problems calling for nothing more than arithmetic and a little ingenuity." Morgan went on to write eleven novels, three plays, and published poetry and essays. After codebreaking at Bletchley, Strachey, a brother of the writer Lytton Strachey, went to Ottawa in December 1941 to develop the Canadian equivalent of BP. Whatever the previous occupations of this new generation of cipher scientists, the Bletchley codebreakers faced a daunting task; they needed to think irrationally.

Unlike in the First World War, secret messages no longer resulted from humans using code words. Bletchley's unorthodox ensemble first had to learn a new language: how to organize a muddle of incoherent letter groupings into a semblance of consistency, and then make lucid an ever-changing confusion of letter combinations.

In overcoming every obstacle to attain a goal many thought impossible, at first the codebreakers solved a trickle of only fifty messages each week from fifty thousand encrypted messages sent by the entire Nazi military and civilian leadership each day. By 1943, the trickle became a torrent of solutions of three thousand daily decrypts, with the two-hundred-person staff exceeding eleven thousand. When human means became inadequate, electro-mechanical systems adapted from the Polish "bomba" machines and renamed "bombes" were installed. When the slow, geared, bombes fell behind, Colossus, a sixteen-hundred-tube electronic programmable computer, reputedly the world's first, reliably read enemy encoded messages at speeds of up to two thousand characters per second. Even the privileged messages between Hitler and his military and civilian leadership were read with ease, sometimes hours before they reached Rommel, Guderian, or Göring.

Supporting the codebreakers were layers of typists, file clerks, radio-intercept operators, translators, machine technicians, mechanics, dispatch riders, telegraph and radio operators, cooks, guards, typex and teleprinter operators, messengers, and drivers. Even homing pigeons were pressed into service. As the war progressed, so did the enemy's abilities advance to further muddle for codebreakers the workings of an ever-improving Enigma. An entry on only one of the keys now wouldn't repeat itself for seventeen thousand entries. Even more daunting, when the enemy changed the key's starting positions, and then augmented the device with a *steckerbrett*—a plugboard with twenty-six lettered sockets and interchangeable insulated wires—up to 159 trillion starting positions were possible. Adding interchangeable rotors with sixty more settings produced 7,576 more rotor positions, further confounding the complexity given to the codebreakers to decipher even one message.

The naval Enigma, the most difficult to unravel, had up to eight spare rotors. Combining three rotors from a set of six with the additional variations possible from the plugboard gave Enigma approximately 159 quintillion (one followed by eighteen zeros) different settings. During the time when the added complications tormented the codebreakers, it at least had the benefit of reassuring the Germans that Enigma remained unassailable. Now convinced of the device's invulnerability against cyberattack, the German high command, *Obercommando der Wehrmacht*, furnished at least one machine to every ship, U-boat, air and naval base, to Organization Todt, the civilian construction arm, to army groups and divisions down to the company level, and to *Gestapo* and SS headquarters. Even the still punctual railway system had its own Enigma network. By the end of 1942 at least 100,000 machines were in use. Enigma operated until the last day of the war, the high command unwavering in its belief that the "thousand-year Reich's" continuity had been safely entrusted to a machine. From the enemy input operator through the entire chain of command, Enigma's presumed invincibility and the mulish Nazi belief in the inability of Allied codebreakers to penetrate its defenses remained unchanged throughout the war.

BREAKING AND ENTERING—INSIDE ENIGMA

For a German operator to send a ciphered message and for a receiving operator to decrypt the same message, an intricate process began with picking the indicated rotors, followed by setting the rotor order and ring

Codebreakers at Bletchley using manual methods. AUTHOR

settings (*ringstellung*). Then came the exact order of plugging (*stecker*) into the lower panel plugboard (*steckerbrett*). The rotor start positions (*spruch-schlussel*) were assigned from printed code books changed monthly. Each military sector had a unique network with individual procedures and code-names. For added security, the rotors were switched every eight hours.

MAKING THE BOMBE TICK

Inside Bletchley's bombe huts, an eight-hour-on, eight-hour-off watch included periods of concentrated tension as operators first plugged a bombe in the hope, but by no means the certainty, of learning Enigma's rotor order. They also needed to determine the starting position and how Enigma had been "steckered" or plugged by the enemy operator into one or more of twenty-six A–Z plugboard sockets. Then they sat at the machines, tried to shut out the heat and noise of the grinding gears in what they called—out of earshot of supervisors—"the hell-hole," and waited for it to stop.

A bombe's limited abilities meant that it functioned only as a mechanized means to search for logical and repeated consistencies or uniformity in an Enigma message. As a mechanical tool, it lacked the ability to make numerical or mathematical calculations as did a computer. But with luck the bombes were capable of furnishing hints or "cribs," potentially leading to an Enigma setting for a twenty-four-hour period.

After about eighteen minutes a whirring and clanking bombe came to a shuddering stop, with a relieved "job's up" call from a watchful Wren. It meant that a "crib" had resulted, potentially leading to an entry but not a decrypt, into an Enigma's rotor order, start settings, and stecker positions. After analysis in another hut or in the mansion, a "crib" could lead to a "menu"—a diagram showing the relationships between letters in the crib. Converted into an electric circuit, an operator "plugged-up" the menu with corresponding cables inserted into sockets behind the bombe. It could lead to the clue needed to penetrate a network or a single device. From an office in Hut 8, Alan Turing developed a working hypothesis to learn the symmetrical relationship of the letters in a menu. By diagramming how they related to each other it could lead to a "good stop"—the rotor order and input settings aligned—or a "false stop" when the settings were wrong. As codebreaker skills improved, a growing database revealed the fatal flaws in Enigma's design, and even more errors in its use by the enemy.

In considering the possibility of a compromised system, German engineers constantly expanded and multiplied the increasingly tortuous ways to deceive the codebreakers. This included changing key entries every twenty-four hours or varying sending frequencies during the same message. Cryptanalysts expected changes; with ten bombes operating and their numbers increasing, it only meant added adjustments and more searches to learn entry keys.

The thousands of intercepts that fed the hungry machines originated from a chain of thirty-two coastal and even more overseas Y or listening stations. At the stations, operators intently listened and noted the ten-to-twenty-second transmissions from U-boats to their headquarters in Lorient, France. Deliveries of the handwritten intercepts from the Y

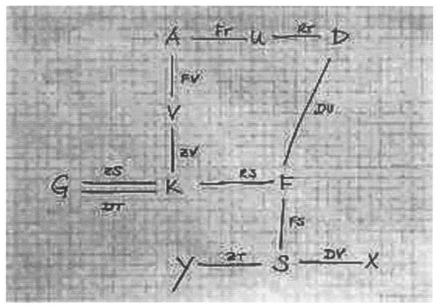

A BP "menu" as a guide to plugging a "bombe" leading to a possible solution.
AUTHOR

Three-rotor Enigma and front plugboard to produce 159 million starting positions.
AUTHOR

stations to BP were first made by motorcycle couriers, and later through secure landlines and teleprinters. After initial sorting, messages went to specialized huts such as ones analyzing U-boat intercepts. Millions of index cards with scribbled cribs and menus were filed in ever-higher stacks for later second-looks or comparisons. With only one of the bombes checking five hundred thousand daily Enigma rotor positions, breakdowns were a regular occurrence. Engineers standing by knew how to adjust machine tolerances, and replace or repair wiring, a relay, rod, rotor, drive cams, gears and wheels, terminals, connectors, switches, or the drive motor. As designed by mathematician masterminds Alan Turing and Gordon Welchman, each of the two hundred bespoke bombe units came from the British Tabulating Company in Letchworth, Hertfordshire. As more bombes were added more BP outstations opened, including in Wavendon, Adstock, Gayhurst, Eastcote, and Stanmore.

DAILY LIFE FOR THE "SECRET LADIES"

Women outnumbered men eight to one at BP, traveling by bus or bicycle to and from billets in private homes or hotels within a twenty-five-mile radius. The lucky ones were assigned to stately homes vacated for the duration, including Woburn Abbey, residence of the Duke of Bedford. Others lived in drafty cells above crossroad pubs. Roommates spent the war together without knowing each other's duty station, or what was taking place at the opposite end of their hut, or on the other side of a wall, or even at the next desk. Everyone signed the Official Secrets Act. Divulge anything about Ultra, even after the war, and death could result.

Working conditions in the huts were wartime spartan, with plank floors, trestle tables, poor lighting, constant drafts, and small oil stoves for area heating. The uniformed services of Army, Navy, and Air Force wore no distinguishing badges or markings of rank. An admiral looked like a seaman, although the wise ones knew better. When on duty, the women Wrens wore flat shoes, dark hose, Royal Navy–blue serge skirts cut just below the knee, and long-sleeved, rolled to the elbows white shirts with dark blue ties. When turned-out on parade, they added double-breasted blue serge jackets with plain brass buttons, and smart berets. The civilian staff dressed casually in tweeds and corduroy. Interviewed by the *London Telegraph* in 2010, former BP Wren, Joanna Chorley, then eighty-eight said: "You knew the work was worthwhile, but it was challenging and there was always a sense of urgency and a need to get things done as quickly as possible."

Distractions and relaxation also had their place. Regular three-to-five-day leaves made possible overnight trips to London on the adjacent rail line. Numerous clubs attended to interests in drama, bridge, dance, and, of course, chess. Lifelong friendships were made. Romance resulted in more than a few marriages. Many other men and women met years later, to learn that each had been stationed at BP at the same time but never met. During a rare visit, Churchill met off-duty staff on the lawn outside the mansion headquarters. With unaccustomed humility, he called the codebreakers "my geese that lay the golden eggs but never cackle," and ordered the building of tennis courts that remain today.

DINNER WITH A CODEBREAKER

Not long after declassification of the Ultra secret, the author had dinner in London with one of the Bletchley Park "secret ladies" and her husband. Betty Warwick (nee Boyd) volunteered to be a Wren in 1943 at age nineteen. Her father had been assigned to 630 Fifth Avenue in New York, the British Security Coordination (BSC) headquarters of Intrepid, William Stephenson. From August to July 1944 in BP's Block F, she sorted and prioritized miles of incoming tape for winding on Colossus, considered to be the world's first semi-programmable computer, and then delivered its decrypts to various huts. "I lived at Woburn Abbey with other Wrens.

Rebuilt from notes and spare parts, "Colossus" at Bletchley Park, the first electronic codebreaking machine. AUTHOR

We never spoke of our assignments; our friends didn't ask, and our parents didn't know, including my father who was himself involved in espionage." Reflecting as if from a long distance she said, "I never wanted to learn what was taking place there, but I did know that it was important to the war effort. To this day, I know very little about Bletchley."

Margaret Mortimer (nee Broughton-Thompson), another Wren technician at BP, remembered the effort needed to operate Colossus at the correct belt tension. "We had to be at least five feet ten to reach high enough to wind the tape around the maze of pulleys. When the whole thing was put into motion, there was much clicking and whirring and heat from all the valves (tubes)." She also remembered the Americans at BP, one being Army captain Elmer A. Van der Wall. He enjoyed special popularity with the women, especially when he came on duty with unobtainable treats, such as a pair of black silk stockings or Nescafe.

PART TWO

THE AMERICAN BOMBE PROJECT AND LORENZ

On July 8, 1942, with an improved version of the same bombes as at BP and other locations in Britain, the US Signals Security Agency (SSA) began decrypting cipher traffic at Arlington Hall, an appropriated girls finishing school at 11 S. George Mason Drive, in Arlington, Virginia. One of two US bombe locations, its codebreaking staff quickly grew to fifty-seven hundred civilians and 2,250 military personnel, including one thousand WAVES.

After each twenty-minute "bombe run," a WAVE gave the printed result to a supervisor who logged the decrypt, then sent the crib by pneumatic tube to cryptanalysts located in Building Two. As at Bletchley, none of the WAVES knew how or if their efforts related to the cryptanalysis process and were also silent about their work to the end of the war. But they also knew that by May 1944 most of the once-feared U-boat fleet had been sunk. The joint Army and Navy intelligence units eventually moved to Fort Meade, Maryland, to form the nucleus of the present-day National Security Agency (NSA).

In late 1943, after initial training at Arlington Hall, Bletchley welcomed the first contingent of American codebreakers. The eighty-five officers and enlisted men of the 6813th Signals Security Detachment served alongside their British counterparts in Huts 3 and 6 as technicians, signals analyzers, and cryptanalysts. As with BP's military their uniforms had no designation of rank, with American personnel given the same billets and tasks as the British. Several would later advance from the obscurity of Bletchley to well-known positions. William Bundy became a Defense Department official and CIA analyst under John F. Kennedy. Lewis Powell became a US Supreme Court justice. Telford Taylor became chief counsel at the Nuremberg war crime trials and an author. None ever spoke in public or published details about the Ultra secret.

A second US codebreaking facility and recipient of the first US bombe operated from the US Navy Communications Annex on Nebraska Avenue in Washington, DC. As an improvement on the British design, the National Cash Register Co. (NCR) built 121 American units in Building 26 at their large Dayton, Ohio, campus. Mounted on pairs of two-wheel casters, each unit weighed five thousand pounds at seven feet high, ten feet long, and two feet deep. By February 1944, approximately three thousand WAVES were stationed at the Annex. With overall direction by Joseph Desch, director of NCR's Electrical Research Laboratory, Alan Turing made two consulting trips to the top-secret NCR facility. As with the BP staff, the US personnel were told that violation of their oath of secrecy could mean the death penalty for treason.

HITLER'S CIPHER MACHINE—THE "SECRET WRITER"

Seeking a way to use a wireless teleprinter as a cipher machine, in 1940 the Berlin-based Lorenz company developed an improved version of Enigma called *"geheimschriber,"* or "secret-writer," a high-grade cipher device limited to the highest ranks of the German leadership. Lorenz AG, one of Germany's largest electrical manufacturers, had experience making telephone and telegraph equipment for the World War I German military.

It operated independently as a subsidiary of its American parent, International Telephone and Telegraph Co. (ITT). The SZ40/42 and later models had twelve rotors, each with twenty-three to sixty-one unique positions and 501 cams or "pins," each operating separately. The device attached to an in-line military grade teleprinter, to randomly insert on perforated paper tape pseudo or virtual characters mixed with the intended message. To send a message, the outgoing operator connected his unit to the circuit and entered the key settings. The message received by the incoming operator had no relationship to the original text. In its function, Lorenz had the same features as Cold War spy favorite, the "one-time pad."

By 1942, Lorenz became the principal manufacturer of high-grade intelligence equipment for the German military. Instead of using the German twenty-six-letter alphabet, Lorenz utilized the thirty-two-symbol Baudot Code, with an output over five channels of data bits or "impulses." With each letter separately encrypted, messages went over twenty-five different frequencies, the sending operator changing frequencies at least once during transmission. Trusting in its infallibility, Hitler's signature began to appear on many Lorenz-generated messages. For weary BP codebreakers, the added complexity meant the need to learn how to decipher another six billion (one billion is a thousand million) starting positions on the revolutionary device.

As with Enigma transmissions sent with Morse code, Lorenz messages also had fatal flaws. The codebreakers quickly found one. Early in its use, an enemy operator sent parts of the same message twice, which meant that he also repeated the same start position both times. Both the sending and receiving operators then needed to identically reset the message start positions, giving BP the all-important start order. By unknowingly changing parts of the original text, the sending operator then made another major error in the same message. This made it possible to compare both messages side by side, and in two months discover its internal configuration. The breaking of Lorenz, the war's major advancement in signals intelligence, allowed the codebreakers to inspect and defeat a device they never saw using the skills of another innovative strategy, the Colossus programmable, electronic, digital computer, that in postwar years became the portal into a new world of personal computing.

ENTER COLOSSUS—THE WORLD'S FIRST
PROGRAMMABLE COMPUTER

Before a Lorenz transmitted message could be deciphered, it first had to be recovered. To intercept and read the decrypts, BP developed a project code-named "Tunny." To receive the Lorenz-produced messages required that six hundred operators listening on thirty receiving radio sets were ready inside an expanded Y station at Knockholt in Kent. Their single assignment: constantly test twenty-five frequencies; wait for the distinctive sound or pulse indicating the sending of Lorenz-originated communication; then intercept the average ten-second message and dispatch it by motorcycle couriers to BP. (As the war progressed, delivery changed to teleprinters over secure landlines.)

Many of the Y station operators were amateur radio enthusiasts, who took time off from other duties or leisure time to volunteer their skills. With headsets tightly pressed against their ears, they had to overcome interference common to radio messages, including in-out fades, whistles, static, storms, electronic jamming, and normal sounds such as music or dialogue. If they missed only one pulse, it would corrupt the entire message.

Utilizing the slow and imprecise bombes would never succeed in deciphering Lorenz messages. A battle would be over or a ship sunk long before a bombe would decrypt a message. To decipher Lorenz a much faster entry into the "secret writer" labyrinth had to be devised.

Over a ten-month period at the General Post Office (GPO) Research Station at Dollis Hill in northwest London, engineer Tommy Flowers and mathematician Max Newman designed and built the prototype of an electronic deciphering computer of such extraordinary abilities that an awed BP staff called it a "colossus." Revolutionary in appearance and operation, it had sixteen hundred vacuum tubes or valves in the first version, increased to twenty-four hundred for the nine operating copies built by 1945. Custom designed to decipher Lorenz messages, Colossus stood seven feet high, seventeen feet wide, eleven feet deep, weighed two thousand pounds, and consumed eight kilowatts of power. On February 5, 1944, it began operating with immediate results. Lacking a stored-memory capability, it optically read five thousand characters per second from eight photo-cells. Operators monitored a paper tape transport that whirred around, over and under pulleys at thirty miles per hour, looking and sounding like a game in an amusement arcade. When the cycle finished, results were printed on an IBM electric typewriter.

For more than thirty years after the war, the existence and historic success of Colossus remained as secret as the other BP accomplishments. This gave the 1945-completed, eighteen-thousand-tube ENIAC, the thirty-ton US Army computer invented to calculate ballistic tables, an unearned distinction. Instead of Colossus being hailed as the first electronic computer, ENIAC received the tribute of being the first of its type, while Colossus developers suffered in government-mandated silence. For decades it had no reference in works describing the history of computing, or its essential contribution to winning the war.

PART THREE

ALAN TURING—THE ENIGMA

Peculiar practices clung to Alan Turing like layers of moor mist. To his Bletchley Park colleagues, he was "the Prof," often seen distractedly hurrying to or from the mansion and Hut 8, the section struggling to break the German U-boat cipher. To his neighbors in nearby Shenley Village, he was the odd one on the bicycle who wore a gas mask to and from work, the best thing for relief of chronic allergies, he believed.

Iconoclastic and contradictory, he avoided eye-contact with fellow codebreakers who considered him to be eminently mysterious and unapproachable. Few would know of his achievements in his lifetime, but in the last years of the twentieth century the fundamental logic of the Universal Turing Machine—central to the science of computing—would finally confer on Alan Turing the long-delayed recognition as "intellectual father" of the modern computer and artificial intelligence.

His mind constantly occupied itself with calculation. In determining that a loose bicycle chain would come off after fourteen turns, he would stop to adjust the chain after thirteen revolutions and then continuously repeat the process day after day. For him, this was merely a practical application of the same logical deduction needed to solve the Enigma riddle. The chain of inferences necessary for breaking Enigma ciphers led to either a contradiction (you were wrong and moved to the next position on the rotor), or a confirmation as the likely letters became words and then a solution. Scientists used the same method in determining the probability of any assumption: observe, question, and conclude.

Alan had few friends, stammered in speaking, and had unrefined manners. His mother regularly wrote reminders to buy items of basic apparel. "Buy at least one suit a year," she prompted. His

Alan Turing, at home only in his world of numbers and computing. AUTHOR

trousers were held up with string, and he often wore a pajama top under his jacket. Fearing that Britain would lose the war, he converted most of his funds into silver ingots, buried them, and then forgot their location. The more discerning of his Hut 8 colleagues saw deeper personality layers of subtlety and erudition, although it was difficult to understand the need to attach his tea mug to a radiator pipe with a combination lock.

Oft-repeated anecdotes about the Prof's peccadilloes leavened otherwise somber conferences in the mansion, where most of the senior administration had offices and ate in the large dining room. His parents had learned to accept the eccentricities, concluding that his genius far surpassed the peculiarities. Years later, his mother marveled, "at twelve and a half he was trying to learn organic chemistry all by himself."

Born in Paddington, London in 1912 to Julius Turing and Ethel Sara Stoney, his English parents met and wed in India. The senior Turing worked for the Madras civil service; his mother was the daughter of the Madras railroads chief engineer. Until Julius retired in 1926 when the couple returned to Britain, Alan and his brother were raised in a series of English foster homes. Disconnected from family and with few friends, Alan wrote his mother that he was "hopelessly miserable" as he began

studies at Sherborne, a private boys' boarding school in northwest Dorset, England.
At Sherborne he became a marathon run-
ner, leading to acceptance by classmates and
faculty, and built a replica of the Foucault
Pendulum in the dormitory stairwell.

Awarded a major scholarship to King's
College, Cambridge in 1935, he read the-
oretical mathematics and became a Cambridge Fellow. Brilliance in chess made him
a two-time British chess champion, helped
by devising two notable strategies: "The
Dutch Defense," and "The Petroff Defense."
In 1936, he presented his first paper, *On
Computable Numbers*, to the London Mathematical Society. It proved the theory that
some mathematical problems were inca-
pable of solution by using fixed, formal

Alan Turing comfortable in his
world of numbers but seldom
anywhere else. AUTHOR

processes. Instead of proving the evidence with a formula, Alan verified
the theory by proposing an abstract "universal computing machine." The
unconventional and original "machine" had a head and moveable paper
tape divided into frames, not unlike a roll of film. He showed that the
head acted as a scanner and could be preprogrammed with instructions.
Each frame had a symbol, such as a 0 or 1, or could be left blank. Each
square could be separately read, the paper could be moved left or right,
and the symbols changed, rewritten, or erased.

With its function of program input, output, memory, and the suggestion of information processing, the visionary automatic problem-solving
theory defined in every way—except by name—the operating system of
a modern digital computer. At age twenty-four, he had unintentionally
advanced the principles of the "analytical engine" proposed by Charles
Babbage in 1833, affording insights into the new world of computing
that he would never know.

After two years in America to earn a Princeton PhD, war clouds were
gathering when he returned to Cambridge in July 1938. On September

4, 1939, the day after Britain declared war on Germany, Alan reported to BP during the darkest period for British intelligence. Not one Enigma-ciphered message had been solved in almost ten months. The U-boat menace had grown from one submarine in 1935 to fifty-seven at the outbreak of war. Britain could not long survive if the sea lanes were not made safe. But with Turing's arrival the codebreakers had an immediate advantage: During the initial assault on Enigma's riddles, he was BP's only mathematician.

One sleepless night he composed in his mind without paper or pencil a palindrome that astonished Hut 8 colleagues who were competing to devise the longest set of words in a sentence reading identically backwards or forwards: DOC, NOTE: I DISSENT, A FAST NEVER PREVENTS A FATNESS. I DIET ON COD.

To solve Enigma, he reapplied existing mathematical principles to create a mechanized approach to tease out the "probable words" common to all secret messages, even those enciphered on Enigma. These included reports by U-boat commanders to headquarters, such as, "need fuel," "nothing to report," "engine problems," and weather reports, ships sunk, and other words used in sentences. Soon after Alan's arrival, the bombes went from decoding only fifty messages a week in 1940 to three thousand per day in 1943.

After the war he quietly returned to academic obscurity, accepting a position at the National Physical Laboratory in London to design an electronic computer based on his Universal Turing Machine. In 1947, he resumed the King's College fellowship, began research into computer development at Manchester University in 1948, and in 1950 developed the "Turing Test," the game to forever link him with the origins of the fast-developing science of artificial intelligence. At the dawn of the computer age, Alan Turing had become accepted. Then it suddenly ended.

A LIFE CUT SHORT

In Manchester on February 11, 1952, he was arrested for "gross indecency with a nineteen-year-old male person." The same draconian 1895 ordinance used to imprison Oscar Wilde had brought Alan's long-closeted private life into public view. In lieu of two years in prison, he agreed to a course of "organo-therapy"—chemical castration with female hormones. He wrote hopefully to a friend: "It is supposed to reduce sexual urges whilst it goes on, but one is supposed to return to normal when it is over. I hope they're right."

With the disintegration of his life almost complete, his government security clearance removed, and his reputation in tatters, on June 7, 1954, the housekeeper found him dead at age forty-two at home in Wilmslow, near Manchester. A partially eaten cyanide-laced apple lay next to the bed. Loyal to the end, his mother insisted that it was an accident. The national press took little notice. Misunderstood in life, neglected in death, he left a legacy that included unfinished works on plant life, artificial intelligence, physics, and computer theory. Almost a century after its formulation, his Universal Turing Machine, the mathematical equivalent to a digital computer, continues as the most widely used model to understand the origins of mathematics and computer science.

PART FOUR

THE SPIES AMONG US

A curious coda completes the Bletchley saga. In 1942, Kim Philby, one of five members in the notorious Cambridge-based spy ring, applied for a position at BP. Found to be deficient in analytical skills, he instead advanced to positions of increasing importance in British intelligence, while also acting as an undercover "mole," an NKVD (later KGB, now SVR RF) double agent. In 1946, Philby married Aileen Furse, the second of four wives and one of Bletchley's "secret ladies." In the most intimate of relationships, she never told the secret of the century and he never knew. But another spy penetrated Bletchley's layers of secrecy much more successfully.

In 1942, John Cairncross, the elusive "fifth man" in the Cambridge spy ring called the "magnificent five" by the KGB (the others were Kim Philby, Anthony Blunt, Don MacLean, and Guy Burgess), arrived in Hut 3 to analyze Wehrmacht and Luftwaffe decrypts. After a stint in the Foreign Office in 1936—receiving the highest test scores—he was then recruited by the NKVD and given the code name Liszt. For most of his one-year BP assignment, using a fluency in German to aid in message decrypts, Cairncross also had an active second life as a spy. He covertly removed Enigma solutions being organized for destruction by hiding them in his trousers. At the Bletchley train station after duty hours, he transferred the paper strips to a bag, and then boarded a London train to meet Yuri Modin, his KGB controller. (In 1994, Modin wrote *My Five Cambridge Friends*, crediting the Cairncross-developed intelligence as the most reliable.)

The Cairncross-produced decrypts, all resulting from Lorenz intercepts, included the location of Luftwaffe airfields in Russia, and plans for the summer 1943 Battle of Kursk, the largest armored clash of the war. Its loss cost Germany the strategic advantage of forward movement on the Eastern Front, a defeat from which they never recovered. German losses included 250,000 men, one thousand tanks and assault guns, and at least 850 aircraft. The decrypt delivery earned for Cairncross the postwar Kremlin Order of the Red Banner.

After the war and two years of investigation by MI5 and MI6, Britain's domestic and international counterintelligence services, Cairncross admitted to spying, but on the advice of his Soviet control confessed to only a careless handling of classified material and was never prosecuted, but lost his professional reputation. The KGB archives later verified that Cairncross gave Moscow Center 5,832 documents stolen from Bletchley Park.

With financial help from Moscow, Cairncross moved to Chicago and a position at Northwestern University as an expert in Romance languages and the works of Pascal and Molière. He then relocated to Rome for a United Nations position. There, in December 1979, journalist Barrie Penrose knocked on his door. The unexpected interview became a confession and front-page news exposing his role as a Soviet undercover agent at BP. He died in 1995, after penning a memoir published after his death, openly telling his role as a spy. Although he never knew how Colossus operated or the purpose of the other huts, he had deeply penetrated Bletchley and the reason for its existence, leading to the belief by some that the British government covered up his role.

PART FIVE

ULTRA'S WAR-WINNING LEGACY

Months before the D-Day landings, the Colossus revelations armed Eisenhower with crucial intelligence describing with precision enemy plans, positions, and intentions for the battle ahead. The Nazi high command, as unknowing about the Allied exploitation of Lorenz as they were with Enigma, lost the strategic and tactical initiative, the battles, and the war, never knowing that Colossus had decoded up to 90 percent of Lorenz messages.

Directly resulting from breaking Enigma and the further solution of Lorenz, the "secret writer," Ultra spared untold thousands of Allied and enemy lives. Battles were won or avoided, wolf-pack lanes attacked or skirted. Ultra knew enemy intentions, orders of battle, situation reports, fuel, ammunition, spare parts, troop shortages, and gaps in Rommel's supply lines. Messages sent by Hitler at lunch in the Chancellery were read, often word for word, by Churchill as he sipped brandy that evening in London. Ultra learned the state of readiness of every unit in the German armed forces, even the amount of men, planes, and tanks committed to a battle. What the Germans didn't know about Allied strategy was as vital as what Ultra did know about enemy intentions. No detail was too small. The operating depth of U-boats had high value for Allied destroyers and submarines. By knowing the grid location of the U-boat's refueling "milk cows," nearly the entire tanker fleet went to the bottom. Because U-boats then needed to return to base for refueling, hundreds of thousands of tons of Allied shipping reached Liverpool or Murmansk. Knowing the location of Atlantic U-boats allowed Europe-bound troopships to steer different courses, with not one of the hundreds of Allied troopships sunk in the war. The Ultra advantage also worked to the disadvantage of Allies in the battles that were fought and then lost, fearing that an easy Allied victory would lay bare the open book of the Ultra secret.

Among the reasons why D-Day happened in 1944 instead of 1945 was Ultra's knowledge of enemy confusion about the actual landing place, causing troop diversions to different locations. Ultra deduced that nineteen German divisions awaited an attack from a nonexistent army fictitiously commanded by Gen. George Patton at a never-intended landing area, the Pas de Calais. By preventing a British defeat and giving America additional months to rearm, in its war-winning totality Ultra became history's greatest intelligence bonanza.

AFTERMATH

After the war ended and knowing how awareness of the codebreaking devices and their process could benefit a future adversary, especially Soviet Russia, Churchill ordered that all the mechanical bombes, electronic Colossus machines, and their plans and parts be reduced to a size "no larger than a man's hand." All were consumed in a huge bonfire. American bombes and electronic codebreaking machines had the same fate, ensuring that the machines that never officially existed no longer un-officially existed either.

In 1990, Tony Sale, director of the Bletchley Park Trust, set out to rebuild a Colossus from parts of existing circuit diagrams, photos, and a few spare parts. Six years later a switched-on Colossus again decrypted the original enemy messages, but this time for curious visitors. The author viewed and listened to the whirring sounds of the rebuilt Colossus shortly after its successful rebuild.

Bletchley experienced a remarkable transformation from its tatty appearance when first viewed in 1997. The changes came not a moment too soon, with wreckers close to destroying the huts and mansion for a housing estate. From few visitors, scant public awareness, and varying deterioration of the twenty-to-twenty-five remaining frame huts, a major infusion of lottery and Bletchley Park Trust matching funds resulted in rehabilitation of some huts and the installation of special exhibits. On view are over two hundred coding machines, including a rare Lorenz SZ42 cipher device—the fabled "secret writer-" a rebuilt and operating Colossus computer, and the largest display of Enigma machines in the UK. Alan Turing's office is in its wartime appearance, including his tea mug chained to a radiator and pet bear Porgy. The mansion's exterior is nearly identical to its appearance in the few wartime photos available. Its interior is also in its original room config-uration. The archives and library comprise five hundred thousand documents and images, including original index cards, Enigma decrypts, and engineering drawings for the bombe. The separate National Museum of Computing traces the history of computing from the development of Colossus to the present. Bletchley Park welcomes over 150,000 visitors annually and is easily reached from London's Euston Station over the same rail tracks taken by the codebreakers. BP is open every day except for Christmas holidays. Admissions charged. Limited parking.

In 1990, years after his 1956 release from a ten-year sentence in Berlin's Spandau Prison as a war criminal, former grand admiral Karl Doenitz, commander of the U-boat forces and, briefly, Hitler's successor, gave an interview to a German journalist at a time when details about Ultra were being revealed. The journalist informed Doenitz that Ultra had been decisive in winning the U-boat war. "So, that's what happened," he said. "I have been afraid of this time and again. Although the experts continuously proved that there were other reasons for the suspect observations, they were never able to dispel my doubts completely . . . well, now you historians will have to start right from the beginning again."

Of the approximately 318 Enigma devices still existing, two are in the Deutsches Museum in Munich. Two M4 naval Enigma devices were captured in June 1944 and are part of the U-505 exhibit in Chicago's Museum of Science and Industry.

CHAPTER NINE

U-Boat Sanctuary

If we lose the war at sea we lose the war.
—ADM. DUDLEY POUND, FIRST SEA LORD, ROYAL NAVY

The only thing that ever really frightened me during the war was the U-boat peril.
—WINSTON CHURCHILL

The tonnage war is the U-boat's main task, probably their decisive contribution.
—ADM. KARL DOENITZ

PART ONE

CRUCIAL TO VICTORY—
WINNING THE BATTLE OF THE ATLANTIC

HONORING THE LION WHO LED THEM

OUTSIDE THE VILLAGE CHURCH OF AUMUHLE NEAR HAMBURG, IN THE damp of an early January morning in 1981, twenty-five hundred mourners and admirers gathered to pay their respects at the burial of the man who led history's largest and most powerful fleet of combatant vessels. His warships commanded such fear and loathing within Allied forces that the battle he began on the war's first day lasted until it ended, meriting from Churchill its name, the Battle of the Atlantic. Many of the mourners were veterans from the same battle, there to salute the memory of Grand Admiral Karl Doenitz, who had died at eighty-nine on Christmas Eve a week earlier. The undersea navy he formed grew from one U-boat in 1935 to fifty-seven at the outbreak of war, expanding to 1,154 by the end of the war. The forty thousand sailors he led had near-reverence for the stoic leader they called *der Lowe*, the lion.

The ribbons on the funeral wreaths heaped in the snow expressed pride for what the aging U-boat veterans stamping their feet against the cold had almost achieved when they were young and victory seemed near. A wreath in gold Gothic letters on a black and white ribbon said: "To our Reich's President." Another read: "From the survivors of U-309, *Alles fur Deutschland*, Grand Admiral Karl Doenitz, in honor and fidelity." Many of the vets resolutely said that except for the West German government prohibition against it, they would have worn their uniforms to the funeral. The admiral had earned their high regard. His strategies transformed the conduct of the war at sea. What his young men achieved had taken Britain to her knees.

But the lion they respected so devotedly also served the perverted political cause of the Nazi regime in its last twenty-three dying days as its *führer*—the last führer. In his 1958 memoir, *Ten Years and Twenty Days*, published two years after his release from a Nuremberg trials—imposed ten-year prison sentence, a defiant Doenitz avowed to have no knowledge of Nazi atrocities and declined any guilt. He wrote: "Those who were in Germany in September 1939 know that the people showed no enthusiasm for war. But war nevertheless came and demanded sacrifice after sacrifice. The German soldier fought with unsurpassed devotion to duty. The people and the armed forces marched shoulder to shoulder, in victory or defeat, to the very end." As for the young men he led, their average age only twenty-two, almost twenty-eight thousand of the forty thousand who served in the "iron coffins" never returned to the fatherland.

A GIFT FROM GREAT BRITAIN TO NAZI GERMANY
Rapidly increasing from only one in 1935, by the end of 1936, another thirty-five U-boats were illegally launched in the shipyards of AG

Weser in Bremen and Blohm & Voss in Hamburg. Eventually, nineteen shipyards built 1,154 U-boats, with every shipyard and the surrounding cities where they were built to later suffer the consequences. The 1919 Treaty of Versailles officially ending World War I prohibited Germany from having any U-boats, giving Great Britain and France the dominant positions at sea. However, unexpected British generosity resulting from the June 18, 1935 Anglo-German Naval Agreement allowed Germany a navy equal to 35 percent of Britain's navy. The pact between Joachim von Ribbentrop representing Hitler, and Foreign Secretary Sir Samuel Hoare, acting for an appeasing British Cabinet, directly placed a resurgent German navy in competition with Britain and France. The bilateral agreement in which France had no representation allowed Germany "the right to possess a submarine tonnage equal to the total submarine tonnage possessed by the British Commonwealth of Nations." At a stroke, this brought Germany to near parity with Britain. Inexplicably, the British government went further in its generosity. The agreement also allowed Germany to surpass the allowance of what had been a nearly equal submarine allocation merely by expressing its intent "to give notice to this effect to His Majesty's Government, and agree that the matter shall be the subject of friendly discussion before the German government exercises that right." Germany could now build as many submarines as it wished without violating the agreement, and do so with the chivalrous acquiescence of the British Parliament.

Equally amenable to Hitler and the Nazi revolution over which he presided in 1935, the agreement allowed Germany to shift unused tonnage from one shipbuilding category to another: "It may be necessary," the agreement helpfully proposed, "that adjustments should be made in order that Germany shall not be debarred from utilizing her tonnage to the full." In elated reaction, Hitler proclaimed the signing as "the happiest day of my life." Germany would again have a blue-water navy and it would be perfectly legal. Britain had directly supported Germany's breaking of the Treaty of Versailles.

Upon learning details of the 1935 accord that would cost Britain immeasurable lives, treasure, and nearly the war, an out of government Winston Churchill begged to differ: "If the figures of the expenditure of Germany during the current financial year could be ascertained, the country (Britain) would be staggered and appalled by the enormous expenditure upon war preparations which is being poured out all over that country, converting the whole mighty nation and empire of Germany into an arsenal virtually on the threshold of mobilization." Only eleven days after signing the agreement, the first U-boat went down the ways, with another thirteen under construction, and fifty-seven ready when the war started.

The pact also legitimized completion of two battleships which also violated the Treaty of Versailles (*Scharnhorst* and *Gneisenau*), and allowed Germany to begin construction the following year on battleships *Bismarck* and *Tirpitz*. All would make their mark in the war ahead.

The bilateral agreement between an appeasing British Parliament and a rearming Nazi Germany angered an unaware French government, which reproached a trusted ally for its treacherous act in concluding a separate accord. The Treaty of Versailles, the French believed, had been intended to impose strict limitations on German naval growth. By allowing its conditions to be subverted, Britain allowed Hitler's appetite to grow larger.

When the war began four years after permitting if not encouraging a rapid expansion of Germany's navy, the presumed superiority of the Royal Navy had proved to be a near-fatal self-deception. The prewar British Admiralty evaluated the U-boat threat as negligible, doing little to endorse much less authorize the construction of modern warships for anti-submarine warfare and convoy escorting. The mistakes of the first great war of the century again were repeated, as an inspired but anachronistic British navy readied to fight again the glorious surface engagements of the past. Soon, they would learn that the mighty dreadnoughts in this new war would be akin to highly polished carriages being suddenly thrust into the new automobile age. Throughout Germany, unrestricted construction of a massive undersea navy would soon bring terror to the world.

THE BATTLE OF THE ATLANTIC BEGINS

The influence of the U-boat menace on the war at sea began on the evening of the same day that Britain declared war on September 3, 1939. Lt.

Fritz Lemp, in command of U-30, took easy aim on SS *Athenia*, a 13,465-ton Glasgow-registered transatlantic steamer en route from Liverpool to Montreal. Included on the 1,103-passenger manifest were 469 Canadians, 72 British subjects, 500 Jewish refugees fleeing Europe, hundreds of children, and 311 United States citizens. The order "*torpedoes los*" sent two torpedoes streaking toward the slogging 15-knot ship, killing ninety-eight passengers and crew, including twenty-eight Americans.

On orders from Berlin to mask the source of the attack, every sailor aboard U-30 signed an oath never to disclose how the *Athenia* had been sunk. To avert an undesired entry by the United States into the war, German newspapers were told to report that it was Britain not Germany that sank *Athenia*. Although Hitler knew he would eventually confront America, it was a nation he was not yet ready to oppose.

Fourteen days later, also in the fertile Western Approaches, another U-boat's crosshairs brought a much worthier target into focus, and it was only three thousand yards distant. Two of three torpedoes from U-29 hit the aircraft carrier HMS *Courageous*, sending to the bottom 519 men, half of her crew.

Thus began the seventy-two-month Battle of the Atlantic, history's longest and deadliest sea battle. Before it ended, U-boats would sink 2,603 merchant ships in 684 convoys, carrying 13.5 million tons of shipping. With the ships were also taken the lives of forty-five thousand British, American, and Allied sailors, merchant seamen, and passengers. In only the war's first nine months, U-boats sank 701 ships carrying 2.3 million tons of cargo. The concessions allowing Germany to build U-boats without restraint would nearly lose the war for Great Britain.

By the end of the first year at war, U-boats (with fewer than ten at sea at any one time) sank more than one thousand ships loaded with four million tons of armaments, tanks, trucks, crated airplanes, provisions, aviation fuel, and oil, most of the cargo originating from Canada and the United States. The loss of 25 percent of the entire British merchant fleet in only the first year of the war could not be sustained. With two-thirds of raw materials and half her food imported from abroad, Britain needed at least one million tons of imported shipping each month merely to exist. But by mid-1940 reserves of bunker oil were already at risk. Without oil, Royal Navy ships would be idle in their ports, vulnerable to attack from the rapidly expanding Luftwaffe.

On June 21, 1940, the nightmare of every British admiral and general from the time of Napoleon came true. France fell after a mere six weeks of mostly uninspired fighting. The humiliating armistice also forced the surrender of its five major channel and Atlantic naval bases. Existing U-boat bases in Wilhelmshaven and Kiel immediately became subordinate to the Bay of Biscay ports in Brest, Lorient, St. Nazaire, La Pallice, and Bordeaux. Almost overnight, German capital ships, surface raiders, and the rapidly expanding U-boat flotillas would have bases averaging 750 miles nearer the dense shipping lanes leading into Liverpool, Britain's second largest port. A long and dangerous voyage through the North Sea and around the top of the British Isles had been replaced with a short trip into the open Atlantic. U-boat flotillas would remain on patrol longer, saving thousands of tons of fuel oil and at least a week in transit from German bases. With possession of the French bases, U-boats would penetrate more deeply into undefended convoy routes. The outflanked Royal Navy could no longer contain the growing U-boat fleet by simply blocking the North Sea exit.

Control of the French ports meant that the big German ports could be converted into shipbuilding, instead of time spent refitting U-boats. Severing the crucial convoy routes would accelerate the blockade of the British Isles and hasten the start of Operation Sea Lion, the invasion of England. As to potential American intervention, German war-planners viewed the United States as no threat to Nazi expansionism. Aware that isolationism had divided Americans, they knew that the country had no appetite to send their boys back into European combat only a generation after the first great war of the century. German war planners also knew that America's military had been allowed to wither, and it no longer could field a modern army, much less confront one in battle. After occupying Europe and defeating Britain, Germany would of course keep the spoils of victory and then negotiate with America from a position of massive strength.

As beleaguered Britain confronted defeat, Germany tasted early victory. Atlantic Wall preparations were reduced as expanding the U-boat fleet and building the French bunker bases became the top priority for the entire military. Much sooner than expected the Thousand Year Reich would be more than a Wagnerian fantasy.

———

PART TWO

HIGH TIDE FOR THE U-BOAT FLEET

Into the Gray Wolves' Den

Less than two days after the formal French surrender in the Compiègne forest outside Paris, a long train left Wilhelmshaven, Germany, continuing without pause through the French capital on the way to the Brittany coast and Lorient. Aboard the train were the commander-in-chief U-boats, newly promoted Vice Admiral Karl Doenitz, and his personal staff. The train also contained torpedoes, spare parts, radios, navigation gear, optical instruments, food and drink, and skilled maintenance personnel. The taciturn forty-nine-year-old commandant was held in high esteem by the "gray wolves," who he would personally debrief after each patrol. In addition to the respect held by the U-boat sailors for their commanding officer, the elite crews fighting for *Volk und Vaterland* viewed him as their father figure and the architect of their young lives.

Like an indulgent father, the admiral returned their adulation. After the long and dangerous patrols, many exceeding sixty days at sea, and surviving relentless depth-charge attacks, chartered trains brought his boys home to Germany for generous shore leaves. He made sure that the *Kriegsmarine*, the war navy, were paid nearly twice that of the other armed forces. The crews had the military's most abundant rations, including fresh fruit and vegetables, bread, meats, beer, and wine. For sailors on shore leave in the French ports, pleasure followed the peril in the beds of the often-compliant women. While their U-boats were being overhauled, the crewmen had thirty days off to relax in "U-boat sailor's pastures"—commandeered French seaside resorts. Officers and men lived equally close to the edge. Why not? Most of them would pay with their lives soon enough.

As each U-boat returned to port after battle, white victory pennants fluttering like washing on the line, shipyard workers and other crews mustered on the pier or on the fortified bunker roofs to cheer the gaunt, grimy sailors with their salt-encrusted gray leather jackets, unshaven faces, and reeking of diesel fuel. As a military brass band thumped, a bearded, white-capped captain, only a few years older than his crew, inspected a steel-helmeted honor guard mustered on the heavily fortified pier. Nurses in white tunics and girlfriends from town scattered fresh flowers in their path. A swelling of pride and more than a little arrogance arose from their ranks. Who could say the crews hadn't earned it? Lorient was then "the base of the aces." In 1942, the heyday of the U-boat's Atlantic offensive, a dozen Biscay-based U-boats each accounted for more than one hundred thousand tons sunk. No navy in history ever had or would ever again achieve such results.

"HAPPY TIME" FOR THE U-BOATS

The offensive against US shipping began in early January 1942 with a captain's briefing in the "museum" of the admiral's spacious headquarters in an appropriated chateau in view of the Lorient base. If the Allies only knew it, his headquarters, two adjacent chateaux, and guard bunkers, stood alone and openly visible to British and American bombers increasingly appearing overhead.

As the admiral waved the U-boats out to sea from the terrace of the chateau's purpose-built communications bunker, his Alsatian shepherd Wolf close by, Operation *Paukenschlag* (drumbeat) began. Later, when the war turned against them, those who survived dreamily remembered the "happy times" of the "American Turkey Shoot."

Operation Drumbeat began only twenty-seven days after the United States entered the war, when twelve 1,120-ton, 253-foot Type IX boats launched a coordinated, two-phased attack on shipping near American shores. By the end of January, nearly four hundred merchant ships, most flying the American flag, were on the bottom. A simple strategy kept the U-boats submerged during the day, to surface only at night to recharge batteries, send reports to U-Boat Command, and seek targets. They were easy to find. The merchantmen hugged American shores, careless and conspicuous in their own waters, and found repeatedly in periscope sights. They plodded one behind the other like elephants on parade, lights undimmed, crews untrained, ignoring radio silence, their silhouettes perfectly displayed against the bright lights of cities from Hampton Roads to Miami Beach. As another setback to oil-starved England, most of the ships sunk that month were tankers, with the loss of only six U-boats. The Americans had much to learn, beginning with enforcement of a strict blackout of coastal cities.

A combination of long-range aircraft, increased destroyer and corvette production, and improved sonar and radar technologies gradually ended the "happy time" and the U-boat threat in the North Atlantic. By May 1943, the wolf packs were at high tide. That month 423 U-boats were operational, but each month thereafter more U-boats were sunk than merchant ships. In August 1944, forty-four U-boats went down, with another sixty-four sunk in the year's last four months, at a loss of only twenty-four merchant ships. The tables had been turned; U-boats never again dominated the Atlantic.

But that lay in the future; for the first four years of the war, U-boats had their way and no navy could stop them. From the beginning of the war, Allied and enemy commanders alike knew that the European war would be won or lost on the gray waters of the Atlantic. That opinion never changed. The decision to base the U-boat flotillas on the French coast changed the strategic nature of the war, bringing Germany the closest it would ever come to winning the Battle of the Atlantic and the European war.

BUILDING THE BUNKER BASES

Of all the cruel arts and sciences in the Nazi arsenal, only the five Biscay bunker bases were built to last for the regime's boasted thousand-year reign. Their historic accomplishment can be compared with another man-made wonder, the construction of Hoover Dam (known as the Boulder Dam 1933–1947), except for the challenge of building the five mammoth French bunker bases while under regular attack and with constant materiel shortages.

From 1931 to 1936, five thousand men controlled the Colorado River to build a dam equivalent to a sixty-five-story skyscraper. With 4.4

million cubic feet of concrete poured over a 1,244-foot length and 726-foot height, as a two-lane highway concrete in the dam would stretch from San Francisco to New York City. Yet, the construction needs of the five bases easily overshadowed Hoover Dam's accomplishment. The concrete poured for their construction would extend ten thousand miles, the distance between New York City and Sydney, Australia.

The three-section base in Keroman outside Lorient by itself compares favorably with Hoover Dam's entire achievement. Beginning February 2, 1941, fifteen thousand mostly slave laborers and German overseers built three separate enclosures, two thousand feet in total length, 425 feet wide, and sixty-three feet high. The gigantic structures were topped with a seven-section, twenty-three-foot thick reinforced concrete roof, itself a daring work of extraordinary engineering skill. Finished in only twenty-three months, often under relentless air raids, concrete mixers in the hundreds and trucks by the thousands poured 3.4 million cubic feet of concrete. Chicago's Willis (Sears) Tower on its side, for years the world's tallest building, would fail to reach the Lorient pens' total length by six hundred feet. The *Titanic* twice over, with four hundred feet to spare, could occupy the combined Lorient bunkers.

Construction raced ahead as the five Biscay bunker bases swallowed fourteen million tons of concrete and one million tons of steel. Over seven hundred of the 220 to-254-foot-long Type VII U-boats, the most commonly used in the Battle of the Atlantic, were built in ten German shipyards, with most of the U-boats intended for the Biscay pens. To transport enormous amounts of building materials from distant sources to main rail lines, and then to the construction site at the water's edge, separate rail lines were needed to move 150,000 tons each month for almost two years. When sand became unavailable at the Lorient site, Organization Todt installed dredgers six miles from the construction site to suction sand from the seabed. By mid-1942, Allied Bomber Command had awakened fully to the threat the bases posed, but it was too late. Although construction slowed during air raids—three hundred recorded only for Lorient—not one mission succeeded in putting the pens out of commission.

Admiral Doenitz later credited the U-boat success in operating unmolested to British War Cabinet policies. "It was a great mistake on the part of the British not to have attacked these pens from the air when they were under construction behind watertight caissons and were particularly vulnerable. But British Bomber Command preferred to raid towns in Germany. Once the U-boats were in their concrete pens, it was too late."

COMPLETE NAVAL BASES UNDER CONCRETE

Containing every facility and service needed for U-boat shelter, replenishment, and overhaul, the pens were more comparable to being complete naval bases under concrete than simply fortified U-boat shelters. All the necessities and many of the conveniences equivalent to a medium-sized town resided behind solid eleven-foot-thick reinforced concrete external walls and three-foot-deep steel armored double blast doors.

With the three mammoth bunkers at Lorient as examples of similar installations at the other bases, extending for hundreds of feet inside, thousands of personnel could safely work through all but the most intense air raids. Within the vast interiors were complete steam and electric generating stations, air-raid shelters, one-thousand-man capacity crew dormitories, ninety-two private crew rooms, scores of well-lighted drafting and engineering offices, cold storage and food lockers, and mess facilities. Other spaces housed firefighting, repair, and first-aid stations, supply and storage rooms, fully equipped kitchens, bakeries, hospital and dental facilities, radios and communication, ventilators, water purification, even an escape tank to train crews in the use of individual breathing apparatus. Concrete steps in the rear went up to storage facilities and more offices within easy reach of dry or wet docked U-boats. Rail tracks brought materials and equipment directly to docks with U-boats being overhauled. Openings in the rear gave entry to trucks and personnel in offices and shops. Feeding the constant needs of repair, re-provisioning, and refurbishment, underground pipes delivered oil, gasoline, lubricants, fresh water, and seawater. Thirty-ton capacity overhead traveling cranes removed periscopes for recalibration during the overhaul.

Additional concrete bunkers inside the pens gave even more protection to vulnerable electrical transformers, fuel tanks, and stand-by power generators. Dangerous or delicate stores such as torpedoes, ammunition, and optical instruments went to fortified bunkers in nearby towns, each with a thirty thousand square feet capacity. Lorient's three structures with a combined width of 1,266 feet measure as wide as the 102-floor Empire State Building is high. Although Lorient had the most complete defenses, each base had its own abilities to guard against every type of attack, by land, air, or sea.

Seventy-five miles north of Lorient, the base at Brest surpassed even Lorient in total area with fifteen overhaul pens under concrete. Built as two joined structures, it stretched 1,092 feet wide, 629 feet deep, and fifty-five feet high, an area of almost 687,000 square feet. For comparison, at eighty-eight thousand square feet New York's Grand Central Terminal Main Concourse measures 275 feet long, 120 feet wide, and 125 feet high.

In building the bases, famous German manufacturers supplied essential management personnel, materials, plans, and equipment, including MAN-designed and -made pumping units, lock gates, and electric traversers that moved U-boats from a pier to dry dock. Using forced labor, prisoners of war, and concentration camp inmates, Siemens contracted for the concrete works and electrical design. Organization Todt, the Third Reich's giant military and civilian construction subsidiary, had overall responsibility for planning and constructing the five bases, and for installation and maintenance of their equipment.

PART THREE

U-BOAT OVERHAUL—FROM PIER TO DRY-DOCK IN ONE HOUR

A U-boat overhaul at the Lorient base began with passage through a 235-foot protected slipway, the start of a never previously attempted and never again to be repeated five-step process. German engineers designed a multi-step transfer system to move U-boats from a mooring pier to an enclosed dry-dock in only one hour. After completing the slipway transfer, a U-boat entered a dry dock through a sixty-foot-high portal enclosed by two armored doors, each three-and-a-half-feet thick, closed or opened by submersible hydraulic caissons. Each dry-dock had two to four intake pumps for flooding the dock basin, each with a capacity of four hundred sixty thousand cubic feet per hour, and two to four drainage pumps, each with a capacity of one hundred eighteen thousand cubic feet per hour. The Lorient dry docks were so immense that two flotillas of fourteen U-boats each could be inside at one time, although one flotilla usually was on the way to a patrol area as the other returned.

In the final stage, with the U-boat secure in a cradle set on a trolley, a sideways-moving thirty-two-wheeled traverser—an electrically driven mobile platform on tracks—moved laterally across eight rails to stop outside an empty pen to precisely place a U-boat inside on keel blocks set according to its size and type. Each base had multiple docks, some holding two U-boats at the same time, with Lorient's major volume sufficient to contain nine dry docks.

Step by Step—The Overhaul Process

Phase One: A U-boat enters an enclosed slipway. The dock gate is closed. Water is pumped out as the vessel is maneuvered with assistance of an overhead traveling crane, onto a cradle fitted to a wheeled trolley set on four rails. The overhead crane removes the periscope for attachment to the deck. Phase Two: With the U-boat secured, the trolley holding the U-boat is winched up a gradual slope by a 220-horsepower electrically powered windlass to a lateral track system. Phase Three: At the top of the slipway, the cradle with the attached U-boat operated by an independent 25-horsepower traction unit, moves the U-boat onto the bed of a thirty-two-wheel laterally moving mobile platform, or traverser. Phase Four: The traverser, itself driven by an independent electric motor, moves laterally with the U-boat on eight tracks along the dry-dock entrances. Phase Five: The traverser stops at the entrance or "box" of the overhaul dry-dock. Under independent power, the cradle moves off the traverser onto a parallel feeder track, ready to insert the U-boat inside the dry-dock. At

Entrance to a berthing "boxes" in Lorient, capable of dry-docking two U-boats. AUTHOR

the end of the final phase, the U-boat passes through a sixty-foot-high entrance with two caisson-mounted armored doors into the enclosed dry-dock. With the armored doors closed, the overhaul begins. The traverser then continues to its own enclosure—the last entrance—to await the next U-boat. Of 1,149 overhauls at the five bases, each lasting about one month, Lorient completed nearly half.

PART FOUR

FANGROSTEN—
THE IMPENETRABLE ROOFTOP DEFENSES

With one of the most complete roof defense systems of the five bases, the St. Nazaire pens also received the least damage from unremitting American and British air raids. If the flight crews being hounded by fighters and flying directly into walls of flak saw anything at all from twenty-five thousand feet, it would have been the peculiar appearance of the roof construction—the topmost layer. The German engineers who invented the roof defenses called them *fangrosten*, or bomb-traps. The never-before built multi-segmented reinforced roofs gave complete protection to bases with the full installation, or partial protection to unfinished sections.

After a bomb detonated on the topmost layer—a series of inverted U-shaped concrete beams—the concussion went either away from or into a six-and-a-half-foot high open explosion chamber, a void below the beams. The space had concrete slabs set parallel to the U-beams on the rooftop above. If a bomb hadn't already exploded, it continued down to another solid section, then to a triangular space formed by tilting concrete U-beams against each other. Serving as a second bomb-trap, it redistributed immense weight loads from the blast to exterior walls up to eight feet thick.

Below the triangle-shaped gap, additional concrete reinforcement encased a steel-trussed framework spanning each pen's dividing walls. A final corrugated steel layer—the only section visible to viewers looking up from inside—served as a ceiling above the dry- or wet-docked U-boats.

Portion of an unfinished top layer of the revolutionary "bomb-trap" AUTHOR

Fangrost Superstructure

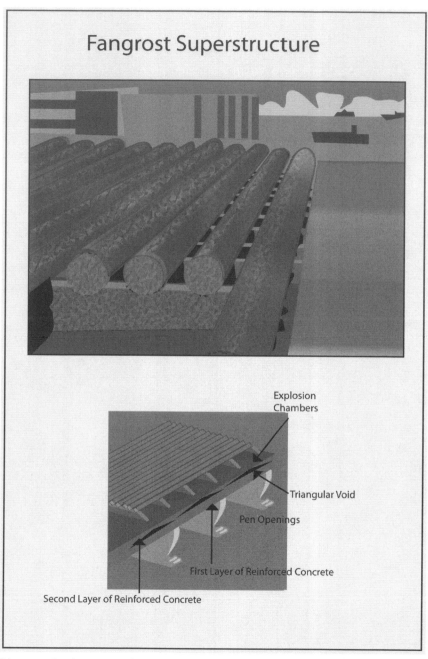

Diagram of unique seven-layer roof construction. N GELBAND O'CONNOR

Combining the effects of the bomb-trap with the open and solid sections, the array succeeded in containing otherwise penetrating explosions. In all, seven anomalous overlays, either dense or open, and up to twenty-three feet thick, protected parts or all of the pens.

After hundreds of raids only indented the pens defenses, a new Allied weapon—a twelve-thousand-pound ballistic bomb named Tallboy—entered the fight. Displaying offset fins for bullet-like torque, its ponderous weight meant that it could be released only from relatively low levels, thus negating much of its penetrating ability. The few Tallboys dropped did little damage.

Another massive bunker-buster, the twenty-two-thousand-pound Grand Slam, nicknamed "Ten-ton Tess," the "mother of all bombs" of its day, entered late in the war against the immense 1,445,000-square-foot, fourteen-hundred-foot-long submarine factory, code-named Valentin, outside Bremen. Up to twelve thousand undernourished slave laborers worked twelve-hour days, garbed in the distinctive striped clothing in which they also slept, helping to complete the factory in twenty months. Unlike the bomb-trap defenses designed for the French U-boat bases, the fifteen- to twenty-three-foot-thick Valentin roof had dozens of steel trusses and reinforced concrete arches made on site. Over 1,640,000 cubic yards of concrete then covered the roof to a thickness of twenty-three feet. Because of production setbacks from a lack of parts made at different sites, only four of 118

Corrugated steel overhead, the lowest of the seven-layer roof defenses. AUTHOR

Valentin assembled U-boats saw combat. The factory's ability to survive benefited from a design by Erich Lachner, one of Germany's best-known civil engineers. After the war, Lachner and numerous engineers and scientists who served the Nazi regime then worked for the Allies to plan repairs to bridges and dams.

On March 27, 1945, two Grand Slams dropped from RAF Lancaster heavy bombers struck a fifteen-foot-thick ferrous concrete roof section of the Valentin factory, penetrating halfway before exploding. About one thousand tons of debris fell into the space below, but failed to significantly damage the factory or its machine tools. Production continued under unremitting air raids to the end. A postwar assessment concluded that the factory's formidable east section roof could have survived even repeated Grand Slam assaults.

Although none of the French bases were destroyed or even meaningfully damaged, penetrating explosions occurred in sections where the innovative roof defenses were incomplete. But even with the super-heavy ordnance dropped, bases with full roof defenses would likely have avoided severe damage from repeated Tall Boy or Grand Slam raids. While only the 1.4-million-square-foot Bordeaux base had the complete *fangrost* array and escaped any type of penetrating damage, each base had some parts of the bomb-trap installed.

ROOSEVELT AND CHURCHILL—"DESTROY ST. NAZAIRE"

On January 3, 1943, led by thirty-six-year old Col. Curtis LeMay, eighty-five B-17s and thirteen B-24 Eighth Air Force Liberators dropped 171 tons of bombs on the St. Nazaire U-boat base without noticeable effect. At the Casablanca conference that began only eleven days later, Roosevelt and Churchill decided that the St. Nazaire base, located sixty-three miles from Lorient, should be destroyed. By early 1944, more than two thousand tons of bombs succeeded in destroying the St. Nazaire docks and most of the adjacent town, but not the 1.3-million-square-foot bunker base.

RAF Bomber Command and the Eighth Air Force then changed tactics to again attack Lorient even more relentlessly, dropping forty-five

Defending troops alongside the St. Nazaire bunker base. AUTHOR

hundred tons of munitions in eight months. After years of attempts by over three hundred missions with thousands of sorties launched against only Lorient, no bombs ever fully penetrated its roof, or any base with the full *fangrost* defenses. As the largest and most complete of the five bases, Lorient withstood up to twenty attacks per month, but remained operational until the last day of the war.

An American Airman vs. the U-Boat Bases

After years of relentless bombings, how could the bunker bases survive and even thrive without significant damage or destruction? One Eighth Air Force pilot had an answer echoed by many of the Americans who flew the perilous missions from scores of bases in England. 1st Lt. (later Capt.) Edward J. Hennessy, a Chicagoan, 1940 Notre Dame graduate, and, later, the author's employer, flew twenty-five missions as a 306th Bombardment Group (H) command pilot of the B17F, "Little Audrey," while based at Thurleigh near Bedford in east England.

At La Pallice, the undamaged entry to the fortified overhaul berths. AUTHOR

On his third mission over the pens at St. Nazaire, Hennessy's luck almost ended when flak took out an engine. "We had damage from Fw-190s [Focke-Wulf] and Bf-109s every mission. Our fighters didn't have the range, so in those early days we always flew without fighter escort," he said. "Everything was tried against the sub pens without results. One time we loaded two-thousand-pound Navy sixteen-inch battleship shells fitted with tail fins, hoping to hit the 'garage doors.' They bounced off just like the others. It convinced us that nothing was going to take out the pens, and we were right—nothing did."

Operation Chariot—"The Greatest Raid of All"

On March 28, 1942, a force of 611 Royal Navy and British commandos launched a land attack against the heavily defended St. Nazaire base, intent on destroying its celebrated 1,150-foot-long *Normandie* dry-dock, one of the few able to service Germany's small fleet of capital ships, such

Part of the traverser system that moved a U-boat from pier to enclosed berth in one hour. AUTHOR

The nearly complete explosion chamber at St. Nazaire U-Boat base. AUTHOR

as *Bismarck* and *Tirpitz*. With HMS *Campbeltown* (the former USS *Buchanan*) as a battering ram, the raid succeeded in damaging beyond repair for the balance of the war and five years after both the lock gate and dry-dock. Fighting their way out of the town, commandos destroyed machinery and structures, but at a cost of 169 killed, 215 taken prisoner, and only 228 returning to Britain. Five Victoria Crosses, eighty-nine decorations, and thirty-eight battle honors were awarded to the raiders.

No Combat Zone Had Better Protection
Designated by Hitler as "*Festung Lorient*"—one of fourteen Atlantic Wall redoubts to be defended at all costs and with no surrender—the post-war US Strategic Bombing Survey tallied a formidable armory of varied weaponry at Lorient. Two hundred 20mm guns, nine 75mm, eighteen 88mm, forty-three 105mm, twelve twin 105mm, and five 128mm guns were sited only in the pill boxes, armored turrets, firing ports, casemates,

flak towers, and block-houses on the roofs of the three structures. A twenty-six-thousand-man garrison with its own armament added more depth to the already daunting defenses. Of the three thousand artillery pieces defending the entire Atlantic Wall, three hundred heavy-caliber guns were sited in or around Lorient. No combat zone had better defenses. In grudging respect, the postwar US survey team called Lorient "the world's greatest submarine base." Encircled by the US 66th and 4th Armored Divisions, it surrendered on May 10, 1945, two days after VE Day.

Another unsuccessful raid against the Lorient U-Boat bunkers. NATIONAL ARCHIVES

Aftermath

When the war ended only two forsaken U-boats remained within the still intact base, with one scuttled. The other, the still seaworthy U-123, saw reflagged service with the French navy as the S-10 *Blaison*, sailing until 1959 from the same berths built and occupied a few years earlier by the Germans. In 2,160 days of fearless and increasingly desperate combat, nearly three of four U-boat sailors died in the "iron coffins." Their ages averaged only twenty-two years. Lt. Ed Hennessy's 306th Bomb Group, the "Reich Wreckers," the first American bombers over Germany, flew 342 increasingly hazardous missions with 9,614 sorties, at a loss of 171 B-17s.

In thousands of heroic missions, many over the Biscay bases, the Eighth Air Force lost 4,009 four-engine bombers, with forty-seven thousand casualties, including twenty-six thousand killed in action, a rate exceeding by ten times the losses for US ground forces. The American cemetery outside Cambridge, England, holds the remains of 3,812 GIs under Portland stone tablets. Another 5,127 names are inscribed on the rolls of the missing. Matching the ages of the U-boat sailors who died, their ages also averaged only twenty-two years.

Lorient, a once prosperous fishing, naval, and shipbuilding town of forty-six thousand, lost all but three buildings to Allied bombing, while operations at the bunker base in the nearby Keroman area continued mostly unimpeded. Only eleven thousand residents survived or returned after the war. Those who came back lived in temporary shelters shipped as kits and built on site, for as long as forty years after the end of the war. Today, the completely rebuilt town has approximately sixty thousand residents.

CHAPTER TEN

Inside the Lion's Den

IN LATE JUNE 1940, THE DECISIVE MOMENT APPROACHED FOR GER-many. Bled white by the mostly undefended destruction of her merchant fleet, Britain neared collapse. Hitler had approved a major increase in U-boat construction to thirty each month. The Third Reich's armies were triumphant everywhere. Poland, Holland, Norway, Belgium, Denmark, and Luxembourg had all been attached to the Nazi leash. And then came the sudden fall of France. On July 10, 1940, the prelude to the invasion, the Battle of Britain began, as the United States continued to ignore the peril abroad. Its defeat seeming certain, Britain stood alone.

On August 29, 1940, with seven department heads, all U-boat veter-ans, Vice Admiral Karl Doenitz entered the three-story circa 1896 Villa Kerillon, overlooking Lorient from nearby Kerneval and in view of the U-boats departing or returning to the bunker base. The confiscated home of a successful sardine entrepreneur, its isolated location suited him. Along with two adjacent chateaux taken for staff, he would be closer to the needs of his men. It would be U-boat Command until March 1942.

The admiral sat at a small desk in a sunny, windowed room, the grow-ing bunker base only twenty-five minutes away by car. In his analysis of the Allied enemy, the commander-in-chief (BdU) U-boats calculated his moves like a wily chess master. Unlike his inflexible Wehrmacht brethren, Doenitz often changed U-boat strategy and tactics in hours, not days, and had no reluctance in accepting advice from his captains.

Inside a connecting bunker, purpose-built for the chateau, in three eight-hour, twenty-four-hour a day watches, officers and enlisted staff

The appropriated chateau headquarters of U-Boat Command near the Lorient bunker base. AUTHOR

examined overnight *B-Dienst*—the signals interception service—radio intercepts, daily U-boat action summaries, weather conditions, spy reports, and warship movements. The nearly obligatory nightly radioed reports from U-boats—a fatal flaw deeply exploited by Bletchley codebreakers—furnished Doenitz with every known variable and trend. With targets selected and patrol lines secured across likely convoy routes, orders were transmitted from a tall tower out of view of headquarters to U-boats: "attack and report sinkings."

CHECK AND CHECKMATE

Each morning the staff presented the admiral with a "U-Boat Disposition Chart"—an analysis presented as a war-games scenario—of the strategic intent of convoy and U-boat movements as viewed from the enemy's perspective. With role-playing almost identical to the Western Approaches gamers, and placing themselves in the enemy's position as did the British, the staff probed each other: "in the enemy's place how would we react to the same movements, and how would we act on the same appreciations of available assets and intent?" The admiral and staff then decided on the best countermeasures to the enemy's assumed intent. Writing in his war memoir, the admiral described "a game of chess that became increasingly more complicated." But as one of the kings in a game of conquest, winner take all, he must have known that one day he would no longer be making the first move, and instead would be the one checkmated.

At the beginning of 1942, in evaluating the overwhelming success of the war at sea, the admiral took pride in the knowledge that only twenty-two U-boats at sea at any one time had the Allies on their back feet, even as half of his available assets were either going to or returning from patrols.

Although unaware of his British rival's Liverpool location or nearly identical war-gaming exercises, in writing after the war Doenitz expressed admiration for Admiral Horton's tactics, also being constantly refined in the Western Approaches bunker. However, armed with Enigma intercepts, Admiral Horton had far greater abilities to predict U-boat strategies developed in the chateau outside Lorient. Nearly identical in purpose to both the Western Approaches map room and the Cabinet War Rooms, maps and charts papered every surface in the admiral's ground floor "museum." In the adjacent communications bunker, his staff also pinned status reports, maps and charts, reports and sightings, weather and sea states, U-boat locations within grid charts, even sketches of both wolf-pack and convoy maneuvers during attacks.

COMMUNICATING WITH THE U-BOAT FLEET

From the chateau's kitchen past an ornate wooden oriel staircase twisting to the second floor, a narrow stone stairway descends to the basement through armored double doors. Two 10,000-square-foot wood-paneled, ventilated, and well-lighted bunkers connect on both sides of the basement. Another section with shower stalls and tub with fixtures made by a German firm, has private sleeping rooms for watch officers. A two-hundred-man signals staff housed in an outside dormitory communicated nightly with U-boats in quick five- to fifteen-second bursts, and prepared "appreciations" for the operations officers and the admiral. Essential to

The chateau with purpose-built attached command and control bunker. AUTHOR

wolf-pack tactics and organization, but disregarding message discipline and radio silence, torrents of two-way messages maintained contact.

U-boat Command transmissions set operational areas, determined spare parts and torpedo status, arranged refueling with the *milch cows*—the larger refueling U-boats or ships—and arranged personnel or supply transfers. The reports were organized into diagrams, bar graphs, and charts to augment the intricate letter- and number-coded grid squares that identified every U-boat and all known enemy shipping around the world.

Spiked like fever charts, elaborate wall graphics illustrated cumulative Allied losses, which by early 1942 neared forty ships sunk for each U-boat lost. Doenitz told his diary that "the tonnage war is the U-boat's main task, probably their decisive contribution." What he didn't know was that most Enigma transmissions to or from U-boat Command had eager ears listening at British Y stations, with intercepts sent to Bletchley for analysis and decryption. With a U-boat's grid location triangulated by high-frequency direction-finding (huff-duff), its life could be measured in hours.

Numerous one- by three-foot partition openings in the communication bunkers, looking nearly pristine decades later, facilitated efficient distribution of incoming radio messages, decrypts, and intelligence reports. Received or transmitted messages were encoded with Enigma or *Geheimschreiber*, "secret writer," the two presumed to be impenetrable cipher devices used by Germany throughout the war.

A Captain's Meeting at U-Boat Command

Like monks assembling for prayer, U-boat captains reported to the admiral after each war patrol, gathering in a 10-by-12-foot, richly paneled, parquet-floored antechamber opposite the busy Operations Room. They set coffee cups on a low flat table decorated with 15 ceramic tiles hand-painted with emblems of U-Boat flotillas. With an assistant at his shoulder recording exchanges, Doenitz probed persistently. "Describe enemy tactics, strategy, disposition, technology, weapons used," he demanded. "Explain U-boat actions taken, or opportunities missed." If a U-boat returned with torpedoes still in the racks, the reason better be plausible. And like commanders everywhere, the admiral must have asked himself why some captains were more successful than others.

One Last Success Before Retreat

The presumed operational advantages conferred by obsessive attention to detail—a compulsively repeated Nazi need—did little good and much ill

Through the double-doors to Admiral Doenitz's ground-floor office. AUTHOR

for U-boat fortunes. The Ultra code-breakers methodically solved most messages within hours, often before the admiral had returned from a bracing walk in the sea air with his dog. Then, with the Americans and British closing the communications and convoy escort gap, the admiral and his U-boats had one final success before enduring cascades of defeat.

In March and April 1943, U-boats came the closest they ever would to winning the war at sea. In March, the Allies—mostly American and British merchant ships in convoys—lost 120 ships at 704,000 tons, with eighty-two sunk in Atlantic waters, at a cost of only twelve U-boats. In April, U-515 sank four tankers in three minutes and another three tankers within the next six hours. For the

To the Operations Room bunker below and alongside the chateau. AUTHOR

month—the high-water mark for the war—sixty-four Allied ships at 351,000 tons went down, at a still-acceptable loss of fifteen U-boats. Then it changed utterly.

What the U-boat sailors called "Black May" ended the strategic and tactical advantage Germany had exploited since the war began. A combination of improved radar, long-range sub-hunting aircraft, and greatly increased squadrons of convoy escorts with improved sonar resulted in the sinking of forty-three U-boats that month. Admiral Doenitz then suffered two great personal losses. On May 19, 1943, U-954, a Type VIIC, went down southeast of Cape Farewell, Greenland, taking with it all hands and Lt. Peter Doenitz, one of the admiral's two sons.

A week later, with 25 percent of the U-boat fleet sunk in only one month, Doenitz withdrew all Atlantic U-boat forces to regroup, await deliveries of new U-boats with fresh crews, and fight another day. He knew that the advantage had been lost and would never be regained. By mid-1943, most of the Atlantic had air coverage from long-range four-engine bombers, with further benefits from the strategic placement of US aircraft carriers and their anti-sub patrols. While the fortified pens continued to give safe harbor, U-boats were at immediate peril after leaving their protection. From mid-1943 as many U-boats were sunk in the Bay of Biscay after leaving or attempting a return to the safety of the bases as were lost far at sea.

In the fall of 1943, with the odds ever longer, the admiral made a last stand by sending what remained of the U-boat fleet back to the North Atlantic, although in far fewer numbers. Facing an enemy with unlimited resources, U-boats had even greater losses and would never again regain supremacy of the seas. After D-Day and the breakthrough of the First United States Army at Avranches in late July 1944, on orders from Berlin the admiral permanently withdrew all Biscay-based U-boats to fortified bases in Bergen and Trondheim, Norway.

A Final Sacrifice

In considering the effect on the admiral over the loss of his first son, the Berlin High Command withdrew his second son, Klaus, from U-boat duties for studies to become a physician. On his twenty-fourth birthday, May 13, 1944, Lieutenant Doenitz convinced friends to take him on the fast torpedo boat S-141, to observe an attack on shipping near the Isle of Wight. The joyride proved deadly when the Free French ship, *La Combatante*, sank the S boat, taking with it the lives of eighteen of its twenty-four crewmen, including *Oberleutnant zur see* Klaus Doenitz. A two-inch by four-inch Gothic-lettered obituary placed by Admiral Doenitz in a Berlin newspaper ended with a declaration that his only remaining son died *"fur Fuhrer und Vaterland."*

The New Führer and His Fading Fleet

In April 1945, with both the Allied and Red Armies enveloping Berlin from east and west, Doenitz moved his headquarters again after leaving Kerneval, first to Lanke near Berlin, then to Ploen, sixty miles north of

Hamburg. In happier times, with victory within reach, he regularly drove to the nearby but now leveled port city of Kiel to rally his "gray wolves." It had been home to the Fifth U-Boat Training Flotilla, and home port of the now faded Baltic Fleet. With the Eighth Air Force regularly bombing Kiel, on April 20, 1945, the regime in its last dying days, RAF bombers destroyed Kiel's remaining U-boats. Also sunk at the Kiel docks by the RAF, on April 9 cruiser *Admiral Scheer* went down followed by the scuttled cruiser *Admiral Hipper* on May 3.

On April 30, Doenitz received a Lorenz-generated radio message from Martin Bormann, then Hitler's personal secretary. "Grand Admiral Doenitz: The fuhrer has appointed you, Herr Admiral, as his successor in place of Reichmarschall Göring. Confirmation in writing follows. You are hereby authorized to take any measures which the situation demands. Bormann." That afternoon Hitler committed suicide in his thirty-two-section two-level bunker fifty feet under the Reich Chancellery. One of the last messages Hitler read came from SS Brigadier General Wilhelm Mohnke, defending less than a mile away in Berlin's Mitte or central section. He said that his men would use the last of their ammunition that night.

On May 1, seven days before VE Day and Germany's unconditional surrender, Doenitz, now the leader of a nearly destroyed nation, summarized the state of the war in a dictation to his aide de camp. The report had one exception to an otherwise bleak assessment. With the Third Reich only hours from eternal extinction, Doenitz stubbornly held out hope for his U-boats. "The U-boat arm was on the eve of the revival of the submarine war campaign, as, from May onwards, the new types of boat would be coming into service in increasing numbers." Although revolutionary in its propulsion system and ability to remain submerged for long periods with a snorkel, the admiral's reference to the Type XXI U-boat was more hopeful than actual. Only four were operational in the last weeks of the war. No Allied ships were sunk.

END OF THE U-BOAT EPIC

In the last years of the war, U-boat losses far surpassed the replacement abilities of shipyards. In 1943, 244 were sunk, with another 249 in 1944.

With a 75 percent casualty rate in 1943 and 1944, even Japanese Kami-kaze pilots fared better than a U-boat on its first patrol, when only 10 percent returned. From late 1943, one would be sunk on average only three months after commissioning. In total, 765 of 1,154 U-boats went to the bottom, usually with no survivors. Only nine thousand of the once formidable forty thousand member force, most of them volunteers, survived. In comparison, the US Navy lost fifty-two submarines and thirty-five hundred men in the two major war theatres.

In writing about the U-boat menace—the only part of the war that frightened him—Churchill expressed respect for the U-boat crews in the battle that ended on the war's last day. "By stupendous efforts and in spite of all losses, about sixty or seventy U-boats remained in action until the end. Allied air attacks destroyed many U-boats at their berths. Nevertheless, when Doenitz ordered the U-boats to surrender, no fewer than forty-nine were still at sea . . . such was the persistence of Germany's effort and the fortitude of the U-boat service."

AFTERMATH

Decades later, overlooked by history, the five French bunker bases endure as nearly indestructible to both man's war machines and the forces of nature, from a distance appearing as nearly original. As a reminder to the future, they endure as Nazi Germany's most determined intent at world domination, its largest construction project, and the most complete remaining vestige of the war in Europe. Some of the pens show faded remains of crew sketches on walls in the echoing interiors. Several bases have penetrating bomb damage in roof sections with partial bomb-traps, but no base had major damage, and all remained active throughout the war. Mostly located outside city centers, the former bases are reached by TGV high-speed rail from Paris and rental car. Several have seasonal guided tours.

The largest of the bunker bases near Lorient has few visitors and is remarkably well preserved, with close views of the innovative fangrosten construction from both the pens below and the roofs above. The admiral's command chateau in Kerneval is in its original appearance but mostly unavailable to visitors. The pill boxes, guard posts, dormitory, concrete garage, and bunkers to defend U-Boat Command were never attacked and are in a semblance of their original appearance. Drawings by soldiers with time on their hands are visible on walls. Adjacent to the one-time U-boat Command, a chateau used by officers on leave is partially open to the public as a bar.

Among the hundreds of U-boats sunk by the US Navy, only one became a prize of war. On June 4, 1944, off Cape Blanco, French West Africa, Task Group 22.3, led by escort carrier USS *Guadalcanal*, the USS *Pillsbury* (DE 133) forced Lorient-based U-505 to the surface with depth charges. It became the only German submarine boarded and captured at sea during the war, and the only enemy warship of any type captured by the US Navy since 1815. The *Pillsbury's* crew received the Presidential Unit Citation, with the leader of the boarding party, LTJG Albert David, awarded the Medal of Honor. Visited by over twenty-five million since 1954, U-505 is permanently berthed in a recreated bunker deep within Chicago's Museum of Science and Industry.

CHAPTER ELEVEN

Launching the Invasion: Southwick House and D-Day

History does not long entrust the care of freedom to the weak or the timid.

—GEN. DWIGHT D. EISENHOWER

—~

PART ONE

SUNDAY, JUNE 4, 1944: DELAY AND DISAPPOINTMENT

SHORTLY AFTER A 4:15 A.M. WEATHER BRIEFING ON JUNE 4, GEN. Dwight D. Eisenhower stepped out for another smoke under the portico with the eight Doric columns of the immense 1841 three-story mansion near Portsmouth on England's southeast coast. Into the first of up to four daily packs of Camels and fifteen cups of coffee, before dawn he and his subordinate commanders had already completed the first of two daily weather briefings with British meteorologist, Group Captain J. M. Stagg. Within the elegant interior, Stagg and his meteorologists had just recommended a delay to the start of Operation Overlord, the liberation of the European continent from Nazi oppression. Ike had immediate major decisions to make.

Throughout the mansion's spacious gardens were scattered numerous half-cylindered corrugated steel structures named after their inventor,

Peter Nissen. Tents of various sizes and temporary housing extended from the surrounding woods almost to the mansion's entry. For a brief time, the ancestral country home of the Thistlewaite family, Operation Overlord's pre-assault naval communications center, would be the most important place on earth.

From where the stately home resided in the low hills above Portsmouth harbor, Ike could almost see the water and part of the vast armada containing every type of naval vessel afloat. In addition to Portsmouth, eleven other British ports were equally laden with so many ships that it was almost possible to walk with dry feet from one vessel to the other, so closely were they moored. The supreme commander of history's mightiest invasion force knew that every man from general and admiral to mechanic and rifleman, all 156,000 of them and millions more behind, awaited his command to instantly move from camps to landing vessels, or from ships to the beaches. But it wouldn't come that day and it wouldn't come the next.

The first met (meterological) report that June 4—the second weather update would be at 6:45 p.m.—painted a discouraging picture of high winds, low clouds, and reduced visibility predicted for June 5, the date of the invasion. Any one of the expected weather disturbances would hinder accurate naval gunfire and make certain the swamping of LCVP landing craft—the Higgins boats—at the moment of dropping their bow ramps on the beach, if they even made it that far. Without fair visibility, erroneously dropping three hundred paratroopers from the 101st Airborne Pathfinder teams could fatally divert the twenty-three thousand jumpers in the 82nd and 101st Airborne Divisions to follow. Any expectation of air support over the beaches on June 5, Ike had been bluntly told, would be "impossible"—the ceiling would be under one thousand feet. Yet, on June 4 major elements of the naval forces were already at sea, and, as Churchill would later write, "the movement was as impossible to stop as an avalanche."

Based on combined weather expectations gathered from the other services, Stagg summarized at the pre-dawn meeting the forecast prepared for Eisenhower and his commanders informally gathered in the mansion's library, converted into a weather briefing room. It was a disheartening outlook. Captain Stagg reported "no new evidence; the only small change is that the front which was expected to clear the Channel areas of low clouds during Wednesday is now expected in the first part of Wednesday. Winds will be at Force 5 (19–24 mph) in the Channel from Monday morning onwards: clouds 10/10 at 500–1,000 ft. from Sunday–Tuesday."

As Eisenhower asked around the room for opinions, Gen. Bernard Montgomery told Ike of his keenness to go, but none of the others were as eager. Each had a reasoned objection to explain why his part of the invasion force faced operational hurdles if not defeat. On that June 4, 1944 pre-dawn, weather made the decision: the invasion planned for June 5 stood-down as a no go. While a disappointment, it was not yet a setback. At least two, perhaps three days remained within the window of ideal low tide and bright lunar conditions needed to launch the invasion. But if the elements continued sour, the next time the moon and tides aligned wouldn't come until June 19.

Waiting another two weeks came with the potential of defeat at the water's edge. Keeping men already at sea or fenced-in at temporary camps another fortnight risked discovery and a loss of the vital edge needed for soldiers approaching sudden combat. Fresh troops rotating into the camps expected to be vacated by the invading soldiers would have nowhere to go. Miles of prepositioned equipment on roads and at supply depots throughout England would need to be re-situated, presenting a logistical muddle on the narrow roads.

Some of the 6,939 vessels of all types, including fifty-nine convoys stretching over one hundred miles, would need refueling or repositioning. By then, German spies or overhead reconnaissance might have concluded from the evidence of masses of troops at scores of camps and lurking ships in

Only General Eisenhower could make the decision of the century—go or no go. NATIONAL ARCHIVES

all the harbors, that the invasion wouldn't happen at the Pas de Calais as expected. Maybe, the German high command could have concluded, maybe the invasion would begin at an obscure location not as well fortified. *Maybe it would begin in Normandy.*

Ike later wrote about the June 4th delay: "The decision 24 hrs. earlier to postpone had been taken in beautifully clear weather; the decision to go (June 5) was taken in the middle of a heavy storm. But the storm only proved that the weatherman had been right the day before. I thought this to be a good omen for the success of the attack." But he also told his diary what lay deep within the heart of any commander sending troops to battle: "the inescapable consequences of postponement were almost too bitter to contemplate." Indeed, if both a one-day postponement and still another weather delay later in the month further deferred the invasion to July—a real possibility—it would mean campaigning in the European winter. Ike, an avid historian, knew what happened to Napoleon's five-hundred-thousand-member *Grande Armee* retreating from Moscow in mid-December 1812.

Yet, except for the weather, starting from two-and-a-half years earlier every possible contingency had been planned and anticipated by the Allies. Reconnaissance flights filmed every inch of the battlespace. French Resistance spies reliably reported on German troop movements. Deceptions ensured that the main body of the enemy lay in wait at the Pas de Calais for the landing of Gen. George Patton's invented First Army Group (FUSAG), an army of rubber tanks and trucks deceptively based in southeast England. Mechanics made final adjustments as pilots of twelve thousand Allied aircraft painted in the special invasion stripes, tested engines, and waited at scores of East Anglia bases. Troops confined within barbed-wire enclosures inspected equipment still again, exercised, ate, and complained. The entire southeast British coast had been sealed tightly; no man, woman, or child could move for ten miles beyond the restricted area.

Among the ships in Operation Neptune, the crucial naval element, were 1,213 warships, comprising six battleships, twenty-two cruisers, and ninety-three destroyers. Included in the 4,126 transport vessels were 148 LCT (landing craft tanks), fifteen hundred LCVP flat-bottomed landing craft, and 287 minesweepers. All awaited orders to weigh anchor or cast off from docks. The Allied invaders had the latest and best equipment that money could buy and willing hands and machines could make. Yet, and Ike knew it better than anyone, after allowing for advantages in equipment and troop resolve, only 15 percent of the landing force had seen combat. That could be telling against an experienced enemy fighting and winning for five years.

The Longest Day

Convinced that the invasion couldn't possibly begin in such wretched weather conditions, an ailing Field Marshal Erwin Rommel, in temporary charge of beach defenses along the Atlantic Wall, left his headquarters in the castle at La Roche Guyon, France, to be driven in his big open Horch home to Herrlingen, Germany. It would be a surprise birthday visit with wife Lucie and son Manfred. Earlier, in a final inspection of the layered fortifications expected to stop the Allied invasion at the water's edge, Rommel told an aide that "the war will be won or lost on the beaches. The first twenty-four hours will be decisive. It will be the longest day."

The dread implications arising from the delay seized Eisenhower's mind like the stab of a sudden migraine. After the bleak morning forecast and breakfast, Ike boarded the four-door khaki Packard driven by Lt. Kay Summersby for the muddy mile back to "Sharpener," the code-name for his pre-invasion camp in the woods one mile behind Southwick House. The enclave had tents for senior aides, his own weather staff, guards and cooks, a mobile telephone switchboard, a personal office tent with concrete floor, and a trio of trailers designed by an American architect working for Lockheed Overseas Corporation. The vehicles had been custom-made in less than sixty days by a Belfast manufacturer. The smallest of the mobile command post's trailers had been planned as Ike's portable office and sleeping quarters. Just past the Sharpener encampment, a much larger complex known as "Shipmate" held hundreds of tents for over a thousand forward-deployed planning staff moved from the former SHAEF headquarters, known as "Widewing," in Bushy Park two hundred miles away. All were intensely preparing final actions to precede the now uncertain date of the invasion's launch.

Doubts About De Gaulle

Before the June 4 evening meeting at the small desk in his trailer, Ike smoked, drank pots of coffee, told Kay to get the weatherman on the phone, and intended to meet only briefly with Gen. Charles De Gaulle, head of the Free French forces, although it wouldn't happen as expected. When Ike informed De Gaulle about the invasion's site, he suffered a one-hour lecture on the errors of its selection.

Until two days before when Ike briefed him in the mansion, De Gaulle had no knowledge of Overlord or the invasion date, and both FDR and Ike wanted it that way. De Gaulle had made clear that only he had the right to give orders to the French population, and had grandiose expectations, FDR and Ike thought, of becoming "ruler of France." Roosevelt utterly opposed such an intent. "Sovereignty in France rests with the people," he said. The Allies were not entering France to force on its citizenry a dictated government or "ruler." Except for a few French commandos who landed with the British troops at Sword Beach, Roosevelt and Eisenhower ensured that the Free French had no role in the invasion.

Churchill to Ike: 'Include Me in the Invasion Force'

In the operations trailer at Camp Sharpener, Ike met with a deeply anxious Winston Churchill. He had earlier arrived on a private train parked on a siding six miles north of Southwick House. Ike told Churchill all that he knew about the weather, which wasn't much, but the evening's forecast might have better news he thought.

Still chafing from not being invited to join the landing force, a shrewd Churchill informed Ike that instead he would place himself within the assault troops, based on his authority as prime minister. But he first had to sell Ike on its virtues, however oblique on its reasoning: "Since this is true (his control over British troops), it is not part of your responsibility my dear General, to determine the exact composition of any ship's company in His Majesty's Fleet." True enough, Ike knew, as Churchill pressed on: "By shipping myself as a bona fide member of a ship's complement it would be beyond your authority to prevent my going." Resolutely opposed to the prime minister of America's most important ally landing with the troops on an invasion beach, Ike had no choice except to concede Churchill's authority over his own forces, until he was rescued by an unexpected ally, the king himself. Having learned of Churchill's intent, King George VI informed the prime minister that as king he therefore had an equal obligation to be with his troops in battle, as did King Henry V in 1415 at the battle of Agincourt in northern France. A higher authority had outwitted Churchill—the only one higher in rank than himself. Ike heard no further pleas and the king continued to rally his country.

A COMMANDER OBJECTS TO THE LANDINGS

Back in the trailer, Ike mentally reviewed again the egos and objectives among his commanders, and the operational crises needing resolution or avoidance in advance of the invasion. A few days before, Air Vice Marshal Trafford Leigh-Mallory told him, and not for the first time, that dropping Gen. Matthew Ridgeway's 82nd Airborne and Brig. Gen. Matthew D. Taylor's 101st Airborne, the Screaming Eagles, into the Cotentin peninsula would cause glider losses exceeding 70 percent, with American troop losses of 80 percent.

Leigh-Mallory then heatedly told Ike of his objection to the near-certain "futile slaughter" of two fine divisions being dropped in the wrong area. The combination of an unsuitable landing area and expected German resistance, he said, would affect the outcome of the entire assault. Eisenhower later wrote that "it would be difficult to conceive of a more soul-racking problem." Ike told Leigh-Mallory to place his objections into a letter and he would have an answer "in a few hours." He returned to the command tent to think alone and go over still again every piece of the vast puzzle that needed each part to be in the same place at the same time.

If Leigh-Mallory had the correct assessment, Ike thought, then the attack on Utah Beach would also fail, placing at risk the entire invasion, a defeat in Europe, even the loss of the war. But his confidence in the success of the airborne landings, and in Utah Beach and the full invasion, remained firm. At the end of the day Leigh-Mallory made only an assessment, an estimate, while Eisenhower and his commanders had been planning the assault since 1942. "I was not ready to abandon a plan in which I had held implicit confidence for more than two years," said Eisenhower. Leigh-Mallory was wrong in his evaluation. Ike called to tell him that the assault would take place as planned and he would write to confirm it. (After the success of the airborne landings, Leigh-Mallory apologized to Eisenhower for the added burden placed on him during the tense hours before D-Day.)

Also receiving Eisenhower's attention were Bletchley Park decrypts containing Ultra revelations that detected strengthening and movement of Germany's 91st Division directly into Ridgeway's drop zone. The reality of his commitment to battle of the flower of America's youth also pressed insistently on his consciousness while alone in the trailer in the hours before the invasion. If wrong, history would harshly judge his deliberate sacrifice of America's young men on the high altar of inflexibility and expediency. He stubbed out another cigarette and returned to the mansion for the evening's met report.

A CHANGE IN THE WEATHER

As Ike entered Southwick House on the evening of the second weather briefing on June 4, neither he nor any of the commanders knew with certainty when the invasion would begin. He only knew that if it didn't take place on June 6 or two weeks later, it wouldn't happen until early July. The option of a two-week postponement, much less a thirty-day delay, could not happen and it would not happen, and he knew it before the meeting began.

Captain Stagg's evening met summary held out the possibility of a "substantial change" in the overall weather situation beginning that evening, and for at least half of June 6th. "I have some good news for you General," said the usually reserved Scots meteorologist, who opined that planners could expect the likelihood of "rapid and unexpected developments," and soon. He predicted that a front would move much farther south than expected, that it was already approaching Portsmouth, and it would clear the English side of the Channel overnight.

In reply to Air Chief Marshal Tedder, Stagg said that "pressure systems were forming and deepening across the Atlantic at a rate more suitable to mid-winter." Air Vice Marshal Leigh-Mallory then queried the conditions expected for visual bombing by medium and heavy bombers. Stagg told him that "good, though not interrupted conditions for visual bombing by heavy and medium bombers could be expected from Monday evening till early forenoon on Tuesday." Eisenhower, according to Group Captain Stagg's later written summary, was ahead of everyone and asked about expected conditions through the weekend. Stagg said with hope bordering on conviction that conditions "would slowly improve after Friday if the present trend continues." Now Ike had something real but needed full accord from all his commanders.

LAUNCH OR DELAY AGAIN

As horizontal rain continued to shake the house and pelt the windows, Ike went around the room asking opinions to support the invasion tentatively set for June 6. Leigh-Mallory, continuing to be obdurate, urged a delay until June 19. Arthur Tedder expressed equal pessimism. Ramsay reminded Ike of a looming deadline: "Admiral Kirk must be told within the next half hour if Overlord is to take place on Tuesday. If he is told it is on and his forces sail and are then recalled, they will not be ready again until Wednesday morning; therefore, a further postponement would be for 48 hours." Eisenhower, disagreeing: "Conditions are almost ideal up to a point, even if the operations of the heavy air may be held up later." General Bedell-Smith: "Looks to me we've gotten a break we could hardly hope for." Leigh-Mallory, still in opposition: "Bomber Command would have great difficulty in getting their markers down and doing useful bombing." Unnamed other participants disagreed with his assessment. Eisenhower then sharply interjected with Leigh-Mallory: "Don't be so pessimistic."

From General Bedell-Smith: "It's a hell of a gamble but this (the decision) is the best possible gamble." Tedder agreed with Leigh-Mallory's doubts: "The operations of heavies and mediums are going to be chancy." Ike's impatience and the need for consensus showed in a biting rejoinder to Tedder's hesitation: "After all, we have a great force of heavy bombers . . ." Tension in the room flared like a sudden fever; Ike wanted everyone on board, and they weren't there—not yet.

He suddenly turned to Montgomery, poked his chin at him, and asked with a hard intensity: "Do you see any reason for not going

Ike with Adm. Sir Bertram Ramsay outside Southwick House on June 5. NATIONAL ARCHIVES

Tuesday?" Monty looked Ike squarely in the eye and gave a confident reply: "I would say go." Ike had every good reason to further delay and every bad reason that ever existed to back whatever choice became his conclusion. But among the urgent decisions unable to be further postponed was the need as Admiral Ramsay said, for Adm. Alan G. Kirk, commander of the Western Task Force, to depart Plymouth on the USS *Augusta* with Gen. Omar Bradley. He had to sail almost immediately if the ships in Operation Neptune, the invasion's crucial naval landing operation, had any possibility of being on station on time.

Ike paced and paced on the blue carpet and polished wood floor. He heard everyone's best guess, and that's all they were, guesses, and it was now time to decide from within himself in the loneliest and most isolated place any commander ever occupied. Make the right call and the "great crusade" would begin. Get it wrong and history would judge its outcome. Victory or defeat, life or death; it came down to one man in a driving storm.

He stopped pacing to turn and say to anyone and everyone: "If you don't give the instructions now, you cannot do it on Tuesday." The finality of the declaration seemed to suspend itself somewhere above the center of the room. Tedder then spoke an aside to Leigh-Mallory, perhaps to change his mind: "If the later forecast shows a deterioration earlier (Tuesday night), putting on the night bombers at an earlier hour might be considered." Ike, irritably: "The alternatives are too chancy; the question is, just how long can you hang this operation on the end of a limb and let it hang there. The air will certainly be handicapped." Leigh-Mallory, still in doubt: "Hell of a situation; if German night bombers can operate and our night fighters cannot get off. At Dieppe . . ." Eisenhower then firmly interrupted: "If you don't give the instructions now, you cannot do it on Tuesday." Silence and the finality of it all persisted in the cigarette-blue air for what some said were minutes, but that Ike said were seconds.

At 2130 hours on June 4, the supreme commander made a tentative decision: "Well, I'm quite positive that we must give the order; the only question is whether we should meet again in the morning. I don't like it, but there it is . . . I don't see how we can possibly do anything else." After viewing the weather charts again with Stagg, he would have a final decision early the next morning, June 5. Making the call so near the deadline wouldn't have been his preference, but the ships could still be returned to port if the weather stayed gloomy.

An unexpected advantage to the delay was that it allowed still more of the lumbering tank landing ships (LST), derided by the GIs as Large Slow Targets, to be with the invasion fleet. Successfully deployed in North Africa in 1942, the revolutionary flat-keeled, long, narrow vessels could bump directly on the beach with twenty medium tanks, up to four hundred fully equipped soldiers, or twenty-one hundred tons of materiel. With a stern-mounted kedge anchor and windlass, it could even claw itself away from the clutching sand. They would prove their worth soon enough.

That night alone in his trailer, the commander-in-chief of the greatest invasion force the world would know considered the prospect of

Present-day view of Southwick House. AUTHOR

comprehensive failure. He had only nine divisions to land on D-Day. Field Marshal Gerd von Rundstedt waited with fifty-eight divisions in France, Belgium, and the Netherlands, including ten Panzer and Panzer/ Grenadier divisions. In the darkness he remembered Churchill's repeated wariness about the invasion's success. He told Ike: "When I think of the beaches of Normandy choked with the flower of American and British youth, and when in my mind's eye I see the tides running red with that blood, I have my doubts, I have my doubts." He also said, "You will soon have the power of all the Caesars that ever lived."

As the one person responsible for all to follow, Eisenhower felt the heavy weight of responsibility and possible failure, but his superior, US Army chief of staff, Gen. George C. Marshall, remained confident. Marshall had good reason to bring Ike leap-frogging over four hundred senior officers from an obscure colonel in mid-1941 to commander of the European Theatre of Operations (ETO) on June 25, 1942. The stars fell on Ike's 1915 West Point graduating class, and his was one of them.

Fifty-nine generals resulted from 164 graduates that year. In nominating Eisenhower to President Roosevelt as Overlord's commander, Marshall had picked a born leader.

At 3:30 a.m., the clock alarm rang at Ike's bedside in the trailer. He had already awakened in anticipation and could both hear and feel the still buffeting weather. Urged by loops of lashing wind and rain, he entered the Georgian mansion shortly before 4:00 a.m. for the final met briefing in the same twenty-five-foot-by-forty-foot former library with the empty bookshelves and thick blackout drapes. Awaiting Ike over desultory conversation and coffee at long tables or bunched around randomly placed upholstered chairs were seventeen of Overlord's top leaders and their immediate staff. Ike took pride in picking and balancing the senior officers—three American and four British—each a seasoned veteran with over thirty years' military experience. Some had served together in previous campaigns in the Mediterranean, and all knew that success required unprecedented collaboration.

Thin-voiced, vainglorious, Gen. Bernard Law Montgomery, commanding the ground forces, wore his usual corduroy slacks and roll-necked sweater over a casual shirt. Quick-tempered Lt. Gen. Walter Bedell Smith, chief of staff and Ike's gatekeeper, idly conversed with pipe-smoking deputy supreme commander, Air Chief Marshal Arthur Tedder. Seated to one side, Adm. Bertram Ramsay, who led the naval forces that evacuated Dunkirk, had both his headquarters and residence in the mansion, and would command the invasion's naval expeditionary forces. Air Marshal Arthur Coningham controlled the tactical air forces, and regularly would clash with Monty over their use. Impetuous, argumentative, Air Vice Marshal Trafford Leigh-Mallory, former head of RAF Fighter Command in the Battle of Britain, would lead the invasion's air force. Lt. Gen. Omar Bradley, to become "the GI's general," headed the US First Army, initially part of Montgomery's 21st Army Group. Thirteen countries, including token remnants of eight nations under the Nazi boot, awaited the command to land 156,000 troops—seventy-three thousand of them American—six thousand vehicles, nine hundred tanks, six hundred guns, and four thousand tons of supplies, at five beaches on one day along sixty miles of the little-known Normandy coast.

PART TWO

DECISION OF THE CENTURY

Before Ike's arrival at Southwick House early on June 5, several of the chiefs drifted from the weather briefing area in the former library into the connecting map and operations center, previously the mansion's immense drawing room. Powerfully dominating the entire east wall loomed a massive dark green and blue painted plywood map, divided into individual panels marked with letters. Manufactured by a British toy firm, except for one section deliberately left blank it displayed Western Europe's entire coastline from Norway to the Pyrenees. After completing the immense diorama, the two workmen were given the final section to fit into the map's only remaining blank sector—the Normandy coastline and invasion beaches. To prevent disclosure, however remote, of the war's greatest secret to date, the installers were detained until after the invasion.

As the commanders and staff went into the operations and map room, they entered a swirl of activity from the numerous Wrens and British and American officers holding files and clipboards. Typewriters and teletypes clattered over terse telephone conversation in an adjacent room, as personnel stepped over trailing telephone wires clutching decoded messages. With tension rising like a spring flood, all eyes focused on the dominating map, as Wrens perched high and low on ladders plotting positions with crayons and colored markers on transparent plastic, updating the status of underway movements.

On the map's surface, a white clock-like oval displayed a red arrow representing the high-water mark to be eleven feet at Portsmouth at 0600 on D-Day H hour. An identical circle set above Dover showed its high-water mark as eleven feet. A third white ring fastened above the invasion beaches read "HIGH WATER STRAND." The expected high water at the invasion beaches had been estimated at twelve feet. A naval chronometer-type clock with Roman numerals occupied the map's upper center section. On a small black sign attached to the map were chalked the words: "SET FOR D-Day H-Hour 6th June 1944."

Dominating an entire wall, a painted plywood map displayed the invasion beaches.
AUTHOR

Thin, red, lines on the map extended from the invasion ports of Mil-
ford and Swansea, Weymouth, Southampton, Portsmouth, even as far as
Woolwich on the Thames near London, and twenty other embarkation
or supplies ports. Spreading like limbs from the British ports, each line
extended to an assembly area in the English Channel directly east of
Portsmouth code-named Piccadilly Circus. From there the ships would
re-form into five double lines to advance due east to Normandy and five
beaches soon to be etched into history as immortal: Sword, Juno, Gold,
Utah, and Omaha, bloody Omaha.

Promptly at 4:00 a.m., the commanders and staff clustered close as
Ike again summoned Group Captain Stagg. With the storm unabated,
he could have taken a safe route by recommending further cancellation
until June 19 and borne no criticism, especially from those in the room
favoring another delay. He began by reporting that the unfavorable conditions in the Channel predicted for today were now over the landing

beaches. It remained unspoken, but all knew that catastrophe had been averted by delaying the invasion. Stagg forecast that the rain would stop in two to four hours, the winds would abate, visibility would improve, and a thirty-six-hour window of good weather would open. He had correctly predicted the same weather interval last night, and on this pre-dawn his confidence remained undiminished. It wasn't his to say, but the ships now pressing into the Channel toward France could disembark their men as planned. Weather would not delay the invasion.

Hands on hips, Ike again asked the same insistent questions as before with mostly the same terse replies. Monty and Bedell-Smith said go, Leigh-Mallory and Tedder said no. Ike paced in the now silent room. The mighty force, many well underway, compared to moving the entire populations of Kenosha, Racine, and Green Bay, Wisconsin, across Lake Michigan—with all their vehicles—into a heaving storm, and in secret.

No matter his worries, Eisenhower's entire life had prepared him for this one day and this single hour in history. The path that guided him to this house on this day started when he joined West Point's "long gray line" in 1911.

In planning the invasion, he knew that the British army warrior class considered him to be "a mass-produced general," and muttered about his over-emphasis on logistics. Behind his back, Montgomery and Field Marshall Alan-Brooke, Churchill's foremost military adviser, were scornful of his command abilities, telling each other that "he should be kept away from all that business if we want to win this war." But Ike had an awareness they lacked; he knew how to fight a modern war with equipment made by an arsenal of mass production back home. He could arm and move millions of men and fight large-scale campaigns. All who knew him saw something else: He had spine; he knew how to decide.

Some who were there said that the decision took longer, but Ike knew it immediately. He stopped pacing, turned, and said, "OK, let's go." Within thirty seconds the room emptied, leaving only a drift of smoke and a brooding Eisenhower standing alone near a clock on the mantle pointing to 4:15 a.m. on Monday, June 5, 1944.

The Burden of Command

During that longest of nights between June 5th and 6th, riven with the anguish of possible failure, Ike reached for a pencil stub to write on a four-and-a-half-by-seven-inch sheet of paper: "Our landings in the Cherbourg-Havre area have failed to gain a satisfactory foothold and I have withdrawn the troops. My decision to attack at this time and place was based upon the best information available. The troops, the air and the Navy, did all that bravery and devotion to duty could do. If any blame or fault attaches to the attempt it is mine alone." Mistakenly dating it July 5 instead of June 5, he folded the paper into sections, placing it in his wallet for release to the world's press if the invasion failed.

That evening Ike completed a second letter begun in February. Intended as an Order of the Day, on the eve of battle a printed copy went to all the sailors and troops under his command: "Soldiers, Sailors and Airmen of the Allied Expeditionary Force. You are about to embark upon the Great Crusade, toward which we have striven these many months. The eyes of the world are upon you. The hopes and prayers of liberty-loving people everywhere march with you. . . . You will bring about the destruction of the German war machine, the elimination of Nazi tyranny over the oppressed people of Europe, and security for ourselves in a free world. . . . Your task will not be an easy one. Your enemy is well trained, well-equipped and battle hardened. He will fight savagely. Our Home Fronts have given us an overwhelming superiority in weapons and munitions of war and placed at our disposal great reserves of trained fighting men. The tide has turned! The free men of the world are marching together to Victory. . . . We will accept nothing less than full victory."

After the decision, Ike went by car from Southwick House down Portsdown Hill to the Portsmouth piers for visits with British troops of the 3rd Infantry Division about to cast off for Sword Beach. Since June 1940, much of the city's docks and center had been badly damaged from fifty-seven air raids with 2,631 bombs and thirty-one thousand incendiaries. Before boarding, the troops had staged from tents in deep woods near a port city that said farewell to centuries of departing soldiers and sailors. Military traffic choked roads leading to the piers, with so many trailing troops, vehicles, and supplies, that a ten-mile-deep coastal strip had been closed to any movement for days before embarkation. Beginning with Ike's early evening visit, the city and port emptied of men and ships, leaving only numerous chalked "thank you"s on pubs and buildings, and the names of the soldier's hometowns.

Aftermath

Except for the white exterior paint replacing wartime gray, and the long-gone Nissen huts, Southwick House appears as it did during the war. Although differently appointed, the former library—the pre-invasion weather briefing room—remains unchanged. The drawing room—the operations and map room from where the invasion was launched—has the same painted plywood map in the same position, with the same details as set on D-Day, H-Hour, June 6, 1944. Because it is still an active military base, advance appointments are needed for visits.

Walking minutes from the house, the Golden Lion Pub in Southwick Village continues to appeal to thirsty locals as it did to the mansion and tent-based staff and soldiers during the war. As both a pub and brewery it made its own beer and never closed during the war, although the effects of rationing shuttered other pubs. A non-smoking and abstaining General Montgomery reputedly met at least once with General Eisenhower in the rear Gold Room.

Later on June 6 Eisenhower went eighty miles from Southwick House to Bentley Priory near Stanmore, headquarters of RAF Fighter Command. Along with King George VI and Churchill, he observed the invasion's progress from the underground bunker and Operations Room of the converted country house. Maintained in its wartime appearance, the Priory is ten miles from central London on the Jubilee or Northern lines to Stanmore or Edgeware Road, and continuing on the 142 bus to Heathbourn Road. Open from 10:00am Monday, Wednesday, Friday and Saturday.

The D-Day Museum on the seafront in Portsmouth is Britain's only museum covering all aspects of the landings. The same docks used by British forces who embarked for Sword Beach on D-Day are nearby. Fast daily trains connect the London, Waterloo, and Portsmouth Harbor stations.

Golden Lion pub, the unofficial officers' mess in Southwick Village. AUTHOR

PART THREE

AUSTERITY AND OPULENCE—
IKE AND MONTY DRIVE TO THE WAR

Mobile Commanders—Ike's "Circus Wagons" and Monty's Caravans

One mile behind Southwick House, a two-wheeled, single-door hitched trailer resembling a small moving van gave Ike accessibility without ostentation at his forward-deployed headquarters. Painted with a dominant white star on each side, along with two larger and equally unremarkable trailers they allowed communication, portability, and accessibility to his commanders. For obscure reasons, Ike referred to the three-unit olive-drab ensemble as "my circus wagons." The twenty-five-foot towed trailer that in peacetime guise could have been connected to the family car served as a combined office and sleeping area separated into three compartments. With a polished black linoleum floor and walls tinted in a muted pearl gray, its austere interior had as its single-color accent a green-leather bench seat and three green-leather covered armchairs, one at Ike's desk. The desk had a five-by-seven-inch photo of wife Mamie and another of son John in his West Point cadet uniform. A two-row bookshelf contained a selection of western-oriented fiction but was otherwise bare. On the desk were three color-coded telephones. The green telephone connected to Number Ten Downing Street. The black went to SHAEF headquarters in London. A red telephone scrambled calls. A narrow compartment held a chemical toilet, with cold running water in a sink from a forty-gallon roof-mounted tank. A compact galley had utensils, but little else. A narrow bed across the trailer's rear gave Ike no more than four tense hours of nightly sleep. Although he could have resided in the mansion in comfort if not luxury, as did Admiral Ramsay and other key staff, Ike preferred to be near his men, within the enforced solitude that allowed for focused thought on the looming mission.

An adjacent sixty-foot eight-wheel operations van—a mobile war room—had interchangeable battle maps fastened to rollers that recessed into the ceiling, a conference table in the center, and a ceiling-mounted pull-down screen for projection of reconnaissance films. A third trailer to house the portable headquarters operations and service staff included communication equipment, teletype machines, telephone outlets, a dining section, sleeping area, office, bunks, kitchenette, shower, and a single chemical toilet.

Each trailer had fittings for attachment to twenty-ton, ten-wheel, C-2 semi-tractors, with a fifteen-thousand-pound pull capacity, the largest in the US Army. Each had auxiliary power units for lighting, air-conditioning, and communications. The Detroit-made Federal Motors seven-and-a-half-ton army "wreckers," from which the trucks and chassis were adapted, were the workhorses of the war, pulling from ditches or mud many a jeep, truck, tank, and aircraft from Normandy to Berlin.

The rolling war-room's designer, George V. Russell, had prewar experience as a Hollywood set designer and architect of the *Hollywood Reporter* building on Sunset Boulevard in Los Angeles. During the war, in addition to Eisenhower's caravan, he planned air bases and base units in England and Northern Ireland. After the war, Russell designed the Flamingo Hotel in Las Vegas, the master plan for the University of California in Riverside, and a 1976 extension to the Los Angeles Natural History Museum.

By comparison with Ike's understated mobile command post, the interiors of Gen. Bernard Montgomery's trio of command and control vehicles could occupy pride of place as a luxury hotel suite in London's West End or a Hollywood film. Containing a separate motorized bedroom vehicle, an office van, and a bespoke map trailer, part of the mobile headquarters stayed with his command from the victory at El Alamein through Normandy to the German surrender. During his participation in the invasion's final planning at Southwick House, Monty's vehicle assemblage, with an entourage of twenty officers and two hundred enlisted men, had a billet in the woods near the mansion.

Originally used as both a bedroom and office, the trailer became a prize of war, taken after the surrender south of Benghazi on February 8, 1941, from its previous occupant, Italian general Annibale "Electric Whiskers" Bergonzoli, commander of the 23rd Corps. After its capture, the made in Italy body became joined to a British Leyland Retriever six-by-four truck, emerging as a motor home capable of travel through the entire European campaign. At ten-and-a-half feet high, twenty-four feet long, and eight feet wide, its interior had richly burled wood-paneled walls, with a full-size desk facing a two-paned window. Mounted on the wall immediately to the right of Monty's desk, a twelve-by-sixteen-inch portrait of Gen. Erwin Rommel in desert kit resolutely gazed back, serving as an incentive for Monty to enter the mind of the "desert fox" twice beaten by the British Eighth Army at El Alamein, the second battle under his command. Perhaps out of respect for the legendary general, Monty named one of his several dogs, a spaniel, after Rommel. Equally oversize photos of his other adversaries—Generals Model, Kesselring, and Von Rundstedt glowered defiantly back at Monty along an entire wall.

After the defeat of Italian general Giovanni Messe near the end of the North African campaign in May 1943, a second, even more luxurious command vehicle joined Monty's mobile headquarters. Built on a Lancia chassis, it had been captured during the final stage of the North African campaign in May 1943. In an interview after the war, Montgomery told the BBC about its acquisition: "Rommel had gone back to Germany, being ill, and this caravan was being used by his successor, an Italian general called Messe, who was brought to my headquarters as a prisoner. General Messe told me that the caravan belonged to Rommel." Remounted from the Lancia chassis to a Mack frame, it had a deep, Pullman-like single bed, a wardrobe, washbasin, and shower. The four-wheel, wood-paneled motor home throughout, including the ceiling, would be Monty's bedroom for the remainder of the war. He protected its potential use by other commanders—and not altogether in jest—by boasting that he would be turned-out only for Churchill or the king. Indeed, both King George VI and Churchill resided in the vehicle several times during the war. Fastened to its exterior, an eighteen-inch hand-painted heraldic shield depicted Monty's victorious North African campaigns in Egypt, Tripoli, Tunis, and Sicily.

The third caravan, a map vehicle built by the British Trailer Co. in 1944 and donated to Monty without cost, had constant use from soon after D-Day to the end of the war. Churchill, the king, and Eisenhower regularly visited its spacious, squared interior, the maps so dominant that they wrapped around the corners. Two stand-up desks on a raised section, one with a green-handled telephone, led to an open area below completely covered with maps tacked to a plywood backing under clear plastic sheeting. A trail of pinpricks extending from pushpins portrayed the Allied advance. Three round black prominently marked map cases held additional rolled maps.

AFTERMATH

Ike's humble trailers never reappeared after the war, but not Monty's custom caravan. The three-section command extravaganza was returned to Britain for storage in his barn at Islington Mill in Hampshire until four months after his death in 1976. Given in his will to the Imperial War Museum, the vehicles with the same wall-pinned maps and oversize photos of his adversaries are in the Land Warfare building of the Imperial War Museum Duxford, a still-operating former Battle of Britain airfield near London.

THE PRIDE OF OUR NATION

On the evening of D-Day—it was already near dawn in Normandy and occupied Europe—President Roosevelt again turned to the radio, the second time in as many nights, to rally the nation with a prayer:

Almighty God: Our sons, pride of our nation, this day have set upon a mighty endeavor, a struggle to preserve our Republic, our religion, and our civilization, and to set free a suffering humanity.

Lead them straight and true; give strength to their arms, stoutness to their hearts, steadfastness in their faith.

They will need Thy blessings. Their road will be long and hard, for the enemy is strong. He may hurl back our forces. Success may not come with rushing speed, but we shall return again and again; and we know that by Thy grace, and by the righteousness of our cause, our sons will triumph.

THE BEGINNING OF HISTORY

The generals, admirals, and marshals who rushed to telephones and teletype machines to launch the invasion that stormy June 5 pre-dawn at Southwick House set into motion a vast apparatus leading to a result even they could no longer fully control or even imagine. In the implementation of Eisenhower's order, the commanders changed from planners to passengers, becoming part of the same progression and purpose as their troops. What they began in Normandy would change the balance of all the history that would ever be written.

When the war in Europe ended, the US Army—eighteenth in the world in 1940—had 1.9 million military only in Europe in two army groups, five field armies, thirteen corps, and sixty-two combat divisions. By the end of the war, 16,354,000 men and women, over 12 percent of America's entire population, served their country. At the end, after almost six years of war Great Britain had nearly exhausted its reserves, with fewer than twenty divisions in combat. As a hinge to the entire war and to the remainder of the century, everything that D-Day started became the pivot for the world to come, with America's future destiny as the only country to emerge fully intact from the war as its fulcrum.

CHAPTER TWELVE

The Band of Brothers

From this day to the ending of the world
But we in it shall be remembered
We few we happy few, we band of brothers;
For he today that sheds his blood with me
Shall be my brother, be he ne'er so vile
This day shall gentle his condition,
And Gentlemen in England now a-bed
Shall think themselves accurs'd they were not here
And hold their manhood's cheap whiles any speaks
That fought with us upon St. Crispin's day.
—*HENRY V*, ACT IV, SCENE 3, WILLIAM SHAKESPEARE

LATE IN THE EVENING OF JUNE 5, IKE DROVE TWO HOURS ON RUTTED roads from Camp Sharpener to Newbury and the base at Greenham Common in Berkshire. Army Air Force (AAF) and RAF bases carpeted the area. If a B-17 or B-24 pilot returning from a mission on a wing and a prayer couldn't get back to his assigned base—and it happened regularly—another would be in view only a few miles away.

Before they left on the epic mission, Ike had an almost reverent need to see the men of the 101st Airborne who, along with the 82nd Airborne, Air Vice Marshal Leigh-Mallory had declared, would be "futilely slaughtered." They were making final equipment checks, applying lard mixed with soot to camouflage their faces, and, as Ike later wrote, "were in fine fettle." They cheered him and he cheered back, joking, and laughing:

"Where are you from son?" "Anyone from Abilene?" "Don't worry sir" they assured him, "everything is in good hands." He knew it; he could see it; the men were confident; they were ready. They were gung-ho.

From 10:30 p.m. at scores of bases, 2,395 aircraft including 1,087 Douglas C-47 Skytrain and Dakota transports, and 867 towed gliders finished loading their "sticks" of American and British jumpers—eighteen per plane—then took off to claw for altitude. With moistened eyes, Ike saw every flight into the sky before returning to camp about 2:00 a.m. on June 6. He later learned that losses for the 82nd and 101st for the entire Normandy campaign—well beyond the invasion—were 868 killed and less than three thousand wounded or taken prisoner. Overall casualties were far less than Leigh-Mallory predicted for only the single day of June 6.

At Upottery air base one hundred miles from Newbury, expecting the invasion order at any moment, two thousand men of the 506th Parachute Infantry Regiment (PIR) of the 101st Airborne Division sat on the ground next to their assigned aircraft. As they boarded eighty-one C-47s, fifty of them towing Horsa and Waco gliders, one trooper pushing another up the ladder, the jumpmaster checked their equipment for the two-hour flight into battle. Some had thirty-five to seventy-five-pound British-made leg bags, immediately torn from them in the slipstream after jumping. Most carried up to one hundred pounds of equipment. No one had less than seventy pounds. The men were issued a three-day supply of food and ammunition, although most added more ammo, cigarettes, and gum. Also at Upottery, among 15,500 airborne troops boarding C-47s throughout England, were the 140 men of E-Company, 2nd Battalion, 506th PIR, 101st Airborne Division. They were the men of "Easy" Company, a group made immortal by history. Like avenging angels the brothers would descend from the heavens into "fortress Europe." They had trained two years for a single flight with a single mission on the most important day of the twentieth century.

JUNE 6, 1944: WE STAND ALONE

As with everyone in the US armed forces, the airborne trainees who would become the storied Easy Company of the 506 PIR came from

Ike with 101st Airborne shortly before they launched the invasion from the air.
NATIONAL ARCHIVES

throughout the country. Their names resonated with the authenticity of America's diversity: Heffron, Toye, Lipton, Compton, Malarkey, Powers, Foley, Guarnere, Blithe, Nixon, and Winters. Easy Company's Executive Officer, 1st Lt. Richard "Dick" Winters, from tiny New Holland, Pennsylvania, population 2,153 in 1940, deep in Pennsylvania Dutch country, would soon make his mark in history, as would his men. All would first train at Camp Toccoa deep in Georgia's Blue Ridge Mountains.

The 506th commanding officer, Col. Robert Sink, read somewhere that a Japanese battalion had achieved a world record by marching one hundred miles in seventy-two hours. "My men can do better than that," he said, and proved it by marching 118 miles with his men from Toccoa to Atlanta in only seventy-two hours. To further instill team spirit and harden his troops for combat, the regiment regularly ran with packs up and down Currahee Mountain's 1,753 feet. "Three miles up and three miles down," became an almost defiant challenge. Adopting the Cherokee name, Currahee, "(we) stand alone," as their battle cry, they would need all their earned endurance and shared brotherhood for the battles ahead.

THE JUMP INTO HISTORY

Approaching the drop zone near Sainte-Marie-du-Mont soon after midnight on June 6, 1944, the C-47 with E Company's commanding officer, 1st Lt. Robert Meehan, took a hit from German antiaircraft fire. An engine exploded before any of the men could jump, consuming in flames the aircraft and everyone in it. Shrapnel sliced through Lieutenant Winter's plane killing the co-pilot, causing the pilot to switch on the green jump light before reaching the drop zone. It meant an immediate exit. Eighteen paratroopers were in the slipstream in less than ten seconds.

On the ground behind enemy lines, his company scattered and unaware of its location, Lieutenant Winters, now E Company's commanding officer by default, gathered available men including twelve from Easy Company, to assault a German artillery battery at Brecourt Manor. Defended by sixty troops with two machine guns, the GIs saw a four-gun 105mm howitzer battery raining accurate fire on Utah Beach and the exposed troops of the 4th Infantry Division. In neutralizing the battery, Winters's squad killed most of its defenders, earning for him a Distinguished Service Cross, and for the squad three Silver Stars, eleven Bronze, and three Purple Hearts, with a loss of four killed and two

2nd Lt. Richard Winters in 1942.
US SIGNAL CORPS

wounded. As an example of the ideal use of small unit tactics and leadership, the textbook assault would be taught to decades of soldiers.

Easy Company expected to be in battle for three days but stayed until June 29, beginning with the liberation of Carentan the next day, June 7. When they returned to England three weeks later for rest and refit, only seventy-four remained of the original 140 officers and men who jumped on June 6. In the spirit of "we stand alone," when the men returned to combat, several of the wounded still in the hospital "discharged" themselves to rejoin their friends.

In support of Operation Market Garden, the flawed attempt to capture bridges over the lower Rhine and bring the war to an end, the 506 PIR jumped again on September 17, 1944. Although surrounded, they defended fifteen miles of the road called "hell's highway" that went to Arnhem. With only thirty-five men led by Winters, E Company repelled a German force of three hundred, losing only one of their own. Made executive officer of the 2nd Battalion, newly promoted Major Winters and Easy Company were ordered with the 101st Airborne to beleaguered Bastogne, arriving on December 19, 1944, four days after the start of the siege in the Battle of the Bulge.

A ONE-WORD REPLY TO THE ENEMY DEMAND

Taken by surprise twenty-three thousand Americans, short of artillery, armor, ammunition, and air cover, fought a desperate battle in the final offensive of the war, surrounded by fifty-four thousand attackers from all or parts of seven German divisions. Confidently expecting victory, on December 22 Gen. Freiherr von Lüttwitz, commander of the XLVII Panzer Corps, sent a surrender demand to his counterpart, Brig. Gen. Anthony McAuliffe, commanding the 101st Airborne Division. "To the USA Commander of the encircled town of Bastogne. The fortune(s) of war is changing. This time the USA forces in and near Bastogne have been encircled by strong German armored units. More German armored units have crossed the river Our near Ortheuville, have taken Marche and reached St. Hubert by passing through Hompre-Sibert-Tillet. Libramont is in German hands. There is only one possibility to save the encircled USA troops from total annihilation: that is the honorable surrender of the encircled town. In order to think it over a term of two hours will be granted beginning with the presentation of this note. If this proposal should be rejected one German Artillery Corps and six heavy A.A. Battalions are ready to annihilate the USA troops in and near Bastogne. The order for firing will be given immediately after this two hours term. All the serious civilian losses caused by this artillery fire would not correspond with the well-known American humanity. [signed] The German Commander."

Shortly after receiving the surrender demand, General McAuliffe wrote a short response: "To the German commander. NUTS. The American commander." After considering the meaning of the American slang word for *no*, the German commander correctly concluded that it meant "go to hell." ("Nuts"—a declaration of defiance and determination, not only in the Battle of the Bulge, but for the entire war, lifted the army's spirit and gave new resolve to the nation. It became the war's most repeated word.)

Elements of Patton's Third Army began to lift the siege the day after Christmas. Expecting to be replaced, the 506th and Easy Company instead resumed the attack on January 17, pushing back the elite of the German army to Bourcy, the same location where the offensive

E Company, 2nd Battalion, 506 PIR, 101st Airborne. US SIGNAL CORPS

began. Relieved the next day by other troops of General Patton's third Army, losses for the 101st were 341 killed, 1,691 wounded, and 516 missing or taken prisoner.

On May 4, the German surrender mere days away, E Company, the 506 PIR, and the 101st Airborne captured what remained of Hitler's sprawling Berghof mountain retreat outside Berchtesgaden. They also liberated stockpiles of his fine wines and champagne, while gazing through the big picture window at the Bavarian Alps. From Georgia's Camp Toccoa, Easy Company, the 506th, and the 101st Airborne had traveled from England to France, Holland, Belgium, and Germany.

DICK WINTERS'S PEACE

Long after the war, Dick Winters reminisced about what it was like on D-Day and after: "When I saw others next to me get hit just because they lifted their head up at the wrong time, I knew I could be killed, too. I said, 'My dear God, if I live through all this, all I want for the rest of my life is peace and quiet.'"

His prayers were answered. After the war he married Ethel Estoppy, bought a small farm, raised two children, and started a farmers' feed and supply company, with Ethel managing the small office near Hershey, Pennsylvania, where the family lived. Married for sixty-three years, he died at age ninety-two on January 2, 2011. Ethel died fourteen months later at age eighty-nine. When one of his soldiers, "Wild Bill" Guarnere, learned of his death, he said: "He was a good man, a very good man. I would follow him to hell and back; so would the men from E Company."

Buried next to his parents in the Bergstrasse Evangelical Church Cemetery in Ephrata, Pennsylvania, his grave marker reads, "Richard D. Winters, World War II, 101st Airborne." On June 6, 2012, the sixty-eighth anniver-

Richard Winters in 2004. US ARMY HERITAGE AND EDUCATION CENTER

sary of D-Day, the citizens of Sainte-Marie-du-Mont, the village he and E Company liberated on D-Day, dedicated a twelve-foot-tall bronze statue in his likeness. Informed of the plans before his death, he refused to allow the statue to be built unless it included the names of the junior officers who died in the Normandy campaign. Over family objections, a replica of the same statue was dedicated in Ephrata, Pennsylvania, on September 14, 2015. During an interview for the celebrated miniseries, *Band of Brothers*, Winters looked back at the war and the dedication he had for his men: "Do you remember the letter that Mike Ranney wrote me? Do you remember how I ended it? I cherish the memories of a question my grandson asked me the other day: 'Grandpa, were you a hero in the war?' Grandpa said no, but I served in the company of heroes."

Forty-nine of the Easy Company heroes were killed in action, with scores more wounded. One E Company soldier later said that "the Purple Heart was not a decoration but a badge of office." Richard "Dick" Winters rose from private to major, receiving the military's second highest award, the Distinguished Service Cross.

Brig. Gen. Anthony McAuliffe said "nuts" to the German surrender demand. NATIONAL ARCHIVES

D-DAY ALLIED ORDER OF BATTLE

UNITED STATES: First Army, V Corps, VII Corps, 1st Infantry Division, 4th Infantry Division, 29th Infantry Division, 82nd Airborne Division, 101st Airborne Division, Eighth Air Force, Ninth Air Force, Western Naval Task Force. GREAT BRITAIN: Second Army, 1st Corps, 30th Corps, 3rd Infantry Division, 6th Airborne Division, 50th Infantry Division, 3rd Canadian Infantry Division, Royal Air Force, 2nd Tactical Air Force, Eastern Naval Task Force.

Operation Overlord Landing Beaches

The Allies divided the invasion beaches into five sectors across sixty miles of the Normandy coast. The assault began soon after midnight on June 6, 1944, when the US 82nd, 101st and British 6th airborne divisions landed behind enemy lines on the west and east sectors to secure targets for the amphibious assault. Between 0630 and 0745, elements of the US First Army and the British Second Army landed five US, British, and Canadian divisions, at five code-named invasion beaches.

UTAH BEACH: US 4th Infantry Division
OMAHA BEACH: US First Infantry Division
GOLD BEACH: British 50th Infantry Division
JUNO BEACH: Canadian Third Infantry Division
SWORD BEACH: British Third Infantry Division

CHAPTER THIRTEEN

Air Force Pilot, Hero, and Movie Star— Jimmy Stewart and the Need to Fly

The trumpet sounds retreat; the day is ours.
Come brother, let us to the highest of the field,
To see what friends are living, who are dead.
—HENRY IV, PART 1, ACT 5, SCENE 4

PART ONE

THE FREEDOM IN THE SKY

Not long after his 1908 birth in Indiana, Pennsylvania, already nearing the end of its coal-mining prosperity, Jim Stewart knew that he had to fly. Something about the open environment in the sky suited his nature. Inherently reticent and modest as boy and man, a distinct speech pattern of part stutter and part slight pause showed both strength and vulnerability, an unexpected advantage during his years of success in movies.

Soon after the century's first Great War ended in 1918, barnstormers and flying circuses offered rides at a flat farm field in town to anyone with ten dollars for ten minutes or fifteen dollars for fifteen minutes. The pilots flew in the war for the Aviation Section of the US Army Signal Corps, and now demonstrated to an eager public a new way of warfare, and, soon, mass transportation. The shows had wing-walkers, stunt parachutists, midair wing-to-wing plane transfers, performers, and the daring pilots themselves who did barrel-rolls, breathtaking spins and dives, even top-speed hurtles through open barns, although not always with a safe landing. The Curtiss JN-3 "Jenny" biplanes they trained on during the war cost the government $8,100 each, but were eagerly bought by the same pilots, now civilians, for as low as $1,000 each.

Taking time off from flying model airplanes on the roof of the family home, and building crystal radios with cereal boxes and wires, the reliable Jenny became not only the first aircraft that Jim saw, but the first he flew in as a preteen rear seat passenger. He saved for the first of four rides from wages earned at J.M. Stewart & Co, the hardware store owned by his father, Alexander. Alex served in both the Spanish-American and the Great War repairing ordnance equipment. Service to country ran in Alex's family. His father, uncle, and father-in-law all fought in close combat for the Union in the Civil War.

In his bedroom Jim mapped every rapturous report describing Charles Lindbergh's historic 1927 solo flight across the Atlantic, never imagining that thirty years later he would be typecast as the shy and reserved "Slim" Lindbergh in *The Spirit of St. Louis*. Years later he described the freedom that he found in the air: "It was the ultimate feeling of being in control . . . and being alone. I've always been a loner . . . I enjoy being on my own."

While at Princeton, he joined the Triangle Club, a theatrical company among the first to perform new shows at the university, and then taking them on the road, even to Broadway. Jim joined the club not because he could act, but because he played the accordion and performed in a specialty duet with another accordionist.

DISTANT SOUNDS OF WAR

After graduating in 1932, Stewart did summer stock with a Cape Cod theatrical company and became close friends with Henry Fonda, another aspiring actor. Along with Fonda, and Joshua Logan, to become a celebrated stage and film director, with periodic residency by actor Burgess Meredith, he rented a small apartment on Manhattan's then scruffy West 63rd Street. By January 30, 1933, the day Hitler became chancellor, Stewart made his professional debut on Broadway in *Goodbye Again*, appearing 216 times as a chauffeur, to speak only two forgettable lines. By taking other secondary parts on Broadway he built a solid resume, leading to a 1935 screen test with MGM in New York. Metro signed Stewart to a three-month contract at a very respectable $350 per week and he headed for Hollywood, to become established in 1937 in a series of secondary parts in B films.

That same year, a continent and an ocean away from Hollywood, Hitler had committed Germany to prepare for all-out war. That year Buchenwald opened, the first concentration camp in Germany. It later became an extermination site for anyone who disagreed with the goals of the Nazi revolution. The captive dissidents included actors, artists, doctors, political prisoners, homosexuals, and, especially, Jews in any profession or occupation. By the end of 1938 Stewart had appeared in eighteen films, including the breakthrough Frank Capra directed, *You Can't Take It With You*, which won two Oscars with five nominations.

In 1939, now an A list screen star, Stewart made another Frank Capra film, *Mr. Smith Goes to Washington*, which earned him the New York Film Critics award for Best Actor, and the film eleven Oscar nominations. Britain's second month in its six-year war of survival with Nazi Germany had scant notice at the movie's October 17, 1939 premiere at Constitution Hall in Washington, DC.

When Germany attacked Poland on September 1, 1939, beginning the Second World War, it had 3,180,000 men under arms in one hundred infantry and six armored divisions. A few months later, the highly advanced Luftwaffe already had 3,684 military aircraft, including 1,107 Messerschmitt Bf-109s. Approximating Germany's military prowess in manpower if not in skills, in 1939 France had ninety infantry divisions in metropolitan France alone, plus the military strength of her far-flung colonies.

In the sweltering Hollywood August of 1940, Stewart wrapped *The Philadelphia Story*, starring alongside Cary Grant, Katharine Hepburn, and Ruth Hussey. He played reporter Mike Connor in a performance so highly regarded that he won his only Oscar for best actor. The romantic comedy received six Oscar nominations, including George Cukor for director, and Katharine Hepburn as best actress. (The critically and financially successful film had an even bigger second life as the 1956 musical *High Society*, starring Bing Crosby, Grace Kelly, and Frank Sinatra.)

Something More Than Fame

At age thirty-two, Stewart had reached the heights of stardom and could finally realize his boyhood dream of flight by taking lessons with Henry Fonda at the Bob Blair School of Flying at Mines Field. Located on former asparagus and celery fields on the edge of the city in Westchester and still lively with jackrabbits, it had a single two-thousand-foot runway with hangar space for forty airplanes. (After the war, it expanded greatly into Los Angeles International Airport.) Soloing in only twelve hours, he earned a private pilot's license, quickly logged over one hundred hours, and bought a bright yellow Stinson 105 Voyager, the same aircraft the Army Air Corps used as a trainer. Keenly aware of world events, when Stewart looked at the horizon he saw more than blue sky. As an aviator he also saw war clouds gathering, and intended to be part of the unfolding events by enlisting in the Air Corps. Buying the Stinson, he thought, would show the Army his added skill flying its basic trainer.

President Roosevelt also viewed war as inevitable, advocating on September 16, 1940 for peacetime passage of the Selective Training and Service Act. The draft bill passed Congress with solid majorities. All men between twenty-one and thirty-five were required to register. Thousands of volunteers flooded recruiting centers to pick a service branch before they received draft notices with the branch already assigned. By the end of that same September 1940, Hitler had already conquered most of Europe in preparation for a blockade of Britain as a preliminary to invasion.

In a nationwide lottery drawing held only two weeks later, out of one million men in the draft Stewart's low number, 310, meant a requirement to report for evaluation and classification. "It's the only lottery I ever won," he said. Appearing before a skeptical recruiter and examining physician for prior approval to enlist in the Army Air Corps, he first had to overcome age, weight, and height issues. Nearly thirty-three, he already exceeded by at least ten years the ages of other men in pilot training.

Other disqualifiers were equally discouraging. At 6'3", he was too tall to fit into the seat of a fighter plane. A rail-thin 130 pounds, he weighed five pounds less than the minimum requirement for induction. "You will be informed of our decision," the examining board told him none too expectantly, and he drove home expecting the worst. The letter that soon arrived rated him as 1B, meaning a six-month or longer deferment, instead of a 1A classification needed for induction and training. Stewart had to pack on proteins and do it quickly, then revisit the draft board doctor to plead for reconsideration.

While awaiting the draft board's reassessment, and in-between completing three pictures for Metro and United Artists, Stewart further perfected his flight skills. The extra hours were needed for the commercial pilot's certification he received on March 10, 1940. He could now fly for an airline. In early March, another letter from the Selective Service System had welcome news: "ORDER FOR INDUCTION: The President of the United States to James M. Stewart. Greeting: You are hereby ordered for induction into the Armed Forces of the United States, and to report. . . ." On March 21, 1941, wearing a suit and surrounded by cameramen and popping flash bulbs, he reported to the West Los Angeles draft board. That day, James Stewart, movie star and Oscar winner, became a recruit in the United States Army.

"I Do Solemnly Swear"

The inducting officer read the Oath of Enlistment, unchanged from 1789: "Inductees, raise your right hand and repeat after me: 'I, (James Maitland Stewart), do solemnly swear that I will bear true faith and allegiance to the United States of America and will serve them honestly and faithfully against all their enemies whomsoever. I will obey orders of the President of the United States of America and the officers appointed over me according to the rules of the articles of war, so help me, God.' Congratulations, you're in the army now," the officer informed the draftees. Neither Stewart nor any GI would ever forget his dogtag number. His changed when he became an officer, but as an enlisted man it was 39230721. His life was about to change forever.

Ever Advancing as War Nears

Although assigned as expected to the Air Corps after completing basic training, Louis B. Mayer and MGM made another type of trip to Mr. Smith's real Washington, to petition their contacts to have Stewart assigned to the Motion Picture Unit at Wright Field in Dayton, Ohio. Metro intended to protect its bankable star. If they were successful, he would sit out the war as a Hollywood hero making recruiting films. Stewart had a more direct approach. First, he went to MGM's co-founder Louis B. Mayer: "Mr. Mayer, this country's conscience is bigger than all the studios in Hollywood put together, and the time will come when we'll have to fight." He then met with Col. E. B. Lyon, commanding officer of Moffet Field in Santa Clara County, to prove his merit in requesting flight training. He handed the C/O a flight log with 367 hours, pages of flights, and a commercial rating, rare for any flight candidate, much less a movie star. He told Colonel Lyon that the added flying hours from the Palo Alto airport had further improved his abilities and could only help the country.

The personal plea succeeded. Near the end of training on June 14, 1941, he applied for promotion to second lieutenant and flight status. On November 13, a thirty-five-minute test flight on a North American BT-14 trainer with an instructor grading every stall, spin, figure-eight around pylons, and chandelle resulted in an "excellent" rating. His promotion had a clause; the examining board at the Presidio of San Francisco endorsed service only in public relations and recruiting, away from combat. That set him back where he started until everything changed on December 7, 1941, when the Japanese attacked Pearl Harbor. He became an instructor in twin-engine aircraft at Mather Army Airfield, near Sacramento. It wasn't combat, but now that he had become a part of history's greatest war, Jim knew that somehow, somewhere, he would get into the fight.

Getting Closer to the Action

One of the powerful new B-24 Liberators rolling out of five factories soon became fundamental to both Stewart's life and his future crew. But first he needed additional ground-school training and four-engine

B-17 qualification at Hobbs Field, New Mexico. In February 1943, with one hundred hours logged on B-17s, he graduated with the twin bars of a captain. Eager for combat but transferred still again, he next trained B-17 pilots at Gowen Field in Boise until everyone went overseas. On August 3, 1943, he transferred to Sioux City Army Air Base for a second refresher on B-24s, receiving the top grade of "excellent" on all tests. As one of the Air Corps' best-trained aviators, the time neared for overseas deployment.

The 445th Bomb Group and its four B-24 squadrons needed an operations officer for the 703rd Squadron when they deployed overseas, someone with the potential to become squadron commander. As the previous operations officer at Sioux City, Stewart had ideal qualifications to command a squadron, training daily and sometimes at night to tighten the intricate defensive box formation. In combat, twelve or more aircraft huddled almost wingtip to wingtip to protect themselves and the adjacent ship with their ten guns. Secure in a combat box, a formation then blended into a stream with hundreds of other bombers, each protecting their mates, while always searching for the enveloping Bf-109s or Fw-190s that suddenly appeared like enraged hornets.

After a short posting as operations officer, Stewart became the 703rd's squadron commander. At age thirty-five, having risen from private to captain in two years, and in skills from a single-engine private pilot to a command pilot qualified to fly the Army's two biggest four-engine bombers, Stewart, the 445th BG, and 703 Squadron were ready and eager to enter the fight.

The 445's headquarters staff and ground crew went to New York by train to sail unescorted across the Atlantic aboard the *Queen Mary* with twelve thousand other GIs. At 27 knots or more, the "gray ghost" could outrun any U-boat on or below the surface. In five days she would safely carry them and millions more during the war to Gourock in the west of Scotland and other ports, to board pier-side trains and travel to bases "somewhere in England."

Ready to fly to the British Isles on the southern route from a final staging area at Morrison Field, Palm Beach, Florida, Stewart and the 445th BG taxied the fuel-heavy Liberators to the active runway. Aboard

Stewart as the 703 squadron commander at Tibenham. AUTHOR

the "Tenovus" (ten of us) in the right seat as co-pilot, Stewart adjusted his tie, placed earphones over his crush cap, changed the fuel mixture to auto-rich, turned on the booster pumps, set trim tabs and flaps, released the brakes, and advanced the throttles to full takeoff power. He knew well how unforgiving the B-24 could be, that the controls were heavy, and it needed constant trimming with two hands always on the yoke to keep it from wandering across the sky. He knew it well enough; he had trained two years for this day.

After takeoff, with an initial compass heading toward Puerto Rico, Stewart could finally unseal the orders and trigger the throat mic to tell the crew their destination. As expected, they were headed to East Anglia in England, via Trinidad, Belem, Brazil, Dakar, Marrakesh, and Prestwick in Scotland, to a base named Station 124, close to a crossroads village called Tibenham, wherever the hell that was.

⌐ ⌐

PART TWO

MANY MISSIONS, LITTLE REST, MAJOR LOSSES

On November 24, 1943, the day the 445th and its four squadrons arrived at Tibenham, the runways Stewart and the crew saw from above resembled a triangular "A" frame, as did most of the scores of Eighth Air Force bases under feverish construction. With three converging concrete runways positioned for the prevailing winds, the main runway, or the bottom of the A, extended six thousand feet, with two intersecting forty-two-hundred-foot auxiliary runways. A fifty-foot-wide concrete perimeter track with thirty-six open "frying pan," or at other bases, looping "spectacle" hardstands for two bombers each, were dispersed along the perimeter to minimize damage from attacks.

The 445th settled into their new surroundings for more classroom instruction in tactics and practice missions over East Anglia. They learned how to recognize the difference and locations of the navigational Buncher beacons at each base, and the numbered Splasher radio beacons along the coast. In a pinch, visual landmarks near Tibenham included an adjacent rail line and the bell tower of the thirteenth-century All Saints Church near the end of the main runway.

Off-duty, it didn't take long to learn the easiest route on foot or on a bicycle, of which there were hundreds on base, to the Greyhound Pub and its two bars and log fireplaces. Since its opening in 1713, the solid brick building, always with an abundance of empty kegs near the entrance, had seen many young men off to war.

On December 13, three weeks after landing at Tibenham, Stewart's 703rd and other squadrons in the 445th BG squeezed on to narrow benches in the Ops shack for a pre-dawn briefing. After overnight servicing and arming by ground crews, trucks stood by to bring the crews to their aircraft. One of four simultaneous "maximum effort" missions this day, it would be the first major attack of the European war and the first time that over six hundred bombers would simultaneously hit multiple targets. As another milestone, it would also be the first mission shared by both B-17s and B-24s. For Capt. Jimmy Stewart and the 445th, it would also mark the first time they flew in combat, and it wouldn't be a "milk run."

When the curtains opened in the blacked-out ops room, the lines extending from Tibenham on the big map showed that both the P-47 and P-51 fighters, the much-appreciated "little friends," would escort the bombers, but only as far as the P-47's two internal fuel tanks and the P-51's 255 gallons would allow. The P-51s had longer range, were more agile in climb and maneuver, and had a streamlined look the P-47 lacked, but the pilots who flew the "Jugs" (Juggernaut) preferred their durability in a dogfight.

With thirty seconds between takeoffs and about an hour to form up, the group flew a twisting S to reach altitude, and then a racetrack pattern to await the others. Then they saw their assigned "Zebra," a garishly decorated B-24, one of several stripped-down bombers serving as assembly points for different groups. After joining-up and now forming a combat wing, they flew as one formation 15 miles to the North Sea and across to the tip of occupied Holland, to cross the northern top of Germany. Some of the groups would hit the port of Bremen, while others, including Stewart's 445th, would bomb the *Howaldtswerke-Deutsche Werft* (HDW) shipyard, U-boat factory, and their pen shelters in Kiel. Every crewman knew that the U-boat factories, bases, and aircraft assembly plants were the most heavily defended in the Reich. Early in the war Hitler had correctly concluded that only by severing the convoy lifeline connecting Britain with North America would he have any chance of winning the war. U-boats were essential to that goal.

With ten five-hundred-pound general purpose bombs racked on each Liberator for the long-range missions, the crews could only speculate as to why the U-boat bases remained undamaged mission after mission, although from twenty-five thousand feet they could see the lack of results after direct hits. They didn't know that a kinetic weight of only five hundred pounds exploding against the multilayered concrete roofs of the armored U-boat shelters had an effect akin to fragments being chipped from a pottery container.

A haggard Maj. James Stewart, England 1944. NATIONAL ARCHIVES

On the first day in combat for the 445th, 171 B-17s hit the target at the Bremen ports, with visible damage to port facilities and flak holes in thirty of the big bombers, but no losses. On the mission to Kiel, 367 B-17s and ninety-three B-24s found poor visibility over the principal target, with some diverting to the secondary target at Hamburg. The remaining bombers were over Kiel from 1245 to 1317 hours, as Luftwaffe defenders swarmed the attackers, shooting down four B-17s and one B-24. Escorted part of the way by thirty-one P-38, thirty-two P-47, and forty-one P-51 fighters, they claimed only two German fighters at a loss of one P-47 and one P-51. At the end of their operational range, the US fighters were forced to leave the scene. The loss of five aircraft on the first major mission of the European war was but a prelude to what would follow. The US crewmen would have been even more disheartened had they known that their raids against Bremen and Kiel were not the first.

Eight months before Stewart's first mission as commanding officer of the 703rd Squadron, the RAF had already completed its eighty-first unsuccessful night attack against the same Kiel U-boat factory and shipyard. At least they caught in the open and sank the "pocket-battleship" *Admiral Scheer*, and damaged cruisers *Admiral Hipper* and *Emden*. But after hundreds of attacks and heavy damage to the Kiel U-boat bases, they continued operational.

INCREASING LOSSES PEAK DURING "BIG WEEK"

With only a two-day break, the 445th flew on December 15, then on the 20th, 22nd, 24th, and for the sixth time in two weeks, on New Year's Eve to bomb a power station in Manheim. From arrival at Tibenham until their last combat mission on April 25, 1945, the 445th flew 280 missions with 6,323 sorties in 475 days. Lost were 138 B-24s, with 1,074 crewmen killed, missing, captured, or interned. With forty-eight bombers in the 445th, by the end of the war the entire group had been replaced by almost three times from its initial complement.

Stewart had been in the cockpit as co-pilot of *Tenovus* on February 20, 1944, the first day of Operation Argument or "Big Week," seven days he would never forget. As the first "maximum effort" combining RAF Bomber Command and the Eighth Air Force in England, with the Italy-based Fifteenth Air Force, the mission included the 445th BG and Stewart's 703rd lead squadron. They would hit Brunswick, a distant 450 miles in and 450 miles back, to bomb a parts factory for the Ju-88 twin-engine fighter bomber. The crews knew that factories making aircraft and U-boats were among the most heavily defended, and they would pay a price that day.

On the mission Brunswick Stewart saw six bombers go down, but Allied losses went even higher only four days later when he wasn't flying. Big Week had the purpose of knocking Germany out of the war in five days of overwhelming attacks against four cities containing the country's most vital war industries. Over a thousand bombers and fighters also hit a Messerschmitt plant at Gotha and a ball-bearing works at Schweinfurt. On Friday of Big Week, more than two thousand planes attacked Germany's war industries.

Watching for the 445th to return from Tibenham's tower observation deck, Stewart expected heavy losses, but not as shocking as the few stragglers he saw limping back. Only thirteen of the twenty-five Libs that went out that morning returned seven hours later, most of them carrying wounded. Henry "Hap" Arnold, the Army Air Force commanding general expressed the loss for everyone. "We paid a price for the air; we lost 244 heavy bombers and thirty-three fighter planes during five days." Sharing in the suffering, RAF Bomber Command lost 131 of 823 aircraft dispatched, or 16 percent of all available bombers. But the Luftwaffe lost the most, with 355 fighters shot down and another ninety damaged, about 17 percent of the total available fighters. After Big Week the Luft-

Officers of 703 Squadron, Jimmy Stewart fourth from left in back row. NATIONAL ARCHIVES

waffe still flew, but they never again challenged the skies for superiority or changed a battle's outcome. Knowing how badly they were crippled, on the eve of D-Day a confident General Eisenhower said to his departing troops: "If you see fighter aircraft over you, they will be ours."

ONE OF THE WORST DAYS—AN 88 PERCENT LOSS

On September 27, 1944, Stewart had been reassigned away from the 445th when a navigational error rerouted the 445th from inside a force of 1,192 bombers and 678 fighters positioning to bomb the Henschel Tiger Tank factory at Kassel. Separated from the main bomber stream, lacking ground reference points, and initially without fighter support, the diverted 445th hit the wrong target at Goettingen, twenty-five miles northeast of Kassel. In one of the worst losses of the war, up to 150 Fw-190 and Bf-109s shot down twenty-five B-24s in less than five minutes. Only the arrival of US fighters saved the ten remaining bombers, but more were to go down. On the return to Tibenham, three damaged bombers were forced down in France and Belgium, two made emergency landings at RAF Manston on the English coast, and one crashed near

Tibenham. As base personnel anxiously looked for the group's return, they counted only four aircraft on final approach, an astonishing loss of 88 percent, including 117 killed and eighty-one captured. That evening, 198 fewer meals were served, with an equal number of letters written by squadron commanders to families back home.

PART THREE

A WONDERFUL LIFE

All Eighth Air Force combat stopped a month before the European war ended. No German cities were left to bomb or fighters to shoot down. The Third Reich had been reduced to rubble. For the short time remaining, Stewart, now a full colonel and survivor of twenty missions with the 445 and 453 bomb groups, had command of the Second Combat Wing. Along with a ticket back to the states, he received the Air Medal and Distinguished Flying Cross.

On August 27, 1945, Stewart and fifteen thousand other GIs returned to New York on the *Queen Elizabeth*. He could have agreed to meet with reporters waiting on the pier to interview a movie star returning from war, but it wasn't his way. Instead he waited at the bottom of the gangway until all his men had disembarked to receive his salute. At age thirty-seven, the first Hollywood star to enlist, and one of the oldest combat veterans in the AAF, Stewart had advanced ten ranks from private to full colonel in four years. But he wasn't finished.

If Hollywood would have him he intended to resume making pictures. After being contacted by director Frank Capra, a US Army Signal Corps filmmaker in the war, Stewart starred as George Bailey in his 1946 comeback film *It's a Wonderful Life*, which co-starred Donna Reed and became a cherished annual family holiday classic. Of much more importance than making movies was his re-enlistment in the Air Force Reserve, to retire in 1968 as a brigadier general.

His return to movies firmly established in 1947 with *Call Northside 777*, co-starring Lee J. Cobb and Richard Conte, in his career he appeared

Colonel Stewart receives the French Croix de Guerre. USAAF

in ninety-two movies, television, and radio programs. In addition to *It's a Wonderful Life*, four other of his films are in the American Film Institute's 100 greatest American films: *Mr. Smith Goes to Washington*, *The Philadelphia Story*, *Harvey*, and *Anatomy of a Murder*. In addition to pictures, he appeared eleven times in Broadway plays and made twenty radio appearances. His tearful reading of "A Dog Named Beau" on *The Tonight Show* with Johnny Carson has been seen millions of times. Having lived a wonderful life of duty, honor, and country, Stewart died at age eighty-nine on July 2, 1997, with burial at Forest Lawn Cemetery in Glendale, California.

AFTERMATH

After building thirty-one U-boats in Kiel and thirty-three in its Hamburg yards, the privately owned HDW Kiel and Bremen shipyards survived the war intact. After VE Day, they immediately began reorganizing for the peacetime contracts sure to come. Among them were Aristotle Onassis's luxury yacht, the *Christina O* in 1952; numerous fast ferries; naval frigates for Germany, Malaysia, and South Africa; corvettes for Israel; and, currently underway, Braunschweig-class corvettes for Germany, in fulfillment of its NATO commitment.

Near the former entrance to Tibenham AAF base thirteen miles south west of Norwich, the Greyhound Pub displays a wartime autographed photo and other memorabilia of Jimmy Stewart, a regular visitor. A painted wall on the Tibenham Community Hall depicts a B-24 in flight. Almost hidden near Tibenham's entrance, a black granite memorial dedicated in 1987 by the 445th BG Association outlines the airfield's runways and features the group's "C" identifying tail marker. The Norwich Gliding Club uses part of an original runway. Also remaining are portions of abandoned huts and other structures.

A museum in the Indiana, Pennsylvania, library near Stewart's birth home at 104 N. Seventh Street has artifacts from his life. The library is near the family's former hardware store and his statue outside the courthouse. Still a small town, Indiana, Pennsylvania, gained only four thousand people between 1940 when Stewart enlisted in the Army and 2018, when it had a population of fourteen thousand.

CHAPTER FOURTEEN

The US Army Air Force in Europe

—◆—

PART ONE

FROM OBSOLETE TO OVERWHELMING

IN 1938, WITH GERMANY MASSIVELY REARMING, THE ENTIRE US ARMY Air Corps GHQ had only sixteen hundred officers responsible for recruiting and training personnel, aircraft purchase, development, and flight operations.

Outgunned, outnumbered, and years behind in manpower compared to the dictatorships already plundering in the Atlantic and Pacific, before achieving anything approaching parity with its future foes, the United States first had to climb out of the prewar ditch it had dug, and do it quickly.

In 1939, only 22,387 officers and men were serving in the Army Air Corps. Of the prewar West Point graduates who elected to join the Air Corps before 1939, there were never more than 246 air cadets selected each year. Shackled by congressional budget restrictions, almost all air cadet graduates were commissioned into the Air Corps Reserve instead of the regular army. After a short tour of duty, the Army returned them to civilian status, many to become commercial pilots.

Before America entered the war, the Army Air Corps had fewer than three hundred bombers of all types with the B-17 as the only heavy bomber. Of the thirty-eight made in 1940, half went to the RAF. The

B-24, the war's most produced aircraft, became combat-ready in mid-1942. Not to enter the war until June 5, 1944, the B-29 Superfortress, the third and largest of the war's heavy bombers, saw action only in the Pacific Theatre. In 1941, with fewer than fifteen hundred combat aircraft of all types, only eight hundred were battle-ready, of which seven hundred became immediately obsolete on December 7, 1941. America entered the war nearly defenseless in the air.

THE LUFTWAFFE—READY FOR WAR

Before Germany began the war, its illegal peacetime *Luftwaffe* already had 370,000 men, each trained and equipped in violation of the Treaty of Versailles, and under the knowing gaze of Britain and France. The Treaty prohibited Germany from developing any military aviation, but as one of numerous ways of evading compliance requirements, the *Luftwaffe* arranged for training in secret from Lufthansa, the civilian airline started in 1926.

Shortly before the outbreak of war in 1939, Germany already flew twenty-eight combat-trained bomber and fighter wings, separated into groups (*gruppen*) and squadrons (*staffel*) of nine to twelve planes per squadron. Immediately at the start of the war, its modern Junkers Ju-88A, Messerschmitt Bf-109, and Bf-110, Heinkel He-111, and Dornier D-17Z controlled the skies. With a robust prewar infrastructure already in place, Germany's production of military aircraft, but not the pilots or enough fuel to fly them, continued until the end of the war.

The opportunity to improve the Luftwaffe's formation flying, bombing skills, and its revolutionary tactic of *Blitzkrieg* (lightning war) came with Francisco Franco's invitation to Hitler for the *Luftwaffe* to intervene in the Spanish Civil War, leading to the April 1937 terror bombing of Guernica.

At the outbreak of war, the *Luftwaffe's* forty-two hundred aircraft included 3,260 bombers, dive bombers, fighters, and transports. Led by Reichmarschall Hermann Göring, one of only two *Luftwaffe* commanders, so confident were expectations of victory by the *Luftwaffe,* the invasion of the British Isles had already been given a summer 1940 start date. Eighteen months before America's entry, the *Luftwaffe* had vastly enlarged to 2.2 million men.

One of the war's best fighter planes, the 1,900-horsepower BMW engine–powered Messerschmitt Bf-109, with over twenty thousand made. AMERICAN AIR MUSEUM

THE USAAF—FROM SELF-DEFENSE
TO HISTORY'S DOMINANT AIR POWER

In sharp contrast to Nazi Germany, in 1939 the US Army Air Force ros-ter included hundreds of World War I–era trainers and several hundred portly Brewster F2A (Buffalo), called "Ronsen's" or "flying coffins" by their surviving pilots.

From its beginning as a continental self-protection force, the AAF multiplied in less than four years by more than one hundred times its prewar size. By 1944, it had 2.4 million personnel—one-third of the entire US Army—including over 150,000 in the Women's Army Corps (WAC). Sixteen tactical air divisions and eight support commands, each with separate operational units, flew 2.3 million missions worldwide. By VE Day the USAAF operated from 392 European bases. In England, the Eighth Air Force controlled three air divisions at seventy bases. B-17 manufacturing increased from thirteen on September 1, 1939 to 12,731

on VJ Day. At 18,482 manufactured, the B-24 became the most produced American aircraft of the war.

In the United States, 2.2 million workers, from a few who hand-
finished components in small shops, to multi-thousands in seven-days-a-
week manufacturing and assembly lines, vastly expanded from producing
fewer than three thousand planes in 1939—much of it for the British—
to 324,750 aircraft of all types by the end of the war.

Activated on January 2, 1942 at Savannah Army Air Base, Georgia
under Maj. Gen. Carl Spaatz, the infant air force's first mission began
on the ground in England with a small headquarters staff at Wycombe
Abbey, a herald of the air armada to come. From the desks of its planners and in the factories of American workers emerged an enterprise so
massive in scope that its achievement could not be predicted by even its
most visionary believers. From a modest planning contingent in 1942
came history's dominant air power in 1945.

Origins of the British Bases—
The "Germany First" Decision

To keep Nazi Germany at a distance while the United States rearmed,
Lend-Lease aid totaling $50.1 billion ($675 billion now) continued
until the end of the war. Britain, the Soviet Union, and France were the
major aid recipients among thirty-six countries, although the Lend-
Lease fighter planes sent to England were so inferior to the Hurricanes
and Spitfires defending Britain that most went to support or training
assignments.

Then came a decisive change in political strategy at first to diminish,
then to destroy Nazi Germany's military dominance. On December 11,
1941, four days after the Pearl Harbor attack, Germany declared war
on the United States. Two weeks later at the Arcadia Conference in
Washington, DC, FDR and Churchill agreed to defeat Germany first, a
decision made easier by Germany's declaration of war. The statement by
the two leaders began an immediate and unprecedented construction of
American air bases on the British mainland. To build them, the United
States poured an immense treasure of men and materiel into forging a
world-dominating air force.

Beginning January 27, 1943, when the Eighth Air Force dispatched its first mission of sixty-four B-17s from England against the port of Wilhelmshaven, a bomber crewman could expect to suit up for a maximum of twelve missions before being shot down or returning to base with a damaged ship and crew casualties. By the fifteenth of twenty-five missions needed for a "completed tour of duty" rating, then reassignment to ground status or stateside rotation, bomber crews were living on "borrowed time," with scarcely one in four surviving twenty-five missions. Only the most experienced crews, who were also the luckiest, had the best odds of not "buying the farm."

Later in the war, with increased crew attrition as manpower became scarcer, missions flown before reassignment increased from twenty-five to thirty. A paradoxical "catch 22" meant that every additional hour flown further reduced the odds of survival, especially after twenty-five missions. In a January and February 1944 study, the Eighth Air Force chief flight surgeon, Brig. Gen. Malcolm Grow, assessed that the heavy bombardment missions over occupied Europe were "the most hazardous operations which have ever been conducted over a sustained period." Yet, as combat fatigue or "flak-happy" cases surged because of major increases in aircraft and crews, morale and crew spirits also went up, as evidenced by the low number of mission aborts for real or invented reasons. With a unit cohesion unique to warriors who depend on each other for survival, the crews flew for their friends as much as for their desire to rid the world of tyranny.

⌐ ⌐

PART TWO

THE EIGHTH AIR FORCE THEN TO NOW—A LONG WAY TRAVELED

First headquartered at Bushy Park, then at High Wycombe ("Pinetree"), forty miles west of London, the Eighth AAF, much greater in size but comparable in unit formation and chain of command to a field army, became the centralized command for three ETO air divisions

TOP AND BOTTOM: The B-17 Flying Fortress and B-24 Liberator were the two heavy bombers in the European war, with a total of 30,119 produced.

headquartered in Britain. Each division had separate headquarters and staff, with authority to plan, develop strategy, establish doctrine, and control operations.

In the twenty-first century, only a single division in one of sixteen global air forces would numerically challenge any air force in the world. With scores of airfields in East Anglia and the Midlands, mostly within the counties of Norfolk, Suffolk, Buckinghamshire, Herefordshire, Northamptonshire, and Cambridgeshire, the sparsely populated agricultural landscape had thousands of acres of low flat pastures and fields, ideal for the runways needed by the heavy bombers.

To be envied by major twenty-first century corporations for its twentieth-century organization of tasks and grouping of skills and responsibilities, the Eighth AAF developed, controlled, invented, planned, organized, or improvised tactics, strategies and campaigns never thought possible, for accomplishment by a mostly citizen air force.

After completing scores of thousands of missions, another section within the organizational structure evaluated each mission, even individual sorties, to ensure the best use of resources. At a time before the electronic combining of production and implementation, a Services of Supply Command had staff trained in acquisition, distribution, unit communication, maintenance, and re-provisioning through a supply chain that extended from an air base or a battlefield directly to young women assembling torpedo components in Chicago.

Geographically, East Anglia, in the East of England, the region with the most bases, had the added advantage of its coast jutting like a thumb in Hitler's eye from the mainland to the North Sea, then eighty miles across to the continent. With the cathedral city of Norwich at the center, the bases extended like spokes on a wheel, although periodically subject to Luftwaffe raids causing thirty-four hundred Norwich casualties, with thousands of homes destroyed.

FIRST AIR DIVISION

Headquartered at the 1773 Brampton Grange in Huntingdon, Cambridgeshire, the First Division operated five wings with twelve B-17 bomb groups, one fighter wing, and eleven composite groups. Its 67th

First Air Division HQ at Brampton Grange in Suffolk. AUTHOR

Fighter Wing, with headquarters at Walcott Hall near Stamford, had sixteen fighter squadrons, each with up to twenty-five planes. Among the Division's bases were Bassingbourn, Ridgewell, Nuthamstead, Podington, Chelveston, Thurleigh, Molesworth, Martlesham Heath, Kimbolten, Grafton Underwood, Polebrook, Deenthorpe, and Glatton. The 356th, one of six fighter groups in the 67th Fighter Wing, was known as a "hard-luck outfit." Based at Martlesham Heath in Suffolk they flew 407 missions, first with P-47s, then with the twin-boom P-38, before changing to P-51s. In escorting B-17s on bombing and strafing missions over Germany, the 356th shot down 277 enemy aircraft, but at a significant loss of seventy-two pilots killed in action.

SECOND AIR DIVISION
Six miles southwest of Norwich, Ketteringham Hall, the 1839 Gothic-style former headquarters of the Second Air Division preserves the same country mansion appearance now as when its 750 officers and

Ketteringham Hall Second Air Division headquarters. AUTHOR

enlisted staff, including three hundred Women's Army Corps (WAC) staff, were responsible for over fifty thousand airmen organized into wings, groups, and squadrons. Decades later, scattered remains of Nissen huts and other evidence of Eighth Air Force occupancy extend beyond the mansion. Converted into a prestige office building on thirty-six wooded acres, with a lake and walled garden, the mansion retains its original sculptures, appointments, and stained glass, including a tearoom open to the public. After the war, Ketteringham Hall became the initial planning center for development of Lotus Formula One race cars. The nearby Lotus factory occupies part of the former Hethel AAF base and original hangars, its main runway converted into a track to test sports and race cars.

With fourteen bases, the Second AD had five B-24 wings of fourteen groups, plus one fighter wing with five groups at another nine bases. Each group had up to fourteen squadrons with twelve to sixteen aircraft per squadron. Escorting the bombers, the 65th Fighter Wing had four fighter groups and one scouting group, with sixteen squadrons and one training squadron at eleven additional bases.

2AD headquarters had planning and operational authority for 850 B-24 bombers in fourteen groups at seventeen bases, each base with twenty-five hundred to three thousand officers and men. It controlled five fighter groups at thirteen other bases. Its staff planned 493 missions over Europe, with ninety-five thousand sorties. Six of its groups received Presidential Unit Citations. Five men were awarded the Medal of Honor, four posthumously. The Second Division paid an eternal price for its hard-won victories, with the loss of 1,458 B-24 bombers and sixty-seven hundred men but costing the enemy 1,079 aircraft.

THIRD AIR DIVISION

With headquarters at Elveden Hall, Suffolk, the most magnificently appointed of all the division headquarters, the Anglo-Irish Guinness family loaned the AAF its 1760 mansion with thirty bays and seventy bedrooms. The 22,486-acre estate, the largest working farm in England, remains their ancestral home. Renamed Camp Blainey during the war, in addition to headquarters purposes the stately home and its grand salons were the residences for two generals, fourteen colonels, and 184 officers. Many temporary buildings extended into the grounds.

The Division controlled four bombardment wings (4th, 13th, 45th, and 93rd) with fourteen mostly B-17 heavy bomber groups. Attached to the Third Division, the 66th Fighter Wing furnished air escort and fighter support. Within the Division, the 4th Combat Wing of B-17 bombers at fourteen additional bases had fourteen bomb groups of fifty-six squadrons, with twelve bombers in each squadron. As part of the Third AD the 66th Fighter Wing, headquartered at Sawston Hall near Cambridge, had five fighter groups of P-38s and P-47s and six mixed groups, including the secret "carpetbaggers," four squadrons of black-painted bombers at two bases. In darkness they dropped supplies and weapons to resistance fighters in France, Italy, and the Low Countries. Escorting Third AD missions were five fighter groups of fifteen squadrons at nine other bases. The Third AD bombed airfields, U-boat pens, and German

Third AD HQ at Elveden Hall, Suffolk. AUTHOR

aircraft industries. Parts of the estate, including a small hotel, the Elveden Inn and restaurant, are open to the public.

THE MIGHTIEST AIR FORCE

At its peak in late 1944, the Eighth AAF had 220,000 personnel stationed in Britain, with more than 350,000 GIs serving at different times during the war. The Eighth flew eighty thousand aircraft of all types, able to send into combat up to two thousand bombers at the same time, escorted by another one thousand fighters.

With the RAF conducting tactical night bombing missions and the Eighth AAF in strategic daytime attacks, the entire means of German military organization, command and control, production, transportation, delivery, and operations underwent systematic destruction. Among the targets were the oil and lubricant industry, including synthetic production, refineries, and storage and delivery; U-boat, tank, truck, and aircraft manufacturing sites; transportation on lakes, rivers, and canals; and the interconnected rail and highway network. When the war ended every German city with war manufacturing industries had been reduced mostly to rubble.

With its personnel distributed among fifteen hundred individual units, America's "friendly invasion" of Britain occupied more space and

American WACs on Ketteringham Hall staff receive awards. DAVID HASTINGS

populated a greater area than all the original occupants in the same region for all the previous centuries.

Throughout the world, Air Corps personnel exceeded 2.4 million men and women. In addition to scores of bases and thousands of aircraft in Europe, the USAAF operated over sixteen hundred airfields in every known and many unknown parts of the world, with another 783 bases located in almost every state and region in the United States. In its use of a combined twenty million acres, the AAF occupied more space than the acreage in the states of Massachusetts, Connecticut, Vermont, and New Hampshire combined. By VJ Day, the US military branches had taken delivery of 324,750 aircraft of all types. By comparison, even under almost daily attack, German industries produced 117,077 military air-craft. Even with increasingly limited access to spare parts, Japan produced 79,123 military aircraft.

Aftermath

And how can man die better/
Than facing fearful odds/
For the ashes of his fathers/
And the temples of his Gods.
—Lord Thomas Babington Macaulay

Among the 3,812 buried in the American Cemetery and Memorial in Cambridge, England, are the remains of Eighth Air Force crewmen and Battle of the Atlantic sailors. The names of another 5,127 US military dead who were never found are engraved on the walls of the missing. The ashes of thousands more were repatriated back to the United States. Airmen of the Eighth AAF were awarded eleven Medals of Honor, 226 Distinguished Service Crosses, 442,300 Air Medals, and 2,984 Bronze Stars. RAF Alconbury, Molesworth, Croughton, Fairford, Lakenheath, and Mildenhall are the last World War II bases co-operated with the RAF by the US Air Force.

THEN TO NOW—CAPABILITIES AND DEFICITS

The diminished in size US Air Force continues as the world's dominant air power, prioritizing capability over capacity with some 5,414 fixed-wing aircraft, and 1,840 fighter/multirole aircraft in fifty-five worldwide combat squadrons of eighteen to twenty-four aircraft each. At the time of writing, the US Air Force strategic bomber fleet had 104 B-1A and B-1B Lancer bombers, twenty B-2 stealth bombers, and fifty-six six-decade-old B-52 Stratofortress bombers, with twenty in reserve. The average age of the 414 KC-135 refueling tankers is fifty-four years, with more than half operated by the Air Force Reserve and National Guard. In partial replacement of the KC-135, Boeing will complete 179 KC-46 Pegasus tankers by 2027. The last delivery of the 900-mph bomber, Rockwell's B-1B Lancer, "The Bone," came in 1988 during the Reagan era.

In development, the Northrop B-21 Raider stealth strategic bomber will become operational in the late 2020s, with approximately one hundred ordered.

In 2018, in a 286 ship and submarine United States Navy, were eleven operational 104,000-ton Nimitz class nuclear aircraft carriers, plus nine amphibious assault carriers, at 40,000–45,000 tons, each larger than World War II aircraft carriers, and fifty-two nuclear attack submarines. In late 1941, the US Navy had eight carriers, seventeen battleships, thirty-seven heavy and light cruisers, 171 destroyers, and 114 submarines. By 1945, the United States had ninety-nine fleet and escort carriers, twenty-three battleships, seventy-two cruisers, 738 destroyers and frigates, 232 submarines, and thousands more amphibious, auxiliary, and patrol ships.

In 2018 the Royal Navy, an echo of its former world-dominating abilities, had seventy-four commissioned ships, of which twenty were major surface combatants. They include ten nuclear submarines, with only two at sea at one time. The surface fleet had thirteen Type 23 frigates and six Type 45 destroyers, with up to thirteen regularly out of service "due to a lack of manpower, fuel, and supplies." The sixty-five-thousand-ton HMS *Queen Elizabeth II*, the UK's only aircraft carrier until 2020, entered service in 2018, with full operational capability in 2020. Aircraft carrier, HMS *Prince of Wales* will begin sea trials late in 2019. The UK will not have more than two aircraft carriers until at least 2030. In World War II the Royal Navy had 332 warships including sixty submarines and eleven aircrafts.

According to the defense analysis group HIS Jane's, the RAF "by the end of the decade could be left with a mere 127 combat fighter planes," the fewest since 1918. The Ministry of Defence reported that eight US F-35Bs purchased in 2015 will not be "at full operating capability until 2023." At the start of World War II, the Royal Navy, then the most powerful in the world, had seven aircraft carriers with five under construction, fifteen battleships and battlecruisers, fifty-six cruisers, and 181 destroyers of all types, including sixty-eight from World War I.

The German air force, still known as the *Luftwaffe* but a ghost of its World War II power, in 2018 had 698 military aircraft, including fewer than one hundred deployable Eurofighter Typhoons and 1970s-era variable-sweep wing Tornados, from a force of about 261 fighters.

In 2018, the German navy had five hybrid diesel-electric Type 212A submarines, compared to the 1,154 built in World War II.

Russia, ranked #2 in overall military power, in 2018 had approximately 3,914 military aircraft, including 806 fighters and 1,438 attack aircraft. Of its estimated 180 bombers, Russia relies on the 1956 Soviet-era TU 95, the TU22MB, introduced in 1972, and the TU 160 from 1981. In 2018, the Russian navy had one aircraft carrier, the 1995 steam-turbine driven *Admiral Kuznetsov*.

In 2018, China had approximately three thousand military aircraft, with 2,656 fighter/interceptors and attack aircraft. The rapidly expanding undersea fleet had five nuclear-powered attack submarines, four nuclear-powered ballistic missile submarines, fifty-four diesel-power attack submarines, and eighty-five destroyers and frigates, some already challenging the US Navy for freedom of navigation. With two aircraft carriers commissioned in 2018 and up to six more expected by 2025, a newly aggressive China is on course to potentially displace the United States as the world's dominant military power by 2040. At the 2017 opening session of the Chinese Communist Party Congress, President Xi Jinping said that it was time for China to become "a mighty force that would lead the world on political, economic, military and environmental issues."

From a register of about 944 military aircraft including fighters, North Korea is estimated to have fewer than one hundred deployable MiG-23 Floggers, Sukhoi Su-25 Frogfoot close air support aircraft, and MiG-29 Fulcrums, purchased from the Soviet Union and China in the 1980s. Its pilots are allowed about ten hours per year of flight training. The navy has 1 Krivak Class frigate and 1 Nanjin Class light frigate bought from the former Soviet Union, six "blue-water" diesel-electric submarines, about forty coastal patrol submarines, and no destroyers, frigates, cruisers, or aircraft carriers.

CHAPTER FIFTEEN

"Little America"—Patriotism and Production Built the British Bases

THE MARCH 1941 LEND-LEASE ACT AUTHORIZED THE GIVING OF FOOD, oil, weapons, and materiel to thirty nations, with no payment required (or received after the war). Much of the authorized $50 billion ($681 billion now), including bulldozers, excavators, rollers, scrapers, tractors, concrete mixers, and fifty-three hundred dump trucks, went directly to British contractors building the new air bases. With priority expediting, the equipment sped by rail from US manufacturers to ports, then across the Atlantic to locations near the under-construction bases.

In a speech at London's Mansion House on November 10, 1941, Winston Churchill said: "The Lend-Lease (Act) must be regarded without question as the most un-sordid act in the whole of recorded history." In 1942, the peak construction year, a new air base became operational every three days. Almost simultaneously, at least sixty thousand structures, mostly half-cylinder Nissen (Quonset) huts, were being assembled on the base sites. The uninsulated, easily assembled huts were covered with corrugated steel sheets over T-shaped ribs on concrete floors, some with wood-framed doors at each end. Other buildings known as Seco Huts were made of prefabricated concrete assembled onsite to house semi-permanent personnel, such as operations officers. Each base had at least two steel-framed hangars for major aircraft maintenance and engine changes. At 120 feet wide, 240 feet long, and thirty-nine feet high, they were wide enough to house a B-24's entire

110-foot wingspan. Made to be semi-permanent for postwar use, the hangars were built to code specifications, including proper roof and wall cladding, solid operable doors, concrete flooring, drainage, electrical connections, interior lighting, and heating. Eight decades later, most of the remaining hangars are used for farming or industrial purposes, with the original use evident in their appearance.

FULLY EQUIPPED BASES

Uncle Sam spared no expense in furnishing the new bases with all the necessities and many of the conveniences available at stateside bases. Officers and men lived in separate huts, with latrine and bathing facilities nearby, heated by coal-fired potbelly stoves. A separate hut served as both a movie theatre and club for crew-developed jazz or big-band nights, with single women and other guests invited from nearby towns. USO shows with major Hollywood stars made regular appearances. Glenn Miller's forty-piece Army Air Force Band performed at almost every AAF British base, with up to seven shows in seven days. (On December 15, 1944, as he traveled with another passenger to Paris on a single-engine UC-64A Norseman airplane, Miller's flight went down in bad weather over the English Channel. Neither his body nor the plane were recovered.) Other huts had separate clubs for officers, non-coms, and enlisted men. Every base had a Red Cross detachment, and a small hospital with medical staff. The Army Dental Corps, with a mere 316 active duty dental officers when the war began, expanded to 15,292 dentists, with a full dental facility staffing each base.

A base Quartermaster Corps detachment furnished laundry and dry-cleaning facilities, office supplies, and everyday necessities. The unit clothed and equipped the airmen for missions, even booking and furnishing chits for rail travel within Britain. Another section known as the Station Complement Squadron had day-to-day operational responsibilities, including maintenance of the base telephone exchange, fire department, post office, ambulance, electrical installations, and other utilities. At each base, an Ordnance Supply and Maintenance Company maintained over three hundred vehicles, from Jeeps to four-thousand-gallon fuel trailers, and a twenty-six-hundred-ton bomb dump with an inventory

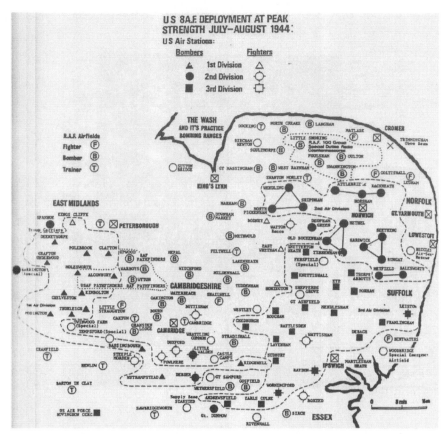

Map of the USAAF bases in England at peak strength in 1944. WWW.IBIBLIO.ORG

of one-hundred- to two-thousand-pound bombs and incendiaries. It warehoused, supplied, and re-equipped the mission-critical ammunition stores, and serviced the hundreds of .50-caliber guns on a group's twenty-four bombers.

The Sub Depot, another unrecognized "back-office" base service unit, had wide responsibilities far exceeding its unspectacular name. It included welders, machinists, mechanics, and instrument technicians, who repaired, cleaned, replaced, or rebuilt battle-damaged aircraft. Their stateside-trained skills and precision tools repaired wings, tail sections, fuselage, and sheet metal, including the rebalancing of an aircraft's aileron, elevators, elevator, and rudder, and the repair and recalibration of

Norden or Sperry bombsights. Sub Depot mechanics tested, repaired, or replaced aircraft starters, generators, pump motors, landing gear, and flap retractors. A special "quick-change" crew could remove and replace an engine overnight in the well-lighted, closed hangars, allowing a bomber to quickly return to the flight line. In permanently removing an engine, they cleaned and restored its propeller for re-installation on another engine. If a crewman's electrically heated suit or oxygen mask needed repair, they were there. Their military skills paid later dividends as they transitioned to becoming skilled craftsmen in postwar America. After specialized training, Quartermaster Corps personnel—not flight crews—rigged crew parachutes. A separate finance and payroll department arranged for the delivery of cash for twice monthly paydays. Separately, they maintained records providing for deductions and allotments, such as war bond withdrawals. At each base MPs guarded entrances and patrolled perimeters in Jeeps.

A Worldwide Independent Supply Command

Learning from mistakes in the care and recovery of wounded from campaigns earlier in the war, the USAAF bypassed established channels to directly obtain supplies and equipment from a depot in Newark, New Jersey, through its own Air Service Command, controlled by headquarters at High Wycombe. Seeking ways to reduce the highest percentage of dead and wounded in the US military, the Eighth AAF commissioned a British firm, the Wilkinson Sword Company, to develop a light armored vest with thin manganese plates, a quick-release pull, and an improved helmet, all intended to protect the head, chest, and pelvic areas. By early 1944, all crews in heavy bombers wore flak vests or suits and steel helmets, reducing by 75 percent injuries and deaths from flak.

Most bases had an abridged hospital unit, with operating theatre, beds, two medical officers, and one surgeon, assisted by eight enlisted corpsmen, a pharmacy, laboratory, and X-ray department. A dental officer with patient chair, lighting, equipment, and a dental technician added to the health and safety needs at the new bases.

Stateside at Wright Field near Dayton, Ohio (today's Wright–Patterson Air Force Base), a vast logistical organization, the Services of

Former hangar at Rackheath AAF base. AUTHOR

Supply (SOS), backed the men at war as an overwhelming in size independent army command. It developed, procured, stored, and distributed an infinite variety of supplies from innumerable sources. To be emulated by twenty-first-century internet retailers, SOS channeled the supplies from a central distribution location in England by the most efficient air, land, and sea method, to the air bases and widely scattered combat areas.

As American crews were training at US bases, simultaneously, 136 British construction contractors, later joined by US Army Engineer Battalions, were building the bases they would soon occupy. They represented every major and most minor contractor in Britain, including Bovis, Taylor Woodrow, George Wimpey, John Laing, Alfred McAlpine, Sir Alexander Gibb, and W. C. French. Given firm deadlines, the contractors were either planning, building, or finishing scores of complete air bases for the AAF and RAF. In addition to constructing the USAAF and RAF bases, the contractors also built additions to sixty-three existing airfields.

The Green Man Pub near Rackheath AAF Base where 467 BG crews gathered after missions. AUTHOR

To set in place only the runways at each base required eighteen thousand tons of dry cement mixed with ninety thousand tons of aggregate, for a continuous concrete slab six to nine inches thick. To acquire enough material to set only the hardcore foundation, every day up to six long trains left London carrying rubble from buildings destroyed in Luftwaffe raids. As increasing numbers of bombers were returning from missions heavily damaged, several already completed airfields were widened and expanded for the many emergency landings.

The civil engineers needed to design the new bases increased from fifty-four in 1939 to 580 in 1944. Unskilled laborers were allowed to work twelve-hour days seven days a week, with many housed in temporary onsite dormitories at nominal cost. Priorities were given to all needed building materials, including timber, steel, cement, tarmac, concrete, bricks, electrical, glass, and roofing materials. As an employment condition, workers could neither resign nor be dismissed without cause.

The sixty thousand employees were prohibited from striking in return for guaranteed wages, no layoffs, and full salaries for overtime. A government commission expedited contract approvals in days instead of months, with bonuses paid for jobs completed ahead of schedule.

At a time of acute shortages in every skill—with most of the trade workers, supervisors, and office administrators already in the military—all civil construction in Britain halted for the six years of the war, as the new air base construction raced ahead. In addition to the uncertainties of delivery arising from linking available manpower with scarce materials coming from thousands of miles away, construction took place in the open on flat land, with the workforce under constant threat of air attack.

From viewing the original plans, most bases included offices, barracks, latrines, bathing, mess hall, recreation, kitchen, bakery, storage, repair workshops, garage, crew lockers, firefighting, blast and bomb shelters, and general maintenance. A distant location held munitions, including separate underground storage areas for fuzes, incendiaries, pyrotechnics, and bombs.

In eighteen months or less, the British built the equivalent of 133 complete airports for 213 bomber squadrons, each with up to three thousand personnel, one hundred buildings, control tower, hangars, hardstands, ambulance service, fuel dumps, recreational facilities, support buildings, and dispersal areas—all in an area smaller than New Jersey.

FARM FIELDS TO AIRFIELDS

To obtain the immense amounts of acreage on which to situate the bases—the land occupied for generations by farmers and their descendants—estate agents descended on crossroads villages to locate the owners or tenants and lease their land or buy it if necessary. Agents spent days at town halls to find and then understand ancient records showing land ownership by multiple farmers on the same fields where the bases would be built. Soon, another endeavor would occupy the same ground, as farmers continued to plow what remained of their land, side by side with aircraft, runways, vehicles, buildings, and thousands of newly arriving men.

After a short period of cultural modification—the GIs never adjusting to the weak ale and warm English beer—the townspeople and American servicemen enjoyed a mutually enriching experience, a

TOP AND BOTTOM: The former Rackheath control tower, repurposed as private offices. AUTHOR

lasting measurement being at least seventy thousand British war brides and the children to follow, who populated every state. One of the greatest migrations of women in American history, the British and later the European and Asian war brides came to America not because they had a free ticket to live in a rich country, but because they followed the men they loved. Churchill declared to friend and foe that Great Britain would fight to the death against fascism, an assertion his countrymen repeatedly acknowledged throughout the war, including the crash project to dedicate every resource and ability to quickly build the bases for their American liberators.

CHAPTER SIXTEEN

Sacrifice and Heroism: Attacking the Heart of Germany

A father broods: "Would I have set him
To some humble trade,
And so slacked his high fire,
And his passionate martial desire;
Had told him no stories to woo him and whet him
To this due crusade!
. . . And the spirits of those who were homing
Passed on, rushingly,
Like the Pentecost Wind;
And the whirr of their wayfaring thinned
And surceased on the sky, and left in the gloaming
Sea-mutterings, and me."
—FROM *THE SOULS OF THE SLAIN*, THOMAS HARDY

THE AIRMEN PREPARE

ON THE EVENING OF AUGUST 16, 1943, BEFORE THE RAIDS AGAINST heavily defended Schweinfurt and Regensburg, scores of B-17 crews at bases throughout the Midlands and East Anglia were told to ready for a "maximum effort" the next morning. In anticipation or in dread they prepared in their own ways, by either sleeping soundly or tossing in the night, knowing that each time they flew the odds of surviving the then twenty-five-mission minimum further increased.

The badly needed fighter escort squadrons were arriving and that helped, but they lacked the range to penetrate deeply into Germany. The enemy already had adapted to the increasing missions by sending up entire lines of fighters for stacking across flight paths. The pilots called in the bomber altitudes to flak batteries below, enabling radar-directed artillery to target the bomber stream with corridors of flak. AAF groups began to return with only parts of squadrons that began a mission.

To begin the mission development, "Frag-O" orders, an abbreviated or "fragmentary" form of an operations order, went from division head-quarters over encrypted teletypes to selected bases between 11:00 p.m. and 3:00 a.m., to prepare for a mission on the same day as the op order. A duty officer receiving the orders then made calls to the group commander and his maintenance and operations officers. The group commander's staff alerted squadron commanders to make a roster of squadrons to fly that day. NCOs then awakened the crews who would fly the mission.

One of the groups in the mass assault on this day, the 100th BG at Thorpe Abbotts AAF Base, had a nickname they preferred would not have been theirs. Dubbed the "Bloody Hundredth," on June 25, 1943, their first mission after arriving in England, three B-17s went down. That began a torrent of losses to reach a prohibitive eighty-five B-17s lost in the war. Nine more would go down in the mission about to be announced.

The men knew how powerfully defended were targets such as Hamburg, where seventy day and night raids destroyed the city but failed to fully knock out the factories, shipyards, and aircraft engine works. For the latest war news, mostly bad in those early days, they read *Stars and Stripes*, and listened to Armed Forces Radio and to the surprisingly informed broadcasts made by Axis Sally, one of two American women in Berlin, both with the same task of spreading Nazi propaganda.* As a direct reminder of how bad the odds were, the GIs only had to see the gaps in the returning formations, and then view empty bunks in the barracks with rolled-up bedding.

---

*Convicted of treason in a 1949 trial in the US, Mildred Gillars was released in 1961 from the Federal Reformatory for Women in Alderson, West Virginia, and died at age 87 in 1988 in Columbus, Ohio. Rita Zucca renounced her American citizenship before broadcasting for the Axis and was barred from returning to the United States.

A BRIEFING AFTER BREAKFAST

Awakened earlier than usual at 0330, the men grumbled as always then made their way to the mess hall for breakfast before the briefing. With fresh eggs, bacon, and pancakes regularly available, the plentiful chow earned high marks, although the men avoided breakfast chatter about the mission. It brought bad luck, akin to a *memento mori* of the fragility of their existence. To turn it aside, crews had a lucky something they carried or a ritual to accomplish, or just a silent prayer "to the man upstairs," expecting in the fullness of youth to return and paint another bomb or swastika on their ship, as a herald of one less mission to fly and one day more to be alive.

After turning in personal belongings and checking out bulky cold-weather gear, they shuffled to attention as the group commanding officer entered alongside the weather and navigations officers. After the C/O pulled back the heavy black curtain, all chat ceased as intelligence gathered from ground sources and air reconnaissance displayed photos or film on a screen or on trailing ribbons from the pinned maps, or diagrams on the board.

It began with the announcement that this mission—the anniversary of the first attack into Germany—would be the deepest penetration to date into the enemy's homeland. With 376 B-17s escorted part of the way by 268 P-47s and ninety RAF Spitfires, the attack had two parts the C/O called a "double-strike." After entering German airspace, 146 B-17s would split from the group to bomb the Messerschmitt plant in Regensburg, with the remaining 230 B-17s hitting the heavily defended ball-bearing works 125 miles away at Schweinfurt.

"Little friends"—the fighter escorts at their separate bases—would be with them and they were essential, but in those early days they lacked range, and couldn't get farther than Antwerp or Brussels before returning. Later they had drop tanks for longer range and could escort the bombers into the heart of Germany, but that was then. For now—for six hours—three in and three back, the bombers were on their own.

IMPORTANCE OF THE COMBAT BOX

"No matter what stay in your combat boxes," the C/O reminded crews at briefings. Everyone knew its importance and they practiced it often

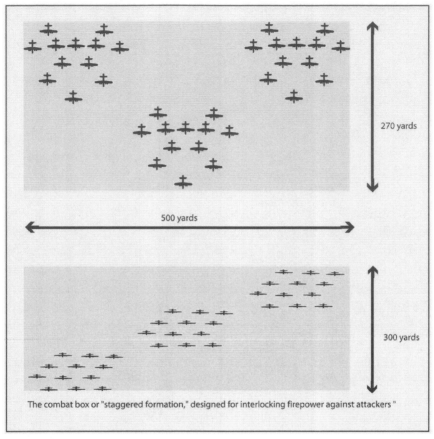

270 yards

500 yards

300 yards

The combat box or "staggered formation," designed for interlocking firepower against attackers "

N. GELBAND O'CONNOR

enough, but the caution needed repeating. Introduced in early 1943, improved mission success depended on exact separations between up to four elements: lead, high, low, and low low. Variations of the tactic could be applied to eighteen, twenty-seven, thirty-six, or even fifty-four heavy bombers. The staggered formation, or what was called Group Javelin Down, maximized everyone's combined firepower by stepping each box diagonally down like a ladder leaning against a garage. Defensively, it intensified the combined firepower into a 360-degree range. Offensively, it placed each bomber in position for an unimpeded release over the target.

As an example, with three squadrons of bombers stepped into lead, high, and low elements of twelve aircraft in each box, the combined firepower from 468 .50-caliber guns wouldn't by itself guarantee a safe trip in and back, but, combined with fighter escorts, tight formation flying, and a great deal of luck, the losses could be reduced. In the combat box, the lead bomber, a position Jimmy Stewart had as commander, went ahead of the others, while the last aircraft in the high flight—a position no bomber crew wanted—became known as the "tail-end Charlie."

The C/O gave a point by point description of the objectives, assembly areas, way-points, radio beacon locations and their codes, and the opposition expected, which this day would be plenty. The weather officer held everyone's attention with blackboard sketches of conditions on takeoff, cloud layers, and weather over the target. Everyone focused with quiet intensity. On missions they were no longer individuals; everyone's lives depended on teamwork. All over England that day, thirty-seven hundred men in sixteen bomber and fighter groups were getting similar briefings. The nearly decimated "bloody 100th" gamely mustered their last bombers and crews. At Thorpe Abbotts and the other bases, pilots in sixty-four squadrons watched the control tower for the green flare, and began to roll for most of the runway's six thousand feet, straining under bomb loads and thirty-six hundred gallons of fuel, to join the group and head to the target. After Antwerp, the RAF Spitfires wiggled their wings goodbye, with the P-47 "Jugs" getting to the edge of Belgium before returning. At twenty-seven thousand feet and a dignified 215 mph, trailing white cones of contrails like a Fourth of July display, they were on their own. But not for long.

The Enemy Had a Say

Luftwaffe pilots came to know the purpose of the combat box as much as Allied crews and adapted accordingly. An Fw pilot approaching an entire wing of fifty-four B-17s in a combat box saw a group spread six hundred yards long, a mile wide, and half a mile deep. In seeking ways to penetrate the formation, the enemy had the advantage of speed over the stately big bomber procession, but also faced hails of hot lead from their combined fire, all turrets it seemed, firing on his approach. Each of the

Unlike soldiers who had choices in movement, bombers flew in formation.
95TH BOMB GROUP ASSOCIATION

B-17's thirteen guns could fire nine thousand rounds of ammunition at fourteen rounds a second, with an effective range up to six hundred yards. With a combined closing speed of over 500 mph, a Bf-109 coming in at a near head-on twelve o'clock high (the favored approach) had only a few seconds to fire a quick three-second burst of about 130 rounds, before diving down and peeling away to avoid the fire from above. Luftwaffe commanding officers took note of their pilots' successes, awarding one point for every fighter shot down, but a generous three points for every bomber downed.

The bombers that hit the Regensburg Messerschmitt Bf-109 plant dropped three hundred tons of high explosives, badly damaging the factory and setting back its production. Not so for the other part of the "double-strike" mission. Because of cloud cover, the B-17s made their bomb run from seventeen thousand feet, ten thousand feet below the plan. Of the 230 bombers in the five-factory Schweinfurt raid, only 183 made it to the target, hounded every mile by enemy fighters jinking around flak bursts, as the highly stressed bombardiers hurried the last minutes of the now straight-ahead bomb run to drop 424 tons, but mostly missing the factory complex.

The holes in the formations gave crews immediate visual results of their losses and the damage below, as they turned 180 degrees away, harassed by bandits who often came down in pairs, having already refueled and returned to the fray. What remained of "double-strike" staggered back to temporary airfields in North Africa or their own bases in England. An astonishing sixty bombers and five fighters went down, with 552 crew members killed or captured. Another ninety-five bombers were so badly damaged that most never flew again. Almost one in two that went out came back heavily damaged or didn't come back at all. Ninety of the men who didn't return were with the 100th BG, "the bloody 100th."

The Regensburg aircraft plant resumed limited production in a matter of weeks, with the Schweinfurt multi-plant ball-bearing complex reduced to an estimated 34 percent output from before the attack. Yet, ball-bearing supplies continued to be delivered from remotely stored stockpiles. The strategy of deep penetration without fighter escorts needed urgent reassessment, beginning with cancellation of a follow-up "maximum effort."

On October 14, 1943, with operational tactics modified from lessons learned after the August losses, a second mission against only Schweinfurt, instead of two targets as before, sent 351 B-17 and B-24 groups from three bomber wings in the First and Third Divisions. As in the failed August mission, multiple squadrons of P-47s escorted the bombers, but still lacked the range to bring them all the way out and back. Unexpectedly, on the way to the target, headquarters diverted one B-24 squadron and its fighters to hit Emden. This left a scattered and reduced force no longer tight in their combat boxes due to poor weather. Once again, the enemy on the ground and in the air were waiting. Flak batteries and extending lattices of Luftwaffe across the flight path shot down sixty B-17s, with 640 men killed, wounded, or missing. Gunners on the bombers and P-47 pilots claimed 186 enemy aircraft, but returning to their bases were only 158 fully intact bombers, 45 percent fewer than at the start.

With seven bombers lost on October 8 and twelve more downed on two other missions the same week as the second Schweinfurt raid, the

Mission briefing before one-thousand-aircraft attack on Schweinfurt. 95TH BOMB GROUP ASSOCIATION

bloody 100th could muster only their last eight aircraft, but this time all returned safely.

The mass AAF and RAF attacks during the week of February 20–25, 1944 known as "Big Week" were intended to destroy all known aircraft production factories and every supply center in Germany. Five separate raids during the assault would take Germany out of the war, planners said. The political, military, and civilian leaderships would sue for peace. Continuing the war would be unendurable, or so believed the Allied political and military leadership.

With protection in and out from fighter escorts, the raids began the night of February 19–20, 1944 with 825 RAF aircraft, including Lancasters and Halifaxes striking Leipzig, Germany's fifth largest city, ringed with powerful antiaircraft defenses. Winds and low cloud cover caused most of the dropped ordnance to miss the target, with an RAF loss of seventy-eight aircraft and their crews. The USAAF Big Week attacks had worse results. With 1,008 B-17 and B-24 "maximum effort" aircraft in thirty-three hundred sorties against five major cities, the AAF lost 226 bombers and twenty-eight fighters.

Protecting the Nazi Manufacturing Centers

Throughout 1944, twenty AAF missions against the IG Farben–owned Leuna synthetic oil refineries near Meresberg in central Germany returned bleak results, partially resulting from excessive reliance on the Norden bombsight's accuracy. As a top priority target for the heavy bombers, the three-square-mile, 250-building Leuna complex had even more formidable defenses than the guns protecting the U-boat pens. In attacking Germany's best-defended industrial target, the bombers flew against seventeen hundred 88mm and 105mm batteries, including over six hundred radar-guided guns. German defenses were deployed in thirty-six-gun groups, with each element able to fire a box barrage into the precise space where ground observers along the flight path had called in reports accurately predicting the bombers' course, altitude, and time of arrival.

Of the Leuna refinery's 62,550 workers, over nineteen thousand were actively engaged in fire protection, making possible a partial return to production soon after the raid. On every mission the bombers met not only massive artillery barrages but also lacked clear target acquisition from the Norden bombsight. The defenders had masked bombardier views of the factories by setting alight thousands of smoke pots on and near the target. Even with rare clear visibility on a given target, only one in three bombs hit within the MPI, the Mean Point of Impact. On cloudy days with radar-guided bombing, 95 percent of the ordnance missed the refinery, instead bombing nearby Meresburg.

It took 6,552 sorties with 18,328 tons of high explosive bombs to finally take out the refinery, except that a lack of awareness of spare parts stored underground nearby resulted in a partial return to production in as few as two days. In repeated attacks against Leuna, the Eighth Air Force lost 119 aircraft and 1,280 crew.

"Black Sunday"—Second Highest Loss of the War

With the Hethel base dispatching one of the B-24 groups, Operation Tidal Wave, an attack on the Ploesti oil refineries in Romania, became one of the most heroic but futile raids of the war. To reduce the round-trip range to twenty-three hundred miles, deployed from forward bases in Benghazi, Libya, 178 B-24s with extra fuel tanks included the Hethel-based 389th

BG, one of five groups in the mission. In daylight on Sunday, August 1, 1943, they flew at treetop level to surprise defenders at the heavily fortified refinery complex. However, alerted by Libyan informants, the defenders were ready, sending up both flak and a black wall of enveloping smoke—that, and scores of Bf-109 and 110 fighters from nearby bases.

With flames and smoke partially obscuring the target, the 389th and other groups twisted around chimney stacks to drop bombs with delayed-action fuzes. Flying directly into thick cords of tracer and cannon fire, the crews were nearly looking into the eyes of the gunners firing directly at the bombers growing ever-larger in their gunsights. In another surprise to the attackers, artillery batteries suddenly emerged from inside haystacks or jutted from buildings with false fronts, to bring torrents of flak and death to the Liberators now committed to the final bomb run. So carefully had the defenders prepared that a train fitted with 88 and 128mm artillery fired point-blank, pacing along with the bombers.

When it ended, the "Black Sunday" mission resulted in the loss of 660 men and fifty-three bombers, the second worst of the war. Another fifty-five damaged B-24s struggled back to the temporary Libyan bases with proof of the mission—epic photos of the raid taken with box cameras. One incredulous crew of a surviving B-24 counted 365 flak holes. The gallant mission earned five Medals of Honor, four awarded posthumously, along with numerous Distinguished Service Crosses and a Distinguished Unit Citation.

The sacrifice had little effect. Air reconnaissance assessed that the raid reduced output by only 40 percent, with some refineries in the widely dispersed complex emerging untouched. Many returned to partial operation within weeks, with overall production in the following months increasing over the pre-attack capacity. An evaluation concluded that the mission produced "no curtailment of overall product output." In a droll comment about the mission, a surviving airman said, "this ain't hell, but you can see it from here."

As aircraft losses grew in the early days, the maximum number of missions flown before reassignment also increased for the Eighth Air Force in Britain, and the Ninth, Twelfth and Fifteenth Air Forces in the Mediterranean, Middle East, and North Africa. Mission minimums first went to twenty-five from twenty, then to thirty, then to thirty-five missions before stateside rotation or ground duties. The crews now had to hope that they could survive up to 45 percent more missions.

NAZI GERMANY—FIGHTING TO THE END

Members of the US Strategic Bombing Survey in the destroyed German cities soon after VE Day estimated that 1.36 million tons of bombs were dropped from over 1.44 million bomber sorties on every city, port, and airfield. Among the findings, as expected after Big Week, German aircraft production indeed slowed, but then quickly returned to near-normal capacities. In overcoming repeated Allied attacks, production increased from 15,596 aircraft in 1942 to 39,807 after Big Week two years later. Near the end, Germany had ample fighter aircraft to continue the war, but few trained pilots and even less fuel for the available aircraft. Allied planners repeatedly underestimated the ability of Germany's major manufacturers to be quickly reconstituted, even if in a reduced capacity. As confirmed by postwar analysis, they equally misjudged Germany's ability to endure years of repeated attacks, a resolve with roots that extended deep into the ranks of ordinary Germans.

SLAVES MADE THE SAME POISONS THAT KILLED THEM

In addition to formidable air defenses and the strategic placement of the vital factories in isolated locations, Germany had good reason to assign twenty-eight thousand troops to protect the Leuna refinery and the adjacent manufacturing complex. The synthetic processes perfected by IG Farben further lengthened the regime's ability to continue the war. Scientists had succeeded in synthesizing oil products made from lignite, known as brown coal in Germany, and still in wide use today. The war-extending artificial products included aviation and diesel fuel, gasoline, lubricants, and paraffin wax, most of it manufactured by the Brabag Co., part of a cartel of mine-owners led by IG Farben. When preparing for war, Germany knew that a lack of crude oil production within its borders mandated new strategies to manufacture petroleum products synthetically.

For operation by Jewish and other forced-labor conscripts with German overseers, a massive synthetic product manufacturing complex extended to within six miles of the Auschwitz death camp. Every day thousands of slaves walked or were transported to the factories. Made in one of the plants, Zyklon-B, the cyanide-based pesticide crystals, soon brought agonizing death to the same prisoners who made it—and to over one million more in Auschwitz-Birkenau and Majdanek.

Under construction in 1942, the IG Farben–invented polymer-based synthetic rubber, known as "Buna," came from the same factories. High-performance fuels made in the plants included aviation gasoline and bunker oil for naval use. Near Auschwitz and its sub-camp, Monowitz, known as Auschwitz III, the Siemens- and Krupp-built manufacturing facilities profited at negligible investment from the ready supply of slave labor.

CHAPTER SEVENTEEN

Living the History—
The Bases Where It Began

O the wild charge they made!
All the world wondered.
Honor the charge they made!
When can their glory fade?
O the wild charge they made!
—"The Charge of the Light Brigade,"
Alfred, Lord Tennyson

PART ONE

HISTORY'S HEROES

As in the failed August mission, the second attack against the Schweinfurt ball-bearing industries had no lasting effect. Production stopped for only six weeks. Large stocks had been sent to isolated locations—enough for the remainder of the war. Due to the mission's failure, until long-range fighter escorts became available bombing missions deep into Germany were suspended for four months.

The bloody but unbowed 100th BG had little left after Schweinfurt but still flew. Including the two missions within days of "double-strike," the 100th lost twenty-eight Flying Fortresses in little more than a week, with nine downed on August 17. On October 8 they lost seven bombers over Bremen. Two days later, twelve more went down over Munster.

One of the most famous if not ill-fated of all the heavy bomb groups, the 100th ended the war with a devastating 77 percent casualties in twenty-two operational months. Only four of the original thirty-eight co-pilots survived. No complete crew of ten finished intact. At least 450 complete replacement crews served with the 100th BG. In total, 177 aircraft were lost in combat, with 785 crew killed in action. Appalling as were the 100th BG losses, they were exceeded by the 91st BG, stationed at Bassingbourn. In 340 missions, the 91st lost 197 B-17s, with the entire group of seventy-two bombers replaced an extraordinary four times including damaged aircraft.

HOODOOS AND MASCOTS
The Air Corps, perhaps more than other services, ritualized their superstitions into behavioral patterns formed before, during, and after missions, such as bringing aboard rabbits feet and other amulets, including lucky charms, mascots, Bibles with metal covers, or silver dollars for placement in a certain pocket or a specific part of the aircraft.

One pilot named his bomber "Boomerang," because the ship must therefore return to its original location—and always carried a real one on each mission. As if to taunt fate, one crew named their bomber "Superstitious AL-O-YSIUS." Every squadron knew about the real or imaginary "clinker" or "hangar queen," a bad-luck bomber that jinxed everyone else. The flight line also had its good-luck airplane, one that got through the fights undamaged, and numerous pilots and crews eager to fly it.

But after adding or deducting the premonitions, jinxes, hoodoos, incantations, and fantasies populating their daily lives, everyone who flew went against the law of averages. When the missions needed for stateside rotation or reassignment increased to thirty and then thirty-five in the fall of 1944, the odds of being killed increased to 71 percent, the greatest by far in all the US military. In jest or in relief, upon reaching the thirty-fifth mission, crews were ceremoniously given a printed certificate of induction into the brotherhood of "The Lucky Bastards Club."

B-17 Superstitious—Al-o-ysius at RAF Bassingboun. DAVID HASTINGS

AFTERMATH: THE AIRCRAFT, THE FLYERS, AND THEIR FATES

The Eighth Air Force controlled 243 combat groups, including 125 bombardment, seventy-one fighter, twenty-nine troop carrier and combat cargo groups, thirteen reconnaissance, and five composite groups. The worldwide Army Air Force included 1,226 combat squadrons distributed throughout the Atlantic, Pacific, and other theatres. Of the sixteen US air forces, the Eighth by far had the most casualties, with 47,483 killed or wounded, 41 percent of the entire AAF in all war theatres. Awarded to the worldwide AAF were thirty-six Medals of Honor, twenty-two posthumously.

Of 99,516 fighter planes made in the United States, only "the mighty Jug" the P-47 Thunderbolt, with 16,231 produced, served in every war theatre. Other famous fighters in the multi-thousands, included the P-38 Lightning, P-40 Warhawk, P-51 Mustang, and P-61 Black Widow. Of an astonishing 107 different US Navy aircraft types made, the carrier-based Grumman F6F Hellcat was the most produced at 12,275 fighters. About fourteen P-47s are in flying condition in the United States, with nineteen on display or in restoration. About three hundred of 15,875 P-51s remain, half in flying condition. Of the twenty-seven remaining B-17s of 12,731 made, about ten are airworthy with seventeen on static display. Of 18,493 B-24 Liberators manufactured—the war's most produced bomber—only eight remain, with two airworthy, *Witchcraft*, operated by the Collings Foundation, and *Diamond Lil*, owned by the Commemorative Air Force. Far surpassing the US and British output were the 30,480 Messerschmitt Bf-109s, and twenty-nine thousand Focke-Wulf Fw-190s from Nazi Germany, and thirty-one thousand Yak-3s, and 36,183 Ilyushin IL-2s from Soviet Russia.

RAF Bomber Command had the war's highest losses of any Allied military. For every one hundred airmen, forty-five were killed, six were seriously wounded, with eight becoming prisoners of war. Of the 120,000 who served in RAF Bomber Command, 55,573 died, including over ten thousand Canadians. Of those who entered combat at the beginning of the war, only 10 percent lived to the end. From March 1943 through February 1944, only 16 percent of British and Canadian bomber crews survived thirty missions. In a five-month period beginning in November 1943, over one thousand British aircraft were lost over Berlin alone. A life-size memorial to Bomber Command in London's Green Park depicts seven exhausted crew members gazing at the sky after a mission.

Although they had immense losses in proportion to the other services, US bombers and fighters took a much greater toll on the enemy than the enemy did on them. Eighth AAF bombers and fighter pilots shot down 6,098 enemy aircraft, and by summer 1944 had nearly swept the skies clean of German fighters.

For the entire war, the Eighth Air Force lost 4,145 B-17s and B-24s. The total of all ETO air losses were 10,561 B-17, B-24, P-47, P-38, and P-51s. Additional losses for medium bombers and other aircraft in the 9th and 12th tactical air forces added to the sacrifices. Within the five ETO air forces, 8th, 9th, 11th, 12th, and 15th, the seventy-six thousand casualties included thirty thousand killed, fourteen thousand wounded, and thirty-three thousand captured.

The fighter squadrons of the Eighth had 261 aces (five or more enemy shot down). Thirty-one of the aces had fifteen or more kills each. Medal of Honor winner, Richard Bong, born in Superior, Wisconsin, became the war's ace of aces, shooting down forty Japanese aircraft in a Lockheed P-38. In appreciation for his daring, Major Bong went home permanently in January 1945. Within days, before twelve hundred guests, he married twenty-one-year-old Marjorie Vatendahl. (Her photo became his aircraft's "nose art," "the most shot-after girl in the South Pacific," he joked.) Reassigned as a test pilot, on August 6, 1945, the day that the United States dropped the atomic bomb on Hiroshima, he died at age twenty-four while testing a P-80 jet fighter at Lockheed's Burbank, California plant (now Bob Hope Airport). Marjorie learned about his death on the radio. Parts of the 100th Bomb Group's epic were incorporated into the novels and films, *Twelve O'Clock High* and *The War Lover*. They were eagles all.

PART TWO

VISITING THE BASES—WHERE THE PAST IS STILL PRESENT

The intrepid and patient time-traveler will be rewarded if not spiritually moved upon discovering numerous remembrances of the East Anglia bases, the least known or explored remains of the war in Europe. Approximately sixty thousand Eighth Air Force air and ground personnel flew or serviced three thousand bombers and five hundred fighters from scores of bases that encircled Norwich for twenty-five miles. With a rental car, GPS, maps of the airfields, and at least three full days, exploration will lead to unexpected discoveries where they are least expected. If lost, inquiring at a crossroads pub, a post office, or a village hall near the expected location of a former base could yield directions to an unmapped country lane leading to an abandoned base, with views of weathered runways, hardstands, hangars, buildings, and control towers.

The Second Division Library in Norwich, started by the division's veterans, has maps and directions to former base sites. Brampton Grange, the First Division headquarters in Northamptonshire, was converted into eleven apartments, its façade otherwise unchanged. Both Ketteringham Hall, Second Division headquarters, and the former Third Division headquarters at Elveden Hall, are unchanged in exterior appearance and may be visited. In addition to memorials and museums at some base sites, major sections or minor parts remain at various of the once thriving bases. The crewmen who remain will remember the names of their bases and how the war forever changed their lives: Attlebridge, Bungay, Horsham St. Faith, Halesworth, Rackheath, Wendling, Shipdham, Deopham Green, North Pickenham, Rodney, Hethel, Tibenham, Seething, Hardwick, Horham, Martlesham Heath, and Old Buckenham.

OLD BUCKENHAM THEN AND NOW

The spirits from the past still populate the once thriving home of the 453rd Bomb Group and its four B-24 squadrons. After being transferred from Tibenham, Jim Stewart came to Old Buck on March 30, 1944, as operations officer and newly promoted lieutenant colonel. With Tibenham an uncrowded five miles away, driving to his new station took only ten minutes. Also stationed at Old Buckenham in 1944, future actor Walter Matthau served under Stewart as a B-24 radioman-gunner.

Walking through the airfield remnants seventy-five years later past an original runway now used for general aviation, a concrete apron reveals the existence of its long-gone airmen. With the concrete still curing, someone on a bicycle incised a long narrow path through the smooth surface, perhaps a GI on the way to a pre-dawn briefing or returning to the barracks in the dark from the mess hall.

A row of two-letter initials comes into view, including one from a kid leaving his mark for posterity with a finger thickly carving his initials and state, "Penna" for Pennsylvania. Per-

A bicycle tire trails into history on the perimeter track at Rackheath. AUTHOR

fectly formed shoeprints left by someone with size nine feet casually if not
defiantly trail into the distance, as if
saying to the future: "see, it's me, and
those prints will stay even if I don't."
Maybe the spectral traces of their
war-winning achievement were made
by crew members laughing on the
way to the chow line after a mission,
glad to be alive and counting down
the remaining missions. In the early
days when they flew without escorts,
one in three never made that walk. As
with all the groups, Old Buck's 453rd
had sizable casualties. In 392 days in
the European Theatre, they flew 259
missions, with a loss of fifty-eight air-

Footprints made circa 1944 in the
concrete at Old Buckenham. AUTHOR

craft and 366 men. From when they first arrived in England, their aircraft
were replaced by more than twice the original complement. Adjacent to
its original main runway, Jimmy's Café pays homage to Jimmy Stewart,
even then Old Buck's most famous resident. Next to the restaurant, a new
museum in a reproduction of an original hut has thousands of uniform
parts, many donated by reunion groups visiting the base. On the former
technical side, portions of original huts remain, including a derelict but
still formidable brick Norden bombsight storeroom.

Dedicated in 1990 by the four squadrons of the 453rd Bomb Group
Association, a black granite memorial in the shape of a B-24 vertical
stabilizer resides at the one-time entrance to Old Buckenham. With the
East Anglia and Midlands bases returned to their former agricultural
purposes or partially converted into industrial estates, similar memorials
are positioned at the entrance to many of the former bases.

HORSHAM ST. FAITH

What remains of the original USAAF Base #123 is within Norwich
International Airport, with three of the original hangars used for aircraft

They *were* there—initials in the concrete at Old Buckenham. AUTHOR

maintenance. Portions of the original control tower remain. Other war-time buildings and the Norwich Aviation Museum (admission charged) with wartime exhibits are within an industrial area opposite the terminal, accessed by auto. A display alongside the terminal has photos and paintings of the original base, home to the 319 and 458 BG, and 56th Fighter Group, and a memorial plaque.

HORHAM

Located in Denham, four miles southeast of Eye in Suffolk, Horham was both the home and headquarters at different times for ten AAF units and the 13th Combat Bombardment Wing of the Third Air Division. Horham also housed the 95th, 47th, and 323 BG. Light aircraft currently use part of the original runway. A memorial to the 95th BG is opposite St. Mary Church. The Red Feathers Club—the former NCO mess—has exhibits and original crew art on walls. The former guard room became the village hall. Parts of outlying buildings and blast bunkers remain.

With 318 missions, the 95th BG became the first group to bomb Berlin in daylight and the last to lose a bomber: 156 B-17s were downed

TOP AND BOTTOM: The former Catholic chapel at Hethel and crew-painted art.
AUTHOR

TOP AND BOTTOM: The repurposed crew quarters, and hangar at Rackheath.
AUTHOR

Memorial to 453 Bomb Group at Old Buckenham. AUTHOR

in combat, thirty-six lost in non-combat missions, with 425 enemy aircraft destroyed. On May 7, 1945, the last day of the European war, assured safe passage by German forces, B-17s dropped 475 tons of food and supplies to impoverished Dutch civilians. On the return to Horham, a German flak battery heavily damaged one of the aircraft, causing a forced landing in England with the loss of eleven crew and passengers.

RACKHEATH
Once home to fifty-eight Liberators of the 467th Bomb Group, rated as the most accurate bomb group in the Eighth Air Force. From March

1944 to VE Day, the 467th flew 212 combat missions from Rackheath with the loss of forty-six B-24s and 235 airmen. Located five miles northeast of Norwich, significant portions of the base remain, including the perimeter track and parts of the main runway.

The former technical side of the base has several recognizable wartime buildings now used by light industry. The restored control tower named Witchcraft honors one of the war's most famous B-24s and its Rackheath base. It may be viewed and photographed from the exterior only. The base environs have four memorials to the US airmen, including one at the entrance. In recognition of their presence, the official village sign at its entrance has a depiction of a B-24 in flight. Holy Trinity Church has a memorial gate, bench, plaque, roll of honor, and a room with exhibits about the base and its occupants. Colonel Albert Shower Road salutes the 467th commander. The Green Man pub frequented by US servicemen is opposite the airfield site.

TIBENHAM

Located 13 miles south/southwest from Norwich, Jimmy Stewart's first station and the former home of the 445th BG retains most of its main and secondary runways. Several derelict huts remain on the technical side. During the February 1944 Big Week offensive, the base lost thirteen of its twenty-five B-24s on one mission. Even worse, in September 1944, the 445th lost thirty aircraft on one day, the largest single-day loss of the war. In September 1944, they flew almost every other day, to total 280 war missions. As squadron commander, Jimmy Stewart flew ten combat missions from Tibenham. Base personnel are remembered on a plaque in All Saints Church, which has thickly upholstered kneelers given by individual crew members or their families. Hand-painted drawings on knitted kneelers depict aircraft and the names of some who served at Hethel. One kneeler has the inscription, "I'll be seeing you," woven above a B-24 in flight.

HETHEL

Home to the 389 BG, part of the main runway is used by the Norwich Gliding Club, although overgrowth partly obscures the other two original runways and perimeter track, which may be walked for much of the

Seventy-five years later the still solid Norden bombsight hut at Old Buckenham.
AUTHOR

length. Parts of low concrete buildings remain in scattered locations. A former chapel is the most significant building remaining, with a 1944 crew painting on a wall depicting Christ on the cross.

MARTLESHAM HEATH

The church of St. Michael's and All Angels has a "Roll of Honour," with names of those killed who were stationed at the base. The former control tower has exhibits describing missions flown by the 67th Fighter Wing. Major sections of the runways, taxiway, original hangar, underground fuel tanks, revetments, and several derelict concrete structures remain.

In June 1946, a plaque placed in the fifteenth-century rural church of Carelton Rode, five miles from the former base at Attleborough, honors the twenty-eight crewmen who died in separate midair collisions over the village in 1944 and 1945. A stained-glass window is dedicated to the crews killed in the collision.

Chapter Eighteen

A Boy on the Fence

. . . Up, Lad, up, 'tis late for lying:
Hear the drums of morning play;
Hark, the empty highways crying,
Who'll beyond the hills away ?
. . . Clay lies still, but blood's a rover;
Breath's a ware that will not keep.
Up, lad: when the journey's over
There'll be time enough to sleep.
—From "Reveille" by A. E. Housman

He first heard the distant sounds as a single irregular drone, *thrum thrum*, and knew that it was time to get on his bicycle, call for his friend, and pedal furiously the few miles to the main gate at Horsham St. Faith. As they neared the base, the overhead sounds separated into the individual roars of four engines powering a bomber inward bound. It then appeared low in the mist in final approach, others following, and watching them take form seemed to him a thing of awe and wonder. By early 1944, American bombers and crews with their B-17s, B-24s, and fighters were becoming familiar sights in Norfolk, Suffolk, and throughout East Anglia and the Midlands. The engine sounds gave comfort to the villagers; they were the sounds of victory. The young men who flew the bombers were the same ones they saw in the local shops, churches, and pubs. On this day, B-24s of the 458th BG were completing another perilous mission over occupied Europe. From the control tower balcony or gathered at the perimeter track straining for views of the aircraft identifying numbers, the ground crew and officers with binoculars peered into the sky for the red flares that meant wounded were aboard. Those shot-up planes landed first, with medics and ambulances ready to rush them to the hospital.

The boys at Horsham's main gate waited until after the mandatory post-mission debrief, with the intent to glimpse if not actually talk to the Yanks and ask with big eyes and shy grins for candy or gum. Even discarded wrappers or boxes from the well-stocked BX (Base Exchange) could be traded at school. Then, out they came, poised, smiling, the officers smart-looking in their crush-caps. One went directly to the fence where the ten year old and his pal waited. With a smile he reached in his pocket. "Hi kid, this is for you," and gave him a quarter. It had an eagle with outstretched wings on one side and a profile of George Washington on the other. Boldly visible on the Washington side, so that friend and foe alike would know its meaning, one word dominated: LIBERTY. He knew that the quarter would stay with him for the rest of his life.

Through the years and decades ahead he touched the coin often, knowing that it meant much more than its monetary value; it represented a resolve and determination to succeed against all adversity in a grand cause that would never happen again. Looking back on those years from long into the future, it seemed to have been part of a dream, although he remembered the faces, their voices, and the confidence they had in themselves. It didn't seem so at the time, but some of the tall young men were only eight years older than him.

Living only four miles from Norwich made pedaling to Horsham easy, but so many bases were nearby that they had a choice of airfields where they could get even closer to the bombers and fighters, and especially nearer to the men who flew them. Chums at school said that Rackheath, home to the 467th BG and its four B-24 squadrons, had a back road going directly to the dispersal side where the aircraft and crews were. Unlike at Horsham St. Faith, they needn't wait at the gate to view the flyers from a distance like spectators at a parade. On this day, three boys on bikes were determined to meet the crews at their planes and, if they were lucky, be invited aboard one of the big bombers.

They left Palmer Road to enter the base on a side lane, arriving at the dispersal area where the aircraft, ground crews, and airmen were together at the start and end of missions. Soon enough, they were caught by an MP sergeant, who said that if they trespassed again they would go before the base commander. One of the boys didn't take the threat seriously; "what harm could come to a ten year old," he reasoned. So, not long after, he biked back only to be stopped by another MP and again turfed-off the base. The next time he returned it was with his mother who worked at the American Red Cross Club in the Cathedral Close in Norwich. Items needed to be delivered to the control tower and he tagged along. There he saw the radio equipment with its glowing dials and heard the tense static-filled talk between the tower and the bombers crossing the North Sea from Germany to England. He couldn't explain it, but he felt history both underfoot and hovering above like a low cloud he could see but not touch.

Undaunted, he pedaled back again, only to be collared by a vigilant MP and told "don't come back if you know what I mean." Stubbornly, this boy man who saw the sky dim every morning and evening with the enveloping presence of the giant airplanes returned still again, only to be grabbed by the same MP who stopped him the last time. Hurried into a jeep, they bounced on the rutted road to the office of the 467th Group commander, Col. Albert S. Shower. (Much later he learned that the commander, a West Point graduate, dapper with a Clark Gable mustache, became the only AAF commander to fly from the States with his group and stay in command throughout the war. Colonel Shower didn't lead from behind a desk either; he flew as lead pilot in the exposed forward part of the combat box and did it for one hundred missions in 140 days. After VE Day he went home with the remainder of the group to prepare for deployment to the Pacific.)

Given a stern lecture, with assurance that his father would be told if he trespassed again, his days among the Yanks seemed to be over. Back at school he learned from other boys also being occasional truants that another AAF base at nearby Hethel, home to the 389th BG, had even easier access than at the other bases. At Hethel, he went over only one fence and then took a short if cautionary walk to find himself next to the bombers, close enough to soak in the rich mix of oil, high octane gasoline, and cordite.

As with all the groups and squadrons in the AAF, the 389th had a nickname and insignia painted on the fuselage. They were the "Sky Scorpions," represented by a fierce winged creature facing down, holding a bomb in its talons, flames trailing behind. Up close, he saw how the aircraft boosted crew morale with cleverly worded and designed pinups on the front fuselage, a graffiti they called "nose art."

A smiling crew chief saw him and left a B-24 to come to the fence: "Hi kid, whatya say." John "Pop" Gantus, in his twenties but a few years older than the ground crew, thus had entitlement to the "Pop" moniker. As crew chief for *Pugnacious Princess Pat*, his other nickname of "Gany" had been painted above the bomber's name. Crew chiefs and ground crews occupied a privileged place in the hierarchy of choreographed actions that made every mission possible. They, and not the pilot and crew "owned" the aircraft they serviced all night, and merely "allowed" it to be flown and returned safely so that they could patch it up for the next mission. The fraternal bond between the airmen and their ground crews had an importance equal to flying the mission itself.

What happened next at Hethel, then mostly empty of the aircraft droning their homebound way from Europe, changed the life of David Hastings, the boy on the fence. As told to the author eight decades later in his home on the edge of the former Rackheath AAF base: "On that day I met the ground crew for *Pugnacious Princess Pat*, had my first Coke and a Hershey bar, but first saw the sky suddenly fill with the roar of the B-24s as they returned home in formation." Then, the bomber and its crew, for whom he would develop an increasing dedication, pivoted onto the pad and cut its engines. Mere feet away now, he saw its namesake painted on the side, a glamorous girl posing in her underwear. (She had been named for the pilot's wife, Pat.)

ADOPTED BY THE CREW

When Pop saw David, he first told "Pat's" crew about meeting the boy, and all then left the aircraft preceded by the pilot, 1st Lt. Al Dexter, who went directly to David sitting on the fence. "I hear that you would

Pat's crew. Pilot, Lt. Al Dexter top row, second from left. Bottom row, Flight Engineer Sgt. John "Pop" Gantus extreme right with peaked cap. DAVID HASTINGS

like to see my airplane." Al lifted David over the fence and they walked back to inspect the silver-skinned aircraft. Once again, another MP pulled up in a jeep to demand that David immediately leave the base. The pilot, a slight twenty-three-year old, intervened with the MP, confirming why he occupied the cockpit's left seat. As related by David decades later: "Al told the MP that he had three choices: 'you can shoot me, which I doubt, get me confined to barracks which means no more missions, or you can get the hell out of here.' The MP quickly departed, and Al began what would become a ritual by placing his arm around my shoulder and walking all the way around his B-24, as well as introducing me to his crew."

A truck came to take the crew to the debrief hut, but before boarding Al returned: "David, you can come back anytime." Pop heard it and came over: "He means it; he wants you to come back." Not aware of its importance—that he had become a needed distraction from the torment they faced on every mission but couldn't discuss with each other—David had been "adopted" by the crew as their mascot. He had to return.

At least twenty-five more times he returned, and he would become as much a part of the crew's rites and rhythms as the other routines completed before and after each mission. For them to see David meant that an indefinable continuity with his life had been linked with theirs. The reality that he signified on the ground would transfer to their next mission, while also knowing that every time they went up the odds against returning went up with them.

As the bombers returned from the next mission, looping around the perimeter track to their assigned hardstands, David squinted for the first look at "his" Lib, *Pugnacious Princess Pat*, the one with the identifier D+ on its tail and squadron marking RR code on the fuselage. Then it came to its stand and stopped. Weighed down by gear the crew smiled and gave thumbs up to David, as Al came over to greet him ready to begin their walkaround.

Pugnacious Princess Pat. DAVID HASTINGS

With Al's arm on his shoulder they went around the bomber, always in the same clockwise direction, touching its metal skin to feel the jagged gaps from flak, David wondering but fearing to ask what it was like in the danger-filled air. While the 389th group and Al's 566th squadron were in the debrief hut, Pop let him walk through the ship to collect candy boxes left underfoot. He had school friends waiting for special ones. When the engines needed testing, sometimes Pop took David through the procedure for starting each of the Pratt & Whitney fourteen-cylinder, 1,200-horsepower engines. He would remember those times for later when his own life changed.

THE BOND OF LIFE THEY SHARED

On non-flying days Al and David periodically went to the base chapel to meet the Catholic chaplain, Father Beck, and to the mess hall for treats not enjoyed in years, such as chicken and ice cream. On weekends, Al, Pop, and the crew went to David's home nearby on Coleman Road for visits that meant as much to the Americans as to the Hastings family. Treasuring every moment, David had gained an unforeseen second family, and the men had another truth: the reality of what they were fighting to preserve, and a resumption of the lives with God's grace and good luck they would return to, existed within an English family.

Beginning with the mission on July 11, 1944 against Munich, then repeating it the next day against the same target, the bomber named with the repeated "P" consonant, piloted by Al Dexter, and with the crew who were now part of his family, flew twenty-five missions in only ten weeks. On September 27, the date of the twenty-fifth mission and a stateside ticket, the 389th BG and Al's 566th Squadron hit Hamm in the steel-making Ruhr area. That same day headquarters and the needs of the war increased the minimum to thirty missions. Flying every other day, only two weeks later over Osnabruck, they completed the thirtieth mission and the hoped-for reassignment.

The minimum then went up again—and for the last time—to thirty-five missions. On November 2, 1944, the day of their thirty-fifth mission, Al and the crew of the battered *Princess Pat* flew through flak for the last time to hit Bielfeld and its large rail marshalling yards.

David awaited "Pat's" return from the thirty-fifth mission more anxiously than ever. He knew it would be either their last mission and stateside, or it would be their last mission and eternity. Then, after "Pat's" tires squealed on to the runway he saw the Liberator's tail marking, and knew they were back safe. After they parked Al came directly across the pad to take him in both arms. "Thank God David, we made it, we made it." After the debrief, Al, David, and the crew went to the mess hall to celebrate with a late night and a long sleep. As David related it long after: "The next weekend all the crew came to our home and I presented Al with a wooden model that I made of *Pugnacious Princess Pat*. We all said a sad farewell and that was the end. I still cycled out to be with Pop, but now without a plane to service, he said that he was going to re-muster to aircrew."

OTHER LOSSES

When Al heard about it he insistently told Pop that he had done his duty and didn't need to join an aircrew. "Stay on the ground where it's safe; the war won't last much longer." As did so many unacknowledged men who also volunteered to extend their duty, Pop had a destiny to fulfill and intended to be in at the victory. But it was not to be. Shot down on March 23, 1945 near Munster, Master Sergeant John M. Gantus, Los Angeles County, California, engineer and top-turret gunner on the B-24, *Yankee Doodle Dandy*, died with his new crew.

In eighty-three days of aerial combat, Al Dexter's 566th Squadron flew thirty-five missions, one for every 2.4 days. In 321 missions, his 389th BG lost 116 B-24s and 588 men plus prisoners, in missions over the Ploesti oil fields, the factories at Munster, V weapons sites at the Pas de Calais, enemy gun batteries on D-Day, German positions in the St. Lo breakout, and storage depots in the Battle of the Bulge. They dropped food, ammunition, gasoline, and supplies to US and British troops crossing the Rhine. They were in at the start and they stopped only when it ended. But Al Dexter's gallant B-24 had another ending.

On Sunday, November 26, 1944, *Pugnacious Princess Pat* and her replacement crew left Hethel at dawn to join 1,136 other bombers and 732 fighters in another mission against the heavily defended synthetic oil factory at Misburg, Germany. Two flak bursts tore into Pat's left wing and tail section and she quickly plunged down. Four parachutes were seen. The other six crew members and the pilot were killed. Thirty-three other bombers and nine fighters were also lost that day.

REMAINS OF THE BATTLE

With the arrival of peace, the vast forward movement that won the European war went into reverse to prepare for the trip home or redeployment to the Pacific war without touching American shores. Weeks passed before the boys again returned to Hethel. David and his friends had finally placed school attendance ahead of absence.

The gate at the main entrance to the base swung lazily in the breeze, with no watchful MPs to chase the boys. In the silence they biked to the huts, entered the chapel, mess hall, the three hangars, and control tower. All were empty. Only a copy of *Yank*, the Army weekly sold to the troops for a nickel, and a steel helmet someone forgot to pack remained in a corner.

Decades later at the former base with the same hardstands that once held forty B-24s, nothing remained to tell the story of Al Dexter, Pop

Reunion in 1992: David and wife Jean (right) with Al Dexter and wife Pat (left with officer). DAVID HASTINGS

Gantus, and the 389 "Sky Scorpions" except for layers of black tire skids on the runways. That and a boy on a fence.

The AAF staff in the six mansions that were headquarters for the three air divisions and their attached wings packed and shipped home masses of files for study by future historians. They unpinned from walls the maps, charts, and graphs that recorded the progress of the European war, looked around, turned out the lights, and left forever. The temporary structures extending from the headquarters buildings remained until the returning estate owners had them removed for scrap. Only a wall plaque outside Ketteringham Hall remains as a testament to the heroic achievements of its one-time occupants. The memory of the citizen soldiers and airmen who came from the new world to liberate the old gradually faded into history. America lost part of a generation of its youth to the war: young men who vanished with their dreams for a full life and a new family and the babies that would never be born, and the generations that would never exist.

Aftermath: Forty-Five Years Later, Norwich, England, 1990

Oh, I have slipped the surly bonds of earth
And danced the skies on laughter-silvered wings;
Sunward I've climbed, and joined the tumbling mirth
Of sun-split clouds—and done a hundred things
You have not dreamed of—Wheeled and soared and swung
High in the sunlit silence. Hov'ring there
I've chased the shouting wind along, and flung
My eager craft through footless halls of air . . .
Up, up the long delirious, burning blue
I've topped the wind-swept heights with easy grace
Where never lark or even eagle flew—
And, while with silent lifting mind I've trod
The high untrespassed sanctity of space,
Put out my hand and touched the face of God.
　　　　　　—"High Flight," John Gillespie Magee Jr.

David Hastings, the boy on a fence, amidst the memories of war. AUTHOR

As the bases were returned to agriculture or industry, David never forgot the young men who flew against the odds. Fulfilling a desire to fly, he earned wings in 1964 then received a twin-engine and instrument rating. In the United States, he logged twenty-nine thousand more miles, and in 2013 received Platinum Wings from the Airline Operators and Pilots Association (AOPA). For twenty-eight years, he served as vice chairman and chairman of the Second Division Memorial Trust in Norwich. Over all those years he wondered, 'what happened to Al Dexter'?

In 1990, after another query by David in the *Second AD Journal* seeking the whereabouts of Lt. Albert Dexter, St. Paul, Minnesota, one day he received a call: "David, this is a voice from your past." Forty-six years later, it was Al Dexter on the telephone. At the Second Air Division reunion in Norwich that year, they reunited for the first time since the 389th left Hethel. They flew together on B-24 *Diamond Lil,* one of only two remaining airworthy Liberators, after Northwest Airlines flew Al and his Pat—the same "Pugnacious Princess Pat"—to Norwich on an honor flight. During the 1992 Second Air Division meeting in Norwich, David flew with Al once again at the controls of a B-24. "He hadn't lost his skill," David said. In a rare honor for a non-member, David attended twenty-six Second AD conventions, and served twenty-eight years as Governor and Chairman of the association.

After he displayed the same silvery quarter nearly seventy-five years later, the author had a question. Well into his eighth decade David still had persistent memories of the self-assured young men who faced death daily, now nearly gone along

In 1990, David Hastings, now a pilot, finally reunites with B-24 pilot Al Dexter.
DAVID HASTINGS

with their days of fear and glory: "Why do you do it after all this time; why do you keep the memories alive?" he asked, "I do it because we can never thank them enough for what they did for us."

CHAPTER NINETEEN

The Norden Bombsight and the Myth of Strategic Bombing

AT OLD BUCKENHAM AND AT MOST BASES, ACROSS THE AIRFIELD FROM operations the huts and hangars on the technical side serviced the aircraft and stored underground ordnance and fuel. Maintenance buildings mingled with separate officer and crew barracks, the mess hall, and the recreational hut. A squat fifteen-by-twenty-five-foot brick structure with one door and two small high windows with bars had an armed guard posted outside twenty-four hours daily.

The building once held Norden bombsights for the 453rd's Liberators, the extravagantly praised bomb-aiming device essential to the success of precision daylight bombing. Escorted by armed guards, bombardiers carried in zippered canvas bags what they called "the football"—the sight head of the two-part mechanism—to and from the aircraft to the "bomb vault"—a safe in the bombsight shop. In the building, highly trained technicians repaired and recalibrated the hand-assembled units, laden with gyros, motors, gears, mirrors, levers, and a twenty-power telescope.

Having signed an oath to protect the bombsights with their lives if necessary, bombardiers with sidearms were ordered to destroy critical components of the two-thousand-part electro-mechanical analog computer if shot down. Because useful parts might remain after a crash landing, each bombsight had a thermite grenade attached, the chemical reaction sufficient to melt it into a molten heap. Although Churchill asked FDR to allow its use by the RAF, so secret were its workings that Roosevelt refused his most important ally.

CARL NORDEN, "OLD MAN DYNAMITE"

Central to the strategy of separating both the intent and the time of RAF and USAAF missions over Germany—the US targeting war industries in daylight, the RAF area bombing by night—the gyrostabilized Norden bombsight was designed to give US bombers the ability to pinpoint targets from an altitude so high—at least twenty-five thousand feet—that they would be above the enemy, with fighter escorts unnecessary. As it turned out the Allies were overly optimistic about both the bombsight's claimed reliability and the safety of bombers from attack at high altitude.

Born in Holland, Carl Norden emigrated to the United States in 1904, to experiment in 1911 with Elmer Sperry on various ways to improve ship gyrostabilizers. The testing took place at Sperry Company headquarters, 40 Flatbush Avenue in downtown Brooklyn. After forming his own company, Norden became a US Navy consultant, assigned to improve the primitive bombsights of the World War I era. After many variations, he perfected the fully automatic M-Series (Navy, Mark 15), to become the Bureau of Ordnance's (BuOrd) most tested bomb-aiming device. Called "old man dynamite" (but not to his face) by Navy colleagues because of his trigger temper, Norden developed the war's primary bombsight, to become widely used by the AAF, US Navy, and later by the US Air Force in Korea and Vietnam. In its tested state it overcame, as Norden repeatedly demonstrated to BuOrd, the many variables previously hindering accurate bombing. He boasted that it would hit the "pickle barrel from 20,000 feet," (although the "pickle barrel" would be invisible at that altitude).

THE SECRET STOLEN BY A GERMAN SPY

Tests of the bombsight's accuracy in peacetime conditions were so successful that the ninety thousand Norden units subsequently ordered by the Army and Navy were favored over rival Sperry's S-1 bombsight. The War Department canceled the Sperry contract in late 1943, unaware that Norden's plans had been stolen in 1938. The designs were given to

German military authorities by naturalized German-American Herman W. Lang, a chief inspector with the Norden company. With ready access to blueprints—which he took home from 80 Lafayette Street (today NYU's Lafayette Hall) to copy—Lang voyaged to Germany with the plans on the SS *Bremen*, to be awarded $4,000 by Nazi officials.

A week after Pearl Harbor, the FBI, which had seeded double-agent William Sebold into what became known as the Duquesne spy ring, arrested Lang and thirty-two other German spies. Along with filming and recording the spy ring's activities for two years at Sebold's 42nd Street office, the FBI covertly operated a shortwave radio station, letting the ring feed disinformation back to Germany. Avoiding the electric chair, all thirty-three spies were convicted of espionage with combined prison terms of over three hundred years, although not all sentences were fully served. Given one of the longest sentences of eighteen years, Lang went to federal prison but served only eight years, and in 1950 was deported to Germany. Postwar evidence confirmed that the bombsight partially adapted by the Luftwaffe beginning in 1938, had many of the same features and effectiveness as the Norden device.

The secrecy of the bombsight's existence quickly faded with its removal by the Germans from hundreds of US planes shot down in enemy territory. Well before the end of the war, with the Luftwaffe in possession of the device and its most important parts, feature articles praising its abilities appeared in magazines such as *Popular Mechanics*, and in daily newspapers. Its classification dropped from top-secret to restricted, the military's least secure category.

In gathering results of bombing effectiveness within days to weeks after the German surrender, or sometimes in combat conditions, the little-known 1,150 officers, enlisted men, and civilians of the Strategic Bombing Survey had unfavorable conclusions about the effectiveness of daylight bombing. Inspected were hundreds of German plants, cities, and areas. Members interviewed the surviving political and military leaders, impounding a hoard of documents, with personnel so close to the front lines that four were killed and many wounded. It was determined that "old man dynamite's device lacked its boasted war-winning precision and "pinpoint accuracy," with the whole being much less than the sum of its parts.

Uncertainties About the "Blue Ox"

In an era before computers, microchips, and high-speed robotic assembly, the two-thousand-part hand-crafted precision instrument had tolerances from one thousandth to ten thousandths of an inch. Modified in 1941 by Minneapolis Honeywell and redesigned as the Army C-1 auto-pilot, the device parts were assembled in great secrecy by mostly women at 80 Lafayette Street, New York, and other locations. Women had the patience and steady hands typical of early watch-makers, the intricate parts needing equal exactness. An eventual ninety thousand units at a cost of $1.1 billion or $8,000 per assembly earned the Norden Co. a 10 percent profit from each sale.

Obscurely known as the "blue ox" by bombardiers and pilots, the Norden sight automatically calculated, and immediately corrected if necessary, the changes caused by wind drift and other factors such as the angle of attack. With Honeywell modifications, a bomber's targeting

A mostly female workforce assembled the over two thousand precision parts in the bombsight. NATIONAL ARCHIVES

could achieve previously unheard-of accuracy, although with the need to fly a level course in the final stages of the bomb run. To achieve the illusion of the target always being in the crosshairs, a motor in the unit's telescope slowly rotated a mirror to remove the effect of the ground always being in motion because of the aircraft's speed. Tests showed that with the bombardier in control, the target always in view, a stable platform would produce optimal results.

However, the two-section forty-pound contrivance had a problem unanticipated by everyone, especially Carl Norden and BuOrd: It didn't operate as intended. Actual combat conditions varied greatly from peacetime static tests, including evasions from fighter attacks, pitch and roll, yaw, turbulence, fog and cloud over the target, or smoke screens on the ground obscuring visibility. Even temperature variations and vibrations from the aircraft altered settings of the fragile gears, barometer, gyroscope, motorized mirror, a wheel and disk mechanism, and pulleys. Every part and process needed intense manual bombardier realignment from the initial point to the thirty-second-later bomb release. By March 1943, to

The upper or aiming section of the two-part Norden bombsight. AUTHOR

offset the growing inaccuracies of precision bombing, Col. Curtis LeMay assigned a lead bombardier to toggle "bombs away"—often accompanied by the firing of a flare as a signal to other bombardiers to immediately drop their ordnance. When the lead bombardier dropped, everyone in the box simultaneously toggled their release as a salvo, further leading to wide variations in target results. As another unsatisfactory tactic to achieving accuracy, RAF and USAAF "pathfinder" bombers dropped flares to mark the target for those following.

Promoted as able to hit within a one-hundred-foot circle at twenty-one-thousand feet, instead, in combat conditions, up to 90 percent of the bombs hit outside of a much larger one-thousand-foot radius. Only 50 percent fell inside a quarter-mile radius. Illogically, as increasing numbers of bomber groups arrived in England to target Germany, the percentage of bombs striking the target increased, but only because a greater volume of munitions not only enveloped the target, but also extended to the surrounding area. As after-mission crew debriefings reported—and the postwar Strategic Bombing Survey confirmed—the improved results came not from the success of the Norden bombsight's accuracy, but from the effects of saturation bombing. Inversely, although the AAF intended to be the strategic bomber force by striking specific targets and letting the British saturate an area, later in the war the AAF and RAF both saturation bombed. To the dismay of residents of entire cities below, as blunt gravity munitions the unguided bombs had inherent aerodynamic flaws, to be later overcome by a new era of precision-guided weapons.

LITTLE IMPROVEMENT AFTER CHANGES

After personally flying missions in late 1943 as commander of the Third Air Division, newly promoted Gen. Curtis LeMay, known both admiringly and derisively as "old iron-pants," further modified bombing tactics but with only a slight improvement in precision. Posted in August 1944 to the China India Burma (CBI) theatre, LeMay's B-29 Superfortresses, equipped with the Norden M-9 sight, had an even greater failure rate, with only 5 percent of bombs on target from high altitudes. Contributing to the inaccuracies and unlike European weather conditions were the unexpected Asian jet stream winds that further deflected the angle

Under perfect conditions the atomic bombs on B-29s *Enola Gay* and *Bockscar* struck almost at the grid reference. NATIONAL ARCHIVES

and drift of munitions dropped. Also unanticipated later in the war were increasing factory quality control hitches from high-volume manufacturing. Even a shortage of ball-bearings caused a backup in deliveries of tested units.

According to the US Strategic Bombing Survey, by changing to low-altitude area bombing with incendiaries against Japanese cities, LeMay succeeded in destroying most of Japan's remaining war industry and its cities, but at the cost of 220,000 civilian lives.

Yet, above Hiroshima on August 6, 1945, the blue skies absent of enemy fighters and conditions perfect, from thirty-one-thousand feet bombardier Major Thomas Ferebee dropped an atomic bomb from B-29 *Enola Gay* to detonate only eight hundred feet away from the hypocenter or ground zero. On August 9, to end World War II, Captain Kermit Beahan, bombardier of the B-29 *Bockscar*, dropped the second atomic bomb above Nagasaki, with an error of only fifteen hundred feet. Norden bombsights were used on both missions.

PRECISION BOMBING NO BETTER THAN AREA BOMBING

Completed only five months after the end of the European war, the US Strategic Bombing Survey issued a lengthy report on the entire bombing campaign, day and night, American and British. Another followed for the Pacific war. It had an unfavorable judgment, not overlooked by future war planners, in opposition to the previously unassailable doctrine of daylight bombing's success. The report confirmed what the airmen always knew and reported post-mission: the Norden bombsight had no better results than RAF night saturation bombing with the less sophisticated but equally effective SABS MkXIV bombsight. The survey concluded that neither strategic nor area bombing decided the outcome of either the European or Pacific war. Scores of Norden-guided attempts to destroy the enemy's aircraft industry didn't succeed either. Well into 1943, even under daily air attack, Germany's warplane availability increased 50 percent to 5,570 aircraft. And in examining the hundreds of Norden bombsights removed from downed AAF bombers, German engineers concluded that theirs was better.

AFTERMATH

A Norden bombsight taken from a B-26 Marauder is on display at the National Museum of the US Air Force at Wright-Patterson Air Force Base in Dayton, Ohio. The National Air and Space Museum in Washington, DC, has several models of the Norden sight, including the one aboard B-29 *Enola Gay* that dropped the atomic bomb on Hiroshima. Entire or partial bombsights are periodically offered for sale online.

Carl Norden. WIKIMEDIA COMMONS

Chapter Twenty

Trent Park Tattletales

Introduction: A Conversation About Lives

(German Generalmajor Georg Neuffer, in charge, 20th Flak Division, captured May 9, 1943, in Tunisia, casually conversing with Generalmajor Gerhard Bassenge, in charge, Air Defenses-Tunis-Bizerta, captured May 9, 1943 in Tunisia. Conversation secretly recorded at Trent Park, London, July 10, 1943.)

Neuffer: What will they say when they find our graves in Poland? I myself have seen a convoy at Ludowice near Minsk; I must say it was frightful, a horrible sight . . . It is ghastly, this picture. The women, the little children who were . . . absolutely unsuspecting. Of course, I didn't watch while they were being murdered. The German Jews were also sent to the Minsk district, and were gradually killed off. It was also done like this when Jews were taken away from Frankfurt. They were only notified immediately beforehand . . . allowed to take only a hundred marks . . . and then the hundred marks would be demanded from them at the station to pay the fare. But these things are so well known—if that ever gets known to the world at large . . . that's why I was so surprised that we got so frightfully worked up over the Katyn case.

Bassenge: Yes.

Neuffer: For that's a trifle in comparison to what we have done there.

NAZI GENERALS TALKED OPENLY TO EACH OTHER
AND SECRETLY TO EAVESDROPPERS

During the war 1,026 British prisoner of war camps held over 425,000 Axis prisoners in disused buildings, Nissen huts, and tent compounds in England, Scotland, Wales, the Isle of Man, and Northern Ireland. The United States held an equal number in seven hundred camps in forty-six states. Liberty Ships carried to Europe the cargo needed to conduct the war, and returned with prisoners in the empty holds, to pass the remainder of the war living in far better conditions than Allied prisoners captured by their German comrades.

Of the three locations in Britain where high-value prisoners were confined, only one became the exclusive residence for the highest-ranking German officers captured on the battlefield. They were held in north London in the circa 1780 former grand residence of Philip Sassoon, the son of Aline Rothschild, the daughter of French banking tycoon Baron Gustave de Rothschild. The society pages nominated him as London's most eligible bachelor. When not in residence at 25 Park Lane, he entertained the era's leading luminaries at Trent Park (TP), his three-story Georgian mansion set deeply within 413 acres on London's northern edge.

Among the many personalities visiting the mansion, who, before arriving, passed sculpture, lavish gardens, two lakes, a swimming pool, and a rare indoor tennis court, were the young Princess Elizabeth (the future Queen Elizabeth II), the Prince of Wales (the later abdicated King Edward VIII), Prime Minister David Lloyd George, Charlie Chaplin, George Bernard Shaw, John Singer Sargent, Mr & Mrs Neville Chamberlain, and Lt. T. E. Lawrence (Lawrence of Arabia). An out of office Winston Churchill, himself a socialite, attended parties, then returned to paint in its serene environs. Between the wars, celebrities, politicians, and notables came to see and be seen, but from mid-1942, the house vacant since Sassoon's sudden death in 1939, a different type of "guest" became resident, to be "seen" in an entirely different way.

The mansion would become the luxurious top-secret home for fifty-nine captured Nazi generals.

After six months of wiring and installation of portable recorders using 12-inch double-sided acetate disks housed in a basement room called "the M (for microphone) Room" the house would become fertile ground for intelligence exploitation by unseen snoops, listeners, and stool-pigeons. From US made RCA Type 88-A omni-directional pressure microphones hidden in twelve rooms and parts of the garden, the listeners recorded and reported on casual conversations the generals had with each other. After translation and typing, the intelligence windfall produced 64,427 bugged conversations. Transcripts went to MI9 and other intelligence departments, with the recordings erased and reused, except for talks discussing war crimes or new technology, such as V-1 and V-2 rockets. The multi-thousand transcription disks, able to record up to fifteen minutes on each side at a then non-standard 33⅓ rpm, were made on RCA equipment, including a specially modified switchboard, sent from the United States. Numerous of the original translated and typed conversations were read by the author at the National Archives in Kew outside London, in 2012, from files marked "Do not open until 2021." The reported 500,000 pound sterling cost of the snooping ($11 million today) and the bugging, remained secret for decades after the war.

CONFINEMENT WITH A PURPOSE

Rushed to the mansion in as few as two weeks after capture, the battles and their strategies still fresh in their minds, the generals were immediately placed at ease, and allowed to wear their uniforms and polished leather riding boots, even medals if they preferred. Continuing a deliberate process of imparting feelings of ease and comfort, they had unrestricted access to many of the mansion's lavishly appointed rooms for casual chat or arranged meetings. They were allowed daily newspapers or books in German, many confiscated from the library at the closed German embassy at 9 Carlton House Terrace (now The Royal Society) in St. James. Obliging servants graciously served meals course by course, including whiskey, wine or beer, in a private dining room. The generals received salutes and salutations from guards, attended classes in English, played billiards or table tennis, watched films, were offered instruction in art, and allowed visits to a sundries shop for beer and cigarettes, the payment made in pounds from a monthly allowance. Although letters were censored, they could send or receive correspondence from families. Allowed to play tennis on the adjacent Sassoon-built courts, they were unaware that even the tennis grounds were bugged.

The spacious rooms on the mansion's ground floor connected one to the other, encouraging movement or conversation, perhaps in a quiet corner next to a warm fire, an ideal location for a microphone hidden in the crown molding. They were given a study for reading, painting, or music, and allowed to sit together in a room

Gen. Dietrich von Choltitz, the "savior" of Paris, sang a different tune to the Trent Park listeners. WWW.CHOLITZ.DE

with a radio to hear uncensored German-language BBC news programs. Films were regularly presented, although newsreels were screened to prevent specific knowledge about the war. They enjoyed escorted walking privileges within the estate, or joined excursions to Windsor or Hampton Court, even to the theatre in London's West End, thirty minutes away by car. The highest-ranking officers had private rooms or suites, with the lower ranks sharing rooms. London tailors arrived twice monthly to attend to clothing and uniform needs. They even had a full-time welfare officer, Lord Alberfelty, who asserted to them his direct relationship with the royal family. At times when they needed someone to be a good listener, the lord nodded his head in agreement or sympathetically asked questions, just to keep the conversation going. It almost made them forget their status as inmates, especially with their captors regularly insisting that they were also their hosts, and that they viewed the battle-hardened generals as more comparable to long-term guests than prisoners. But everything had a purpose at Trent Park.

A Stage Set with the Inmates as the Actors

Indeed, the generals were unknowing participants in a carefully planned and meticulously executed ruse—one of the war's most elaborate. The scam's intent? Deceive the generals into a sense of comfort and dependence within the convivial surroundings, all the better for their tongues to loosen when least expected. The expansive house thus became a stage, with the prisoners portraying themselves in their own costumes—the uniforms, while the concealed "audience" of mostly German and Austrian exiled Jews listened intently to the discourse, although without audible reaction.

Regardless of appearance and the structured ambience, the generals needn't look far to see that windows were barred, a guard tower was immediately outside, and two rows of barbed wire surrounded the estate. Bombs could be heard exploding in the distance or nearby, and they regularly saw the sky darken with clouds of RAF and USAAF bombers heading toward their homeland. They were prisoners and they knew it, but that wasn't the point. Place them at ease and comfort; get them to talk among themselves, and hope that odd bits of intelligence would

Class portrait—comfortable in their uniforms and in the secrets told to each other and to eager ears. TRENT PARK MUSEUM

result. As for kindly "Lord Aberfelty," he was MI9 agent Ian Monroe, who reported everything to his intelligence service quartered in the Grand Central Hotel (Landmark Hotel), opposite Marylebone Station.

In the off-limits basement, listeners and recording technicians activated numerous hidden microphones installed in different parts of the major rooms, even in sections of the garden. The basement listeners wearing headsets were uninterested in idle weather chat, but when the conversation changed to talk about the war and their part in it, a tone-arm with a stylus and diamond-tipped needle went into a groove, and the recording began. Translators and stenographers then produced word for word results.

Being part of a regime of deception themselves, the generals had to be suspicious that their conversations were being tapped and could be used against them. But the deceivers—the secret listeners and the visible staff—were so accomplished in managing the ruse, that the generals had no proof that their conversations were being intercepted and thus gossiped ceaselessly, increasingly, and ever confidently.

To encourage information exchanges to potentially yield revealing intelligence, the detainee ranks were regularly seeded with German officers of different services. A seasoned army general discussing tactics with a Luftwaffe general, could—and did—divulge intimate insights into politics, organizational structure, new or failed battlefield tactics, the use of combined arms, and new weapons and their success or failure. One of the few surviving U-boat captains inserted into the group would have eager ears listening to his descriptions of harrowing battles that might include the best depth to evade surface attacks. Essential details then went to Royal Navy and US Navy officials, then to sub-hunting ships for more precise settings on depth charges.

The ages of the generals ranged from thirty-four to the oldest at fifty-six, with most Prussian born and almost all veterans of World War I. Of the over seven thousand Knights Crosses that Hitler awarded, many indiscriminately, forty-six TP generals wore the German equivalent of the American Medal of Honor. (In World War II, the president in the name of Congress awarded a comparatively few 464 Medals of Honor, 266 posthumously.)

As a further aid to intelligence gathering, *General der Panzertruppe* Wilhelm Ritter von Thoma, the first general sent to Trent Park, not only encouraged conversation among officers, but unknowingly assisted listeners by revealing details of the V-1 flying bomb and V-2 programs in development at Kummersdorf outside Berlin, which moved to Peenemunde on the Baltic coast. Although it didn't stop the use of the new terror weapons, the RAF and USAAF exploited the intelligence by bombing production plants and launch sites at Peenemunde and Nordhausen. For good measure they also reduced to a husk the test site at Kummersdorf. But much more than war plans or tactical discussions were overheard by the secret listeners.

WIDESPREAD COMPLICITY IN WAR CRIMES

The political differences between Gen. Wilhelm von Thoma and Gen. Ludwig Crüwell emphasized the widely divergent views between TP's pro-Nazi ideologues and the more temperate moderates. Among various examples of differing views, von Thoma roundly condemned the unexpected German attack on the Soviet Union, Hitler's leadership, war crimes by German troops in Russia, and the deportation and killing of the Jews of Europe. He said: "A long war is impossible for little Germany and it cannot end happily for us. I felt that when America entered the war—and the situation is very similar to when they [America] . . . entered World War I. . . ." Crüwell then interrupted, thinking it "impossible" for German troops to commit war crimes: "The German army is the best in the world," he said. He also said in a July 2, 1942 letter to his children: "Love for the Fatherland is to some extent the religion of our

Gen. Ludwig Crüwell: a Nazi *without* a hint of conscience. WIKIMEDIA COMMONS

The Trent Park mansion, where the Nazi generals talked openly to each other and secretly to listeners. AUTHOR

time. Love this greater Germany so that the struggle continues to the end. Never under any circumstances marry a foreigner."

Reading a cloudy crystal ball, General Crüwell made a hopeful forecast in a recording made on August 12, 1943: "If no decision [is made] by next year—and I see that as our greatest hope—the Americans will get out of the war. After all, what do they want here? What interest do they have in Italy? What has Germany done to them? They've made a mass of money as usual—they've no love for the English—and above all they recognize the Jewish poison at work among their people and realize how they are blackmailing their leaders. We see the Jewish poison in their heavy attacks on Hamburg. [With emphasis.] It is the Jews who want to destroy us down to the last man! They know that the National Socialist doctrine will spread all over the world! They want to save themselves by hook or by crook from their inevitable extinction!"

Four months later on December 14, 1944, as part of a three-way conversation, General von Thoma added to his despair about what the

The generals had the freedom of the house—nearly. AUTHOR

Nazi regime had done to Germany and the world: "I regret every bomb, every scrap of material wasted, every human life that is being wasted in this senseless war. The only gain that the war will bring us is the end of ten years of gangster rule ... the collapse of Germany is inevitable ... they must put Hitler in a padded cell. A gang of rogues cannot rule forever!"

Gen. Dietrich von Choltitz, over-generously lauded as the "savior" of Paris, when Hitler ordered it to be burned, had another side. Recorded from a group conversation on October 27, 1944 with three other generals: "Have you read Churchill's speech? Appalling! Beyond all words! A Jewish brigade to go to Germany! Then the French will take the west and the Poles the East. The hate in that speech! I am completely shattered."

TOP AND BOTTOM: A friendly corner and a welcoming fireplace in the mansion, perfect for hidden microphones. AUTHOR

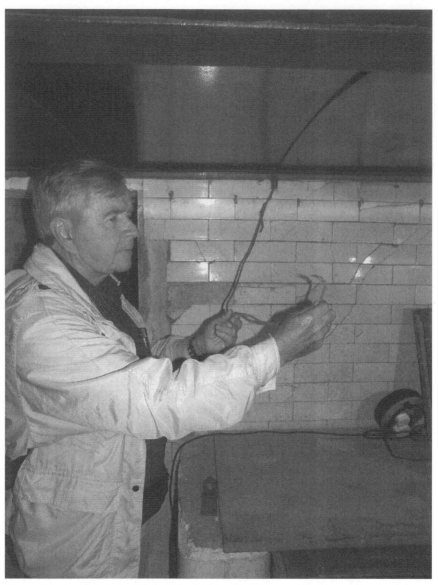

The author locates part of the original wiring that powered the recording equipment. AUTHOR

Part of a vast basement where listeners tapped in to the generals' eager talk.
AUTHOR

Numerous conversations among the generals discussing the fate of the Jews made clear that they, if not the entire Wehrmacht, had, at minimum, widespread knowledge if not outright complicity in knowing that *something* was happening to the Jews of Europe.

In a September 3, 1944 conversation, Generals Muller-Romer and Hennecke were casting-about to assign blame for the atrocities.

Muller-Romer: "Our Gestapo competed with the Russians in their bestial actions. I know the ghastly atrocities committed in Poland since 1939, when those fellows started there.

Hennecke: Did anyone oppose them?

Muller-Romer: Yes. (General) Blasowitz did at the time, but it didn't do him any good. The Wehrmacht had no say in those matters. "That comes under civil administration and is no business of yours." The fact that such things were possible will puzzle world historians . . . the German people shouldn't have stood for all the craziness in 1933.

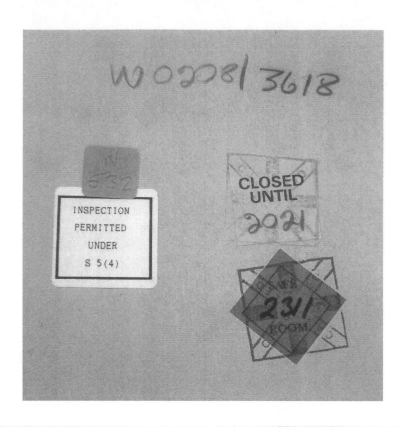

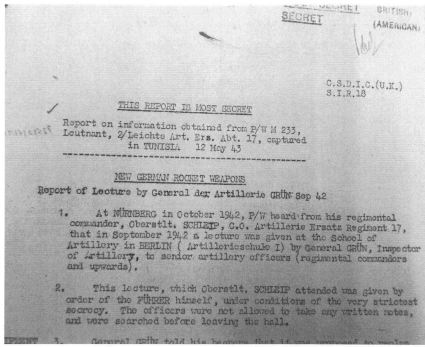

SECRET
BRITISH/
(AMERICAN)

C.S.D.I.C.(U.K.)
S.I.R.18

THIS REPORT IS MOST SECRET

Report on information obtained from P/W M 233,
Leutnant, 2/Leichte Art. Ers. Abt. 17, captured
in TUNISIA   12 May 43

NEW GERMAN ROCKET WEAPONS

Report of Lecture by General der Artillerie GRÜN Sep 42

1.   At NÜRNBERG in October 1942, P/W heard from his regimental
commander, Oberstlt. SCHLEIP, C.O. Artillerie Ersatz Regiment 17,
that in September 1942 a lecture was given at the School of
Artillery in BERLIN (Artillerieschule I) by General GRÜN, Inspector
of Artillery, to senior artillery officers (regimental commanders
and upwards).

2.   This lecture, which Oberstlt. SCHLEIP attended was given by
order of the FÜHRER himself, under conditions of the very strictest
secrecy. The officers were not allowed to take any written notes,
and were searched before leaving the hall.

3.   General GRÜN told his hearers that it was proposed to replace

TOP AND BOTTOM: The declassified files reveal secrets that the Nazi generals told each other. AUTHOR

Hennecke: I never heard about such things before I came here . . . Whenever you asked, "Did you see it for yourself?" or "Did you really know someone?" you got the answer: "No, an uncle of Mrs. so-and-so told me . . ."

In June 1945, with the European war over, all TP inmates were required to view a film showing war crimes and atrocities in death camps. After the showing, Gen. Karl-Wilhelm von Schlieben commented in reference to the death camps: "That's the only thing about the thousand-year Reich that will last a thousand years." Gen. Paul von Selbert, an anti-Nazi: "Yes, we are disgraced for all time." But Generals Dittmar and Holste expressed for history their sorrow that the SS had not destroyed all the incriminating evidence.

Aftermath

In May 2012, on the same day that a part of Middlesex University located at Trent Park permanently vacated the grounds, the author viewed and photographed the mansion's compartmented basement where the listeners were stationed and walked the unchanged high-ceilinged connecting rooms where the generals conversed with each other. The building was closed that evening.

Portions of the land and Grade II-listed mansion were sold to a developer for conversion beginning in 2018 into 262 semi-detached and detached residences at a beginning price of $1,560 million. The historic mansion, its façade unchanged, will be converted into luxury residences to include a small museum describing the overlooked achievement by up to nine hundred staff and listeners. In the interim, located near the Oakwood Underground station in the Cockfosters area, twenty-five minutes from Kings Cross London, the expansive grounds and sculptures are open to the public, with close views of the mansion where Nazi generals talked secretly to each other but openly to the eavesdroppers.

CHAPTER TWENTY-ONE

The Arsenal of Democracy

They have given their sons to the military services. They have stoked the furnaces and hurried the factory wheels. They have made the planes and welded the tanks, riveted the ships, and rolled the shells.
—PRESIDENT FRANKLIN D. ROOSEVELT ON THE AMERICAN
PEOPLE, WORLD WAR II MEMORIAL, WASHINGTON, DC

PART ONE

PREPARING FOR TOTAL WAR

INTRODUCTION: THE SLEEPING GIANT

WHEN INFORMED ABOUT THE JAPANESE ATTACK AT PEARL HARBOR, Winston Churchill envisioned what would come: "To have the United States at our side was to me the greatest joy. Now at this very moment I knew that the United States was in the war, up to the neck and in to the death. So we had won after all!"

Long an admirer of America's industrial abilities and half-American by birth. Churchill had full confidence that America's immense manufacturing potential would lead the world to salvation. It would take three years and nine months to bring victory, but on December 11, 1941, the day Germany declared war on the United States, Hitler also signed his death warrant. The sleeping giant had awakened.

But there were no tools for the machines to be invented, no bullets from the munitions plants that didn't exist, and no skilled workers for the factories not yet designed or for the aircraft, and ships yet to appear on blueprints. Unlike its well-fortified foes, the United States had no war industry or an orderly process to build, assemble, and deliver the goods to sustain a war. All that America had in those early days was a determination to succeed.

Sleepwalking into War

In its prewar absence of readiness, lacking meaningful support in Congress or funds for preparations, before the war the US military functioned as a mostly reactive and improvised home defense force. It had few advocates for rearmament, with inter-service rivalries further hindering cooperation between military branches. Until fired by President Roosevelt in June 1940, the secretary of war, a political appointee and strict non-interventionist, refused to speak with his interventionist assistant secretary of war. In 1939, the United States had a standing army of 180,000, mostly in half-strength divisions, ranking nineteenth in the world, behind Portugal and Romania, and slightly ahead of Bulgaria. The prewar US government operated as it had since the beginning of the Republic, with the War Department (Army) and Navy Department secretaries, usually political appointees, reporting to the president but rarely cooperating with each other. In campaigning for reelection, congressmen on the stump could boast to their constituents—and be rewarded with another term—that they had worked across the aisle to uncover new ways to cut the military budget or deny appropriations.

Having failed to jointly coordinate plans and operations in World War I, a reorganized Joint Board, the predecessor of the Joint Chiefs of Staff, at least mutually agreed to recommend shared interests to Congress, such as modernizing the military. But it had no authority to implement any recommendation. Its proposals were generally ignored.

During the four-month 1898 Spanish-American War, the US Army fielded 171,642 men, nearly identical to its composition at the beginning of World War II. In 1940, the peacetime draft underway, rearmament beginning, and the European war advancing, the US Army continued to train mounted troops for its two horse-cavalry divisions, two horse-equipped artillery regiments, and two mixed horse and motor transport regiments. As late as June 1941—six months before Pearl Harbor—the Army Air Force had a mere 9,078 officers and 143,563 enlisted men. In mid-1941 Army inductees trained with wooden rifles and lobbed painted wood chunks imitating grenades. The Navy sailed a fleet of obsolete warships, many soon to be on the ocean bottom. Until near the outbreak of war, America had no significant munitions industry.

As a self-described "juggler," FDR appeared to be a non-interventionist while secretly aiding Britain, but in public vowed to keep America's sons out of another war. In a plus for Churchill's wants and needs, US voters by wide margins favored giving token aid to Britain—such as exchanging obsolete destroyers for bases—but only if it meant that America would remain on the sidelines and not fight another war. As an advantage for FDR's behind the scenes actions, the four major polling organizations consistently gave him high ratings, averaging 75 percent approval. Yet, when war came, by failing to boldly answer the threat to world order, a sleepwalking America placed not only its national security at risk, but its very existence as a nation.

At the end of 1941, the United States at war only three weeks and rearming barely underway, the air force had only 288 heavy bombers and 2,170 mostly obsolete fighter planes. With 7,340 vintage aircraft assigned to train pilots, the AAF had three times more trainers than fighter planes. That would change as at no other time in history.

The Awakening Begins

With America's sudden entry into the war twenty-seven months after its start, the entire country began immediate conversion of every part and function of its commercial and civil society into a war economy. It started with the mass movement of men and women from civilian occupations into the military. At its peak in 1944, the slender prewar Army Air Corps had massively expanded into 2.411 million personnel including 350,000 women. The air force alone had 31 percent of the entire US Army in its ranks, with another 422,000 civilians in various support capacities.

At the end of the war roughly 12 percent of the American population—16.2 million men and women, almost 39 percent volunteers—served in the military. Three of four were deployed overseas for an average of sixteen months. Nazi Germany, with half the population of the United States, had twenty-two million in the military, 31 percent of its population.

World War II began the movement toward women's equality in the workplace and the military. With an influential impetus from First Lady Eleanor Roosevelt, 150,000 women, all volunteers, had full military status in the Women's Army Corps (WACs). Eighty-six thousand Navy WAVES (Women Accepted for Volunteer Emergency Service) held the same standing as naval reservists, with most officer candidates trained at Smith College, Northampton, Massachusetts. Enlisted women trained at Great Lakes Naval Training Station, Illinois; Hunter College in the Bronx; and other locations. Another 105,000 women served in other

The war brought five million American women into the labor force and 350,000 into the armed forces. NATIONAL ARCHIVES

branches. Over eleven hundred civilians of the Women's Airforce Service Pilots (WASP)—the original fly girls—tested, ferried, towed targets, and delivered every type of military aircraft. It took sixty-five years for the US government to express its gratitude, when in 2010 President Barack Obama awarded the WASPs the Congressional Gold Medal. Almost overnight, an isolationist nation primarily concerned with its own self-interests, began the transformation from a small self-defense military into a world-dominating power, so overwhelming in achievement that its effects continue into the twenty-first century.

A MARATHON OF MANUFACTURING—CONVERTING FROM CIVILIAN TO MILITARY PRODUCTION

To finance, regulate, and control the acquisition, production, and delivery from raw materials to finished product of every commodity needed in the war, FDR reconstituted from its Depression era roots the Reconstruction Finance Corporation (RFC). It financed most of the nation's industrial war expansion, with one department, the War Production Board (WPB), given an authority of such immensity that it affected the everyday lives of every man, woman, boy, girl, and infant in America. Its limitless powers controlled the production from raw materials to finished goods of every product or service needed to conduct the war. Through the Office of Price Administration (OPA), it influenced all aspects of civilian life through rationing and emergency regulations.

All civilian automobile manufacturing ended. Cars being assembled were scrapped or painted olive drab for military use. Unless needed for the war, prohibited were civil projects, home construction, or civilian manufacturing. Multi-thousands of general and sub- contractors converted from civilian manufacturing to war production. As the men marched off to war, twenty-four million other Americans, including eight million women, entered war industries. By 1945, half of all the world's industrial production took place in the United States.

One of the WPB subsidiaries, the Defense Plant Corporation (DPC), vastly expanded existing factories or authorized, built, equipped, and operated new ones. To secure financing needed for their construction, WPB applied to the government-operated RFC for the needed

In November 1944, Harriet Ida Pickens and Frances Wills became the first African-American WAVES officers. NATIONAL ARCHIVES

loans. Investing $9 billion, the DPC quickly approved twenty-three hundred projects, with some in almost every state. In effect, the government owned the war plants, then leased them back to private industry to operate. With the prodigious industrial expansion resulting, the war also ended the Depression. Unemployment plummeted from 14.6 percent in 1940 to 1.2 percent in 1944.

At FDR's request in late 1941, Danish immigrant William S. Knudsen resigned the $300,000 per year ($5,245,191.00 in 2018) presidency of General Motors for one dollar a year as director of the Office of Production Management, replaced by the War Production Board in 1943. Commissioned a lieutenant general and further improving Henry Ford's assembly line advances, Knudsen converted the entire automobile industry into war production. He improved industrial and management practices so much that US war output led to the greatest industrial expansion in history. Asked by his children why he gave up one of the best-paying and most respected positions in the country, Knudsen said, "America gave me everything, now I can pay back some of it."

General Motors became the war's largest defense contractor, shifting production in two hundred North American plants from Cadillacs, Pontiacs, and Chevrolets into $12.3 billion ($215,052 billion today) of war materiel. Included were forty million cartridge cases, 198,000 diesel engines, thirty-eight thousand tanks, tank destroyers, and armored vehicles, thirteen thousand aircraft, 833,000 trucks, and twenty-one thousand of the thirty-one-foot-long, eight-foot-wide, 91-horsepower amphibious DUKWs, known as Ducks.

In addition to the Army Air Forces and Army Ground Forces, the Army Service Forces (Services of Supply), one of three autonomous Army commands, combined sixty-one separate agencies into three war authorities, each reporting to chief of staff Gen. George C. Marshall. Only one of its six massive technical agencies, the Army Corps of Engineers, designed and built over twenty-seven thousand military and industrial projects. They included the management of aircraft, tank assembly, and ammunition plant operations, six ports of embarkation, nine general depots for warehousing supplies, hundreds of fully equipped camps to

house 5.3 million troops, and overall supervision of the air bases being built for the AAF by British contractors.

The Army Corps of Engineers masked the development of the atomic bomb—the war's major secret along with the breaking of the Enigma device—with the industrial code-name "Manhattan Engineer District" (Manhattan Project). On December 2, 1942, after accomplishing the world's first self-sustaining nuclear chain reaction under Stagg Field at the University of Chicago, the Corps of Engineers then managed the project at three major and dozens of smaller sites, to its end in the skies over Japan. In total, over 125,000 worked in secret on the project.

Building the Bombers

The first deliveries of the slab-sided, four-engine B-24s went to the AAF only a few months before Pearl Harbor. Because of the readjustment from autos to airplanes, the auto assembly lines had early problems converting from the fifteen thousand parts needed for cars to the 1,555,000 parts for each B-24. The 80-acre, mile-long Willow Run, Michigan, plant stretched so far into the distance that a mid-point turntable rotated the underway aircraft assembly 90 degrees, to end a half-mile distant with a fully assembled B-24 ready for testing.

By March 1944, Willow Run made one B-24H every one hundred minutes, twenty-four hours a day, seven days a week. The total production from the five plants operated by Ford, Consolidated, Douglas, and North American became so overwhelming that supply began to outpace demand. To slow production three plants were closed, leaving by VJ Day a surplus of four hundred B-24s. At peak production, forty-two thousand workers built the B-24. With 19,256 bombers made by August 1945, the Liberator became the most produced American aircraft of all time, with 70 percent of all production coming from the Ford Willow Run works.

After training at scores of US bases on the newly made aircraft of all types, 72.5 "heavy" bombardment groups, each with seventy-two aircraft and ninety-six separate crews, deployed to Europe. Also sent to Europe were 28.5 medium and light bomber groups, seventy-one fighter, thirty-two troop carrier, and thirteen reconnaissance groups.

Worldwide 1.224 million AAF personnel were deployed—610,000 against Germany and 440,000 opposing Japan. A once in history achievement advanced a third-rate domestic air force to a world-dominating air power in only thirty months.

A "Rendezvous with Destiny"—The American People in the War

Administered by the Office of Price Administration (OPA), a ceiling placed on the value of 90 percent of manufactured goods, including processed and canned foods, limited consumption and spread the available commodities through rationing. Ration books with removable stamps became a second level of currency as "points" were combined with cash to purchase rationed goods. Housewives checked daily papers for the monetary price, then compared it with the "points" price at the market, displayed in red numerals for fresh goods, such as meat, fish, and dairy, and blue points for canned, bottled, or dried foods. Gasoline, heating oil, coal, wood, metals, rubber, plastics, raw materials, coffee, sugar, meats, butter, lard, fruits, jams and jellies, beef, pork, bacon, tires, silk, shoes, nylon, and numerous other manufactured products were rationed, but even as rationed, they often continued to be unavailable. Even 78 rpm recordings were limited, because of a reduced supply of shellac needed in manufacturing.

By learning to do without, ordinary Americans supported a common good shared by all, but if complaints were heard at the dinner table, someone was sure to say, "don't you know there's a war on?" Managing the program from small towns to big city neighborhoods were over eight thousand ration boards, most staffed by neighbors. Except for sugar, which remained rationed until 1947, rationing stopped when the war ended.

Some twenty million Victory Gardens were planted in backyards, on urban rooftops, vacant lots, or open lands in every city, suburb, town, and village from coast to coast. By 1943, the little plots produced 40 percent of the nation's fruit and vegetables, a harvest of up to ten million tons. Produce from the gardens fed not only Americans, but as canned goods went overseas to nourish millions of Allies. Grease saved from bacon and

Saving dinner table fat for conversion into munitions. NATIONAL ARCHIVES

other excess fats became glycerin for explosives. The donors were given four cents a pound for the fat. Urban children prowled alleys for tin cans to earn extra pennies. Scrap drives became community events, with full involvement by the Boy Scouts and other youth groups. Victory posters were pinned in post offices and every public building.

Housewives donated old pots and pans. Waste paper and corrugated box drives were held everywhere. Many car owners donated bumpers and fenders. Melted-down tin, steel, and copper were recycled into numerous war needs. Paper packaging began to replace metal or wood. Pleasure driving became illegal, with a 35 mph limit ("victory speed") for any motoring. Less than sixty days after the war began, over six hundred consumer products were banned from civilian use. Factories made idle then became immediately available for war work, often creating odd industrial bedfellows for a myriad of smaller manufacturers never considered as candidates for conversion into making war goods. Except for military needs, the manufacture of metal furniture disappeared. Silk used in stockings went into parachute canopies until it became scarce, to be replaced with nylon.

Roughly three thousand USO clubs were opened worldwide. The New York Stage Door Canteen and the USO Hollywood Canteen brought the stars and their shows directly to the GIs, with many celebrities working anonymously in the kitchen preparing free food and snacks.

MARITIME AMERICA IN THE WAR—FROM OBSOLETE TO OVERWHELMING

In an immensity of manufacturing and innovation, a third-rate merchant and combat navy converted into a force with global power extending into the twenty-first century. In three years, American shipyards built 6,771 large ships, including twelve hundred major combatant vessels. Also made were scores of thousands of landing craft and small boats to bring the cargo and the men to ports and landing beaches worldwide.

To carry the cargo, oil, ammunition, and, eventually, the troops, 650,000 shipyard workers, including women as portrayed by "Rosie the Riveter," mass-produced in eighteen new East, Gulf, and West Coast shipyards, 2,710 of the 10,850-ton Liberty Ships made. Affectionately called "ugly ducklings" by FDR, they rolled off shipways in an average of forty-two days from keel-laying to commissioning. When their slow-walking 11-knot speeds became untenable, an entirely new class of 531 Victory cargo and attack transports produced an improved 15–17 knots. By 1945, some 290,000 men from sixteen to seventy-eight were in the Merchant Marine. Six thousand officers trained at the Merchant Marine Academy in King's Point, New York. Paying the ultimate price, over ninety-three hundred US merchant sailors went down with their ships.

In fighting a two-front four-hemisphere war, the US Navy won every major battle, with an array of 6,768 ships, including ninety-seven fleet and escort aircraft carriers, twenty-three battleships, seventy-two cruisers, 840 destroyers and destroyer escorts, 232 submarines, and 2,547 amphibious, supply, and auxiliary ships. Bath Iron Works alone (General Dynamics) built eighty-two Navy destroyers, with more "tin cans" com-

Higgins Boats—The Little Boats That Could

In a 1964 interview Dwight Eisenhower said, "Andrew Higgins is the man who won the war for us. If Higgins had not designed and built those LCVPs (Landing Craft Vehicle and Personnel), we never could have landed over an open beach. The whole strategy of the war would have been different." From seven rickety factories in New Orleans and other boatyards, visionary and whiskey-drinking builder Andrew Higgins and an integrated workforce of thirty thousand adapted other types into a mostly wood landing craft, with 23,398 built. Needing a draft of only one-and-a-half feet forward, on D-Day 1,089 LCVPs carried troops directly to the five invasion beaches.

ing from one shipyard than all the warships built by Japan. The Electric Boat Company (General Dynamics) launched seventy-four submarines and 398 PT boats, although ranking only seventy-seventh in the value of military contracts awarded. By VJ Day, 1,051 flat-keeled LSTs (Landing Ship Tanks) brought troops, tanks, vehicles, and cargo directly onto a beach with their wide-opening bow doors. Of the eighteen LST shipyards, many were in unlikely places, including Muskegon, Michigan; Seneca, Illinois; Evansville and Jeffersonville, Indiana; and Pittsburgh and Ambridge, Pennsylvania.

THE COST OF WAR

Every wage-earning citizen paid for the war's $341 billion cost ($4.7 trillion in today's dollars) through increased taxation—$136 billion—and with repeated purchases by eighty-five million Americans of Series E War Bonds, totaling another $167.2 billion, but at only 2.9 percent interest paid over a ten-year maturity. Eight war bond drives between 1942 and 1945 had volunteers going door to door to homes and stores for sales. Contributors were given display stickers for doors or windows. In its response to the patriotism and sacrifice by 65 percent of the US population, the war economy spectacularly grew from 2 percent of Gross National Product (GNP) in 1939 to 40 percent of GNP in 1943.

~

PART TWO

CHICAGO'S ARSENAL OF DEMOCRACY

Long dominant as America's transportation center with six major rail terminals, hundreds of miles of freight lines, and troop trains arriving and departing daily, passengers traveling coast to coast or in-between had to change trains—and often stations—in Chicago. Major hotels, including the three-thousand-room Stevens (now the Hilton Chicago) became military barracks.

Over fourteen hundred Chicago-area companies converted into making or assembling war materiel. Radio Flyer ended production of the "little red wagon" to retool for the "Blitz can"—five-gallon steel containers mounted on jeeps, trucks, and tanks to transport water and fuel. Cracker Jack adopted a patriotic theme, changing the prizes from metal to plastic, then to cardboard. Powdered coffee and other supplements to C and K rations added to their inventory. Kraft Foods made eighteen different ration products including oleomargarine, that fleet sailors claimed "either killed you or made you stronger."

As the most productive engine supplier for the B-17, an 850,000-square foot Studebaker plant in Chicago, and other factories in South Bend and Fort Wayne, Indiana, made 63,789 fully tested 1,200-horsepower Wright Cyclone engines. Each engine had eight thousand parts needing eighty thousand separate machining steps. Three miles northwest, Buick's 125-acre Melrose Park factory made 74,797 Pratt & Whitney B-24 engines. From the factory, they went from spur lines to mainlines and final assembly at Boeing and Consolidated-Vultee plants. Six miles north of Buick's B-24 engine plant in unincorporated Cook County at a tiny airport known as Orchard Field, a two-million-square-foot all wood assembly building—reputedly the largest wood building ever—took only eleven months to complete from August 1942 to July 1943. Operated by Douglas Aircraft, the plant assembled the entire four-engine C-54 transport adapted from the civilian DC4. At the finished end, the aircraft went to one of four adjacent fifty-five-hundred-foot concrete runways for delivery by WASP and USAAF ferry pilots to US bases and then overseas. Douglas-Chicago assembled 655 of the 1,170 Skymasters made, each seating either forty-six passengers or holding twenty-three stretchers. C-54s carried FDR, Gen Douglas MacArthur, and Churchill to meetings, and ended the postwar Soviet-imposed Berlin blockade with thousands of relief missions. Orchard Field lives on with baggage tags marked ORD (Orchard) for O'Hare International Airport, opened in 1955 at the same location.

In downtown Chicago, the entirety of Navy Pier's three-thousand-foot length became both classrooms for teaching US Navy skills and a dock for two converted steamers. They were used as Lake Michigan "touch and go" practice aircraft carriers for fighter planes stationed at suburban Glenview Naval Air Station. On Chicago's far southeast side and in Michigan City, Indiana, Pullman built twenty-four hundred troop sleeper cars, four hundred kitchen, and fifty mobile hospital cars, while increasing its capacity from twenty-three billion passenger miles in 1941 to ninety-six billion in 1945. Accommodating wounded soldiers were forty new Medical Department kitchen cars, spliced between hospital cars in special trains.

For history's most photographed war, Bell & Howell made 16mm gun cameras and the compact, three-lens turret, hand-wound 35mm "Eyemo" camera. Holding one hundred feet of film, it operated for twenty seconds until rewound with a ratchet key, at speeds of twenty-four to sixty-four frames per second. B&H also made the 16mm "Filmo" film projector used at hundreds of bases to show training films made at Chicago's Wilding and other studios.

After first displaying his steam-powered horse-drawn popcorn wagon at the 1893 Chicago World's Columbian Exposition, Charles Cretors made popcorn wagons for stores, state fairs, and carnivals. With the advent of war and lacking supplies or buyers, Cretors left the popcorn business to transition into aircraft oil line fittings and mechanical radio components.

One of the most unlikely candidates for conversion, Chicago Roller Skate Co. retooled to make shell parts and components for bomber nose section guns. Ekco Products went from multiproduct housewares lines to Navy shell casings. David Rockola changed from making the wildly popular Rock-Ola jukebox—with four hundred thousand sold—to machining and assembly of the M1 carbine. With 228,500 rifles delivered at $58 each, Rock-Ola's production still equaled only a scant 3.7 percent of the 6.2 million rifles made, so many that production stopped in mid-1944.

From thirteen acres in Elgin, Illinois, the Elgin Watch Co. moved its production sideways to produce military "hack" watches—a type set to a specific time and then restarted based on a reference timepiece. Elgin also made Navy chronometers, fuzes for artillery shells, aircraft altimeters, and sapphire bearings used in aiming artillery.

Along with twenty-two other pharmaceutical companies given FTC immunity, suburban-Chicago headquartered G.D. Searle, Baxter, and Abbott Laboratories cooperated to mass produce penicillin, the war's "wonder drug." Production increased 500 percent from 1943 to 1945, with millions of units going ashore with the troops on D-Day.

As a harbinger of the future digital age, sixty-three Chicago companies, including Galvin Manufacturing (Motorola), Hallicrafters, and Webcor, made half of the war's electronic equipment. Beginning in 1940, Galvin's SCR-300, a thirty-five-pound, six-vacuum-tube, battery-powered FM backpack transceiver, became known as a "walkie-talkie." By the end of the war forty-five thousand were on battlefields from Normandy to Okinawa. Further advancing portability and battlefield communication, 130,000 of the AM frequency hand-held five-pound dry-cell battery–powered SCR-536 "handi-talkies" came from Galvin's Chicago plant and other factories.

In suburban Forest Park, Illinois, sixty-five hundred mostly women technicians at the new $20 million American Can Co. subsidiary, Amertorp, known as the "torpedo factory," assembled the five thousand intricate parts that went into a single torpedo, completing nineteen thousand in the war. Significant as were these accomplishments, they were among the smallest when compared to one factory that dominated all Chicago war production.

The War's Largest Factory for the War's Most Advanced Bomber

The vast stretches of the Pacific—5,150 miles from San Francisco to Tokyo, 3,862 miles from Honolulu to Tokyo—and an enemy with a powerful navy required planning for an entirely different war than in the ETO. Greatly modified from the tactics and strategies in the European Theatre, planners set different objectives for the Pacific war. An "island-hopping" campaign would bring the US military well within the ring of Japanese island defenses, objectives intended to position the USAAF for direct attacks on the home islands.

Energized by continuous victories at sea and Japanese land losses in the Solomon, Gilbert, Caroline, and Marshall Islands, Navy construction battalions (Seabees) built five major air stations on Saipan, Tinian, and Guam, the northernmost islands in the Marianas chain. Nine B-29 groups at North and West Field (now Tinian International Airport) flew from six parallel crushed coral eight-thousand-foot runways facing east-west. Although the round-trip to Japan remained a twelve-hour journey, a major reason for the Pacific campaign would be realized by constructing air bases within fifteen hundred miles of Japan. Paid for with Marine and Army blood, defeating the island defenders made possible the development of bases and airfields for the war's most advanced bomber.

Developed specifically for the Pacific Theatre, the four-engine Super-fortress had four remotely controlled gun turrets operated by a single GE fire-control system. Forty percent of its pressurized ninety-nine-foot length held two bomb-bays with a twenty-thousand-pound payload. The forty-two-hundred-mile range, up to 9,548-gallon fuel capacity, 358 mph top speed, and a thirty-two-thousand-foot service ceiling allowed it to fly higher and faster than the Japanese fighters retreating to the mainland.

Of all the advancements integrated into the B-29, none had more importance than the four 2,200-horsepower, twin-row, eighteen-cylinder Wright R-3550 Duplex engines powering the fifty-two-and-a-half-ton bomber. A combined 8,800 horsepower had to carry the bomber, an eleven-man crew, the weight of fuel, and the bomb-load three thousand miles round-trip from the Marianas to Japan. At $639,188 per aircraft

One of nineteen buildings at Dodge-Chicago, the eighty-two-acre engine assembly plant. FRANK WERNER

($9.1 million in 2018), nearly four thousand B-29s were built, with nine of ten engines made in one Chicago factory in a crash program surpassing any other war project of its type. To quickly build a factory able to manufacture a complete engine for final assembly at B-29 plants in Seattle and Renton, Washington, Wichita, Kansas, Atlanta (Marietta), Georgia, and Omaha, Nebraska, the WPB approved construction of a nineteen-building, five-hundred-acre, 6.3-million-square-foot complex on the flat prairies near Chicago's Municipal Airport (today's Midway International Airport). Extending from 71st to 77th Street, and 1.5 miles from Cicero Avenue to Pulaski Road, Dodge-Chicago, a division of Chrysler Corporation, led all war construction in combined size and cost. For comparison the Pentagon opened in 1943 with 6.6 million square feet on 583 acres, cost $83 million ($1.35 billion in 2018 dollars), compared to the $187 million ($2.649 billion today) cost for Dodge-Chicago.

Designed by industrial architect Albert Kahn, who planned Ford's Highland Park and River Rouge sites, a steel shortage required that the sixteen thousand workers who completed the plant in only eight months in August 1943 use mostly bricks and concrete for materials. With only reduced amounts of steel available, the arched roof on the eighty-two-acre assembly building—itself extending for almost a mile—needed only 2.6 pounds of steel per square foot—half of a standard design. Thirty million square feet of lumber—enough to build two thousand four-room houses—shaped only the concrete forms. By itself, a separate administration building had 259,000 square feet.

Given extra gas ration stamps, employees with cars had a block-wide, mile-long fifteen-thousand-car lot, with access bridges on either side of the plant. Nearby, seven hundred one-thousand-to-twelve-hundred-square-foot brick single-family, duplex, and row houses were built for employees, priced between $1,000 and $6,000, or rented for $40 to $60 per month.

From Raw Materials to Finished Engines

To begin the thirteen-thousand-part engine-building process, raw ingots of magnesium and aluminum were made into castings in the plant's own forges and foundries. Up to 1.5 million machine tools included jigs, fixtures, gauges, molds, dies, cutting equipment and patterns, many made onsite. Inside the assembly building, which had no interior bearing walls, classroom instruction taught unskilled workers—the women paid up to 50 percent less than the men—how to operate ninety-three hundred metal fabrication machines or cut and finish intricate gears for engine assembly. Assisting in worker comfort and productivity were millions of wood blocks laid over concrete floors. A 250,000-gallon water tower served all manufacturing and firefighting needs. Fifteen lower-level cafeterias equipped to serve hot meals to thirty-five thousand employees at nominal cost connected to the assembly floor above, though a cross-hatching of tunnels, doubling as raid shelters, with periodic openings to the assembly floor above.

At the end of the assembly building, forty-eight separated windowed engine test cells with exterior venting through wide concrete stacks had two rows of meters and instruments, with technicians in each cell measuring engine output for two to four hours each, a sixteen-and-a-half-foot propeller attached to each engine. A large Toledo scale verified the 2,670-pound engine weight. A failed engine meant disassembly, documentation of errors, rebuild, and retesting. Each month the engine tests consumed 2,250,000 gallons of 91 to 100 octane gasoline stored on the site.

A power recovery system converted 25 percent of engine-test energy back to the plant's electrical grid, to operate machinery and motors. Seven

Eight decades later, part of the former engine test cells at the end of the mile-long assembly building. AUTHOR

Babcock and Wilcox coal-fired boilers burned 820 tons of coal every twenty-four hours, producing enough power for a city of three hundred thousand. With testing completed, engines were drained of fluids, wrapped in airtight plastic envelopes, inserted into containers, then loaded into boxcars on one of two sidings, for delivery by rail to a final assembly plant.

The plant soon completed fifty tested and operating engines daily, increasing to sixteen hundred engines monthly. By VJ Day, 18,413 engines—almost five engines for each of the 3,970 four-engine B-29s made—came from Dodge Chicago. No other war factory made fully operating aircraft engines from raw materials to tested engines. The efficiency of the plant and the dedication of its thirty-three thousand employees in two shifts resulted in two price reductions, from $25,314 per engine plus a fee of $1,519 to $11,537 plus fee per engine. The price went down even with 6,427 ongoing engineering changes. Within thirty minutes of the August 14, 1945 announcement by President Harry Truman of victory over Japan (VJ Day) the factory emptied, leaving only a few maintenance workers to dampen the fires and lock the doors. The plant, its inventory of thousands of tools, castings, engine parts, and the knowledge of its historic achievement then went dark for two years.

Preston Tucker—Enter and Exit

In 1947, after working in New Orleans with Andrew Higgins, auto visionary and inventor Preston Tucker leased nearly one million square feet of the empty factory from the War Assets Administration. Given only six days to design the prototype of a new and revolutionary auto, Alex Tremulis drafted plans for what would be advertised as the "Tucker Torpedo." Financial setbacks and fraud allegations led to an October 1949 trial brought by the Securities and Exchange Commission (SEC) and an acquittal. Bad press and a lack of funds ended production and closed the

A sign in a Dodge-Chicago B29 engine cafeteria cautions workers. FRANK WERNER

The tunnel system that served thirty-five thousand employees has twenty-first century uses. AUTHOR

factory after making only fifty-one cars at a then costly price of $2,450 each. Seven decades later, prized by collectors, including Jay Leno and Francis Ford Coppola, forty-seven of the six-tailpipe, three-headlight autos are in museums, such as the Smithsonian Museum of American History, or with private collectors. Judged to be works of art, when rarely available prices are up to $3 million each.

During the Korean War, renamed the Ford Aircraft Engine Division Plant, a modernized factory reopened with eighteen thousand employees, first making Air Force piston engines before converting to the J-57 F-1 jet engine. In August 1959 the factory closed again, until partial conversion into a shopping center named Ford City in 1965.

A Return to Business
As the only major combatant in history's greatest war to emerge undamaged and financially secure, America and its arsenal of democracy quickly reconverted to peacetime manufacturing.

RADIO FLYER Still headquartered on Chicago's West Side, Radio Steel and Manufacturing Co. resumed production of the "little red wagon," with wide postwar expansion into multi-lines.

CRACKER JACK Now part of Frito-Lay, a division of PepsiCo, in 2016 changed to awarding digital "prizes" on a downloadable app and it still includes prizes in an expanded line.

KRAFT FOODS Headquartered in Chicago, Kraft Heinz Company with forty-two thousand employees in forty-five countries is the world's fifth largest food and beverage company.

STUDEBAKER From its start as a farm wagon maker, the company struggled after the war and closed in March 1966, after producing the last Cruiser model, four-door sedan, from its Hamilton, Ontario, Canada plant. Its original headquarters, (Fine Arts Building) on Chicago's Michigan Avenue, still shows its name boldly incised over the entrance

ELGIN WATCH CO. Once employing four thousand, the eleven-block factory closed in 1968, with its main Elgin, Illinois, plant razed. A small two-story former observatory is all that remains. A large vintage clock with the name Elgin accurately displays the time to hurrying commuters at Chicago's Ogilvie Transportation Center (former Northwestern Station).

BUICK–CHICAGO After making B-24 engines, the factory became part of Lisle, Illinois, headquartered International Harvester (Navistar), utilizing the same fifty-acre war plant as its testing and technical center.

PULLMAN With the advent of interstate highways and decline in passenger rail transport, the factory closed in 1957. As a Chicago neighborhood, America's first planned industrial town and its hundreds of residences is virtually intact. In 2015, Pullman became a National Monument and part of the National Park Service.

BELL & HOWELL Headquartered in Durham, North Carolina, changed from cameras and projectors to making a variety of

Women in Daytona Beach learn welding skills for shipbuilding. NATIONAL ARCHIVES

consumer accessories, B&H makes high-speed package-labeling products, utilizing hardware and software information technology.

CRETORS Returned to making popcorn machines, then expanded into bagged popcorn and multiproduct food processing equipment, including pizza ovens and hot dog cookers.

EKCO PRODUCTS Greatly broadening its products, Ekco expanded into numerous lines of non-electric bakeware, kitchen utensils, and molded plastic implements.

ROCK-OLA Accidentally giving part of its name to the music phenomenon of the 20th century, Rock-Ola thrived in the rock and roll era, and continues to make touch-screen and nostalgic juke-boxes in Torrance, California.

CHICAGO ROLLER SKATE CO. After reconverting from making Navy shell casings and aircraft components, it returned to its origins adding quad skates, adjustable boot and in-line skates and skateboards.

SEARLE (Pfizer), BAXTER, AND ABBOTT LABORATORIES Greatly diversifying postwar through mergers and acquisitions, the pharmaceutical giants that joined to make penicillin relocated after the war, although each former headquarters façade is in its original appearance.

GALVIN MANUFACTURING (MOTOROLA) Renamed Motorola after the war, in 2011 the company expanded into diverse electronic fields, splitting into Motorola Mobility and Motorola Solutions. Google acquired Motorola Mobility in 2011, with Lenovo assimilating Motorola Solutions in 2014.

CHRYSLER VILLAGE Built for the B-29 engine works employees to buy or rent at affordable prices, almost all the original housing remains, with most of the residences expanded into second floors or additional rooms. Of special note is that no thought was given to erecting temporary housing for employees, such as Quonset huts. The United States was in the war to win it, and the solid brick houses were built for continuous use after the war.

MUNICIPAL AIRPORT Renamed Midway Airport in 1947 in tribute to the Battle of Midway, it had no war use except as a point of entry by the military and civilian leadership for numerous visits to the giant factories. An SBD dauntless dive bomber, the same aircraft type that won the Battle of Midway, is suspended from the ceiling of the Concourse A.

DOUGLAS-CHICAGO In 1949, with C-54 assembly ended and the factory demolished, the city of Chicago renamed Orchard Field to honor US Navy Medal of Honor winner Edward H. O'Hare, and began a massive expansion. From 178,000 passengers in 1955, In 2018 ORD had seven runways with operations for seventy-eight million passengers, third largest in the United States.

DODGE-CHICAGO/FORD CITY Much of the original development exists both inside and around the still expansive building complex. With over one million square feet removed for a parking lot, and another two million square feet leased to Tootsie Roll Industries, the remaining 1.2-million-square-foot shopping center contains major structural elements of the original B-29 engine plant. In use are the same connecting tunnels under the former assembly floor, with functioning parts of the same electrical transformers, relays, and switches. Outside, almost all the repurposed buildings that surround Ford City were once part of the engine plant. At the north end, easily visible from the street, the engine test stacks are used for storage by Tootsie Roll Industries, which occupies over one million square feet of the original factory and features an assembled B-29 engine inside the entrance. Still in place are the derelict spur tracks that went from the factory where crated engines were loaded, to the nearby eight-hundred-acre Clearing Yard, and delivery to Boeing, Bell, and Martin assembly plants.

Aftermath

Of the 3,970 war-winning B-29s built, only two are airworthy, *Fifi* and *Doc*. Both make periodic appearances at air shows. Among the few Superfortresses on static display are *Enola Gay* at the Smithsonian Air and Space Museum in Chantilly, Virginia, and *Bockscar* at the National Museum of the United States Air Force in Dayton, Ohio. Powered by Dodge-Chicago built engines, *Enola Gay* dropped the atomic bomb on Hiroshima August 6, 1945, with the second bomb on *Bockscar* destroying Nagasaki on August 9, 1945, to end World War II.

CHAPTER TWENTY-TWO

Remains of the Reich:
Intact Traces in Unexpected Places

For they sow the wind and they shall reap the whirlwind. . . .
—HOSEA 8:7

INTRODUCTION: A CRAVING FOR REVENGE

PROMPTLY AT 11 A.M. ON THE ELEVENTH DAY OF THE ELEVENTH month in 1918, the guns fell silent, although there were two thousand casualties in the final morning hours. The last barrages all along the Western Front gave bragging rights to gunners who would claim for the rest of their lives that they fired the last shot in the Great War, "the war to end all wars." They called it the "Great War" because there could never be another one as grotesque as a war with forty million military and civilian casualties, including nearly ten million military deaths and ninety thousand fatalities on all sides from poison gas.

Upon learning of the Armistice while recovering in a hospital in Pasewalk near the Ypres sector from the effects of gassing, a Bavarian army *gefriter*, a lance corporal, buried his head in the pillow on his bed. It lessened the outrage from the "stab in the back" by the General Staff and government. Why an armistice, they weren't defeated? They were decimated in numbers, yes, but his 16th Bavarian Reserve Regiment and most of the German army had ample fight remaining. They marched back to the Fatherland defiant, united, and they weren't defeated, that much he knew.

Later came the humiliation endured by the two forgotten German ministers who signed the formal treaty in the gilded Hall of Mirrors in the Palace of Versailles on June 28, 1919. What stuck in his throat—and in the throats of millions of Germans—was that Article 231 of the treaty flung all the war guilt at Germany. With the forced acceptance of blame also came compliance with the merciless price exacted by the victors, mainly France and Great Britain—132 billion marks in reparations, over $31 billion then ($558 billion in 2018). A "Carthaginian peace" of demilitarization, surrender of territory, and the payment of tribute meant financial and moral decapitation for Europe's most advanced nation. He knew that the debt repayment had been indefinitely postponed in 1932, but it had little effect, the damage had been done. Reparations and world Depression had reduced Germany to indigence. He could see the resentment in the eyes of the swelling crowds at his rallies. And the Mark, once a reliable currency, now went to market in wheelbarrows.

From the *Burgerbraukeller*, *Hofbrauhaus*, and other Munich beer halls, Adolf Hitler, the one-time lance corporal, had eager ears aplenty ready to embrace his undoubted oratorical skills. For Hitler, for millions of Germans and for history, the second great war of the century—a continuation of the first—began on the day of the treaty signing. His time had come. Next would be the revenge.

WEIMAR—WHERE IT GREW

A four-and-a-half hour trip on the fast trains and smooth rails of *Deutsche Bahn* from Munich, the cradle of Nazism, to Weimar, where German classicism flourished, is to see where the Nazi cult grew and spread. With its sixty-five thousand population comparable to 1940, the retelling of the Nazi origins begins at the same rail station where from 1937, a quarter-million political prisoners, dissidents, homosexuals, Communists, Jehovah's Witnesses, and all the Jews of Weimar, boarded trains, each with one suitcase, for a one-way trip to end only six miles away in Buchenwald.

In 1919, the first constitutional assembly of the infant republic met in the State Theatre, giving Weimar's name to a brief experiment in democracy, ending in 1933 with dictatorship. The theatre became a rally point for Nazi meetings, the five high entry windows shutting out the light with garish thirty-foot-high swastika banners.

Weimar saw the birth of composer C. P. E. Bach, son of Johann Sebastian Bach, and the burial of writer, statesman, and poet Johann Wolfgang Goethe. His friend, poet and playwright Friedrich Schiller, lived nearby. Hungarian composer Franz Liszt penned famous works as a seventeen-year summer resident. But the city where the modernist Bauhaus design and architectural movement began also has vestiges of a more recent history it would prefer not to acknowledge. Receiving wide local support and with explosive growth, Weimar is where the nascent Nazi Party had its first rally in 1926, and where it grew stronger and more confident. In its leafy streets, spared from major war damage, are parts of the Nazi beginnings.

Elephant Hotel

During his rise to power Hitler occupied a three-room suite in the ninety-three-room city center hotel, from where he acknowledged adoring crowds from the balcony over the entrance. After dictating *Mein Kampf* in prison, he first stayed at the hotel on July 3, 1926, signing the guest book as "writer," then returned thirty-five more times. Still in use, his former suite has the same wood paneling and a connecting room where he met with Munich henchmen Rudolf Hess, Heinrich Himmler, and Hermann Göring. In a redesign of the hotel, Hermann Giesler, second to Albert Speer among the Nazis' favorite architects, included a cellar escape tunnel, just in case.

Gauforum

Coinciding with the construction of Buchenwald, Giesler also designed an enclosing, five-building, Roman-Fascist styled office and parade ground for Nazi rallies and administrative functions. With wide squares and extending columned enclosures, it became the model for similar unbuilt centers in forty other cities in Germany's sixteen states. The five-thousand-member Hitler Youth and SA or Brownshirt marches passing under Hitler's review at the Elephant House in 1933 grew to forty thousand in 1937, ending at the flag-bedecked Gauforum. The three completed buildings and parade ground survived the war intact, for later conversion into administrative offices and a shopping center.

Gestapo Headquarters in Weimar

On December 14, 1933, eleven months after Hitler assumed power, the state government of Thuringen established a "Secret State Police Office." Steps from the most important church building in Weimar, Saints Peter and Paul, where Martin Luther once spoke, an archway frames the Marstall wing of the *Stadtschloss*, the former lavish residence of Wilhelm Ernst, Grand Duke of Saxe-Weimar-Eisenach, called "a sadist" and "the most unpopular prince in Germany" by his subjects. On November 9, 1918, two days before the Armistice, he abdicated to the family estate in Silesia.

Early in the Nazi era, offices in the castle's Marstall wing became the regional headquarters of the *Geheime Staatspolizei*, the feared Gestapo. Outside each office, printed signs informed visitors of the entrance protocol: "all render the Nazi salute." Late-night fists thudding on doors brought Weimar's remaining fifteen hundred Jews, the "unwanted persons," into the castle's courtyard, down sixteen steps into a damp cellar, and into double-walled, sound-proofed rooms for interrogation and torture. Along a narrow passage, cells with wooden or steel doors and viewing ports held increasingly more prisoners. Always obsessive in its record-keeping, administrative employees in the Gestapo headquarters expanded from thirty-seven in 1938 to 250 by January 1945.

With prisoners packed so tightly that efficient processing became affected, the castle's former coach garage became another confinement space. Expanding again, a temporary courtyard structure built by Buchenwald prisoners held ever-more German citizens in "protective arrest." Steps away, the castle's high-ceilinged riding hall became a "collection camp" where Jewish families, after first signing away on long lists their real estate and personal property, were organized for deportation from the Weimar rail station to Buchenwald, Theresienstadt, Auschwitz, or other camps.

As the US 80th Infantry Division approached Weimar on April 4, 1945, the Gestapo marched the jail's remaining 142 men and seven women across the Kegel Bridge over the gentle river near the house where Franz Liszt once composed, to an obscure forest where they were killed and buried in a communal grave. The castle's Gestapo files were burned, erasing their crimes against humanity. Or so they thought.

Buchenwald

On a gradual rise of the Ettersberg Mountains six miles from Nuremberg, the Nazis built a vast, extending multiple-use concentration, slave-labor, and death camp named Buchenwald—"beechwood." Beginning in 1937 multitudes of Jews and political prisoners from fifty countries were confined in conditions of medieval barbarity in a camp operated by the SS for the Gestapo.

To increase capacity and expedite the transport of slaves and raw materials to nearby armaments plants, prisoners widened a dirt path into a wide three-mile-long, concrete-paved, connecting road, adding an adjacent rail extension from the main line. Paid for with uncounted lives, prisoners called it the "blood road."

Through a permanent gate structure with offices, clock tower, loud-speakers, and machine-gun position above, an eventual 280,000 men, women, and children were confined inside thirty-six 330-foot-long, thirty-three-foot-wide wooden barracks, with four-tier high wooden bunks.

To each his own, the taunt at the entrance to Buchenwald. AUTHOR

Remains of bowls used by Buchenwald prisoners. AUTHOR

A 380-volt electrified barbed-wire fence and twenty-two watchtowers surrounded the prison, with Waffen SS Death's Head Division guards patrolling on an adjacent footpath.

On the white painted gate—the only way in or out for everyone—prisoners viewed a conspicuous red-painted metal inscription, the sign oddly facing into and not out of the camp, its enigmatic taunt a reminder of their fates: *Jedem das Seine*—"to each his own."

To conceal their crimes as the US Sixth Armored Division neared Weimar in early April 1945, the SS quickly evacuated some twenty-eight thousand prisoners, half dying from exhaustion or shot in the process. GIs liberated the remaining twenty-one thousand on April 11. A large American flag then flew above the entrance. When Third Army commander Gen. George Patton learned of the atrocities, he ordered Weimar residents to walk to the camp to see for themselves what had happened to their Jewish teachers, druggists, doctors, shop-owners, servants, neighbors, and fellow citizens.

The efficient Nazis had cards for prisoner transfers from Weimar to Buchenwald.
AUTHOR

Filmed by the US Army Signal Corps and famed *Life* magazine photographer Margaret Bourke-White, after liberation two thousand well-fed, warmly clothed Weimar residents—the women carrying purses and smiling, many of the men wearing jackets and ties—entered the camp. They saw the stacked, emaciated, naked bodies and were made to enter the foul-smelling huts and crematorium to witness for themselves what had been done in their names. When questioned by the press and GIs about the destruction of an entire part of humanity, almost to a person they said, "*we didn't know.*"

Aftermath

The little-known Gestapo headquarters in the basement of the Stadtschloss museum and art gallery appears in no guidebooks and has no opening hours posted. As silent witnesses to the atrocities within, one of the former interrogation rooms has numerous large plastic sleeves hanging from the ceiling, filled with the detritus found after the war, including notes, bits of files, and parts of what may be thumb screws.

The Buchenwald sign with its inscrutable portent of what would come remains at the entry. As further confirmation of the prior kinship between the town and the camp, bus #6 from town is marked "Buchenwald." After holding twenty-one-thousand suspected Nazis in the same huts until 1950, the Soviets then burned the barracks. Black cinders outline their location, with two guard towers and parts of the electrified fence remaining. Views of nearby villages from the camp imply widespread local knowledge of its war existence. Among the survivors was future author and Nobel Peace Prize winner Elie Wiesel, who helplessly watched his father die from a beating in the bunk below his. Fifty-six thousand others also died from starvation, illness, or torture.

NUREMBERG—WHERE IT SPREAD

With its steep, gabled roofs, cobbled streets, and half-timbered homes, for Hitler it was the most German of cities, and his clear favorite. In northern Bavaria, 150 miles south of Weimar and 283 miles north of Munich, with a 1940 population of 425,000, Nuremberg's rail connections extended to Berlin 450 miles away, all the better to increase attendance at the annual rallies. The party rallies and what they represented in prestige and income were eagerly awaited by shopkeepers and hoteliers, who welcomed three times the population of the city to the final turnout in 1938.

Nazi Party Guest House

In researching this book, the author stayed at the former Nazi Party guest house (Park Plaza Hotel). Newly opened for the 1936 rally, its facade, interior travertine marble flooring, and wide staircases leading to meeting rooms are unchanged. The six floors with rare for the time air-conditioning had two hundred rooms for officials and guests, its rooms in use only during the annual gatherings. Narcissistic Reichmarschall Hermann Göring, the dictatorship's second most powerful, occupied Suite #379, then with two-inch-thick white lambs-wool carpeting, and a permanent reservation for him and no one else. Issuing from propaganda minister Joseph Goebbels's office were press releases puffing the regime's exploits, while ignoring reference to the 1935 law passed in Nuremberg making non-persons of German Jews. After seizure by US forces, judges and lawyers prosecuting the nearby Nazi war crimes trials resided in the renamed Bavarian-American Hotel.

Hitler's Dreams of Domination—No Fantasy

At the city's edge, miles of undeveloped land were set aside for the new *Reichpparteitagsgelande*, the State Party Congress Grounds. Planned for an immense area of six square miles—three times larger than Chicago's Loop—Albert Speer designed an assemblage of imposing enormity and fascist magnificence, with separate areas for sports, parades, military maneuvers, camping, and administration. Intended to at once impress and intimidate believers, its considerable remains illustrate Hitler's manic obsession with spectacle and splendor. Nine decades later the grounds and their structures represent the only remaining window into knowing how the dictatorship celebrated itself. Except for the war and its loss, all would have been completed by 1946.

Leni Riefenstahl's 1934 propaganda masterpiece, *Triumph of the Will*, primarily filmed in Nuremberg, featured torch-lit night scenes and light

Nazi leaders face their crimes at Nuremberg trials. NATIONAL ARCHIVES

displays to humble Hollywood's best. The Speer-designed placement of 130 searchlights at forty-foot intervals pointing twenty-five thousand feet skyward encased the stadium and grounds in a dome of white light, or, as said by one awed guest, British ambassador to Germany, Neville Henderson, "a cathedral of ice."

The "Great Stadium"

In 1935, Hitler authorized Speer to build a stadium never to be surpassed in grandeur and size from the ancient to the modern world. At a time when one-hundred-thousand-capacity arenas were the largest, it would seat four hundred thousand within an area 1,815 feet long by 1,518 wide—a volume of eleven million cubic yards. History's largest precedent and its inspiration, Rome's Circus Maximus, held 250,000 spectators. When Speer estimated the cost to Hitler at one billion marks ($500 million), he replied: "That's less than the cost of two battleships of the Bismarck class . . . this building will stand for centuries." Orders were placed for the granite cladding, pink inside, white on the exterior, and work began. With only a foundation pit dug, it became a lake during the war.

State Congress Hall
In 1935, some fourteen hundred workers began construction of a monumental Roman/Fascist–inspired covered arena, topped with a 250-foot free-standing dome, to simultaneously seat fifty thousand party delegates. With about 40 percent finished, construction stopped in September 1939, leaving a dramatically incomplete oval shell replete with crated granite slabs quarried by slave laborers on the ground awaiting installation. Scores of windowed offices extend around the completed exterior colonnade. The unfinished result is so large that only one of its wings contains the performance center for the Nuremberg Symphony Orchestra.

Zeppelin Field
In early 1934, with Hitler having been chancellor for only a few weeks, he assigned Speer to design the first of the rally ground's colossal outdoor structures, a three-section stadium thirteen hundred feet long, eighty feet

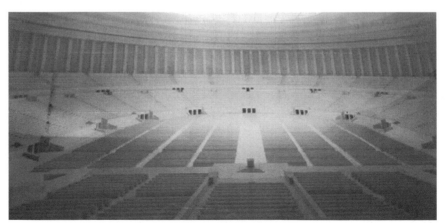

Model for the fifty-thousand-delegate Nazi Congress Hall in Nuremberg. AUTHOR high, with a two hundred thousand capacity. The raised central section, closely modeled on the second century BC Pergamon altar from ancient Greece, gave privileged seating to five hundred officials. The "Führer's rostrum" projected ten feet into the field, bringing Hitler ever nearer to his acolytes in acknowledgement of their devotion. From behind and above the stands, a massive Speer-designed wooden swastika overlooked the proceedings. Extending along the rear, a gallery with sixty high pillars heightened the intended effect of imperial magnificence. Each end of the central stands held an eight foot in circumference cauldron flamboyantly lighted each night. Additional spectator grandstands encircled the field, leaving ample room for precision marches by elite troops, thumping brass bands, and swirling folk dances by young women. Inside the central tribune, a long marble-walled "golden hall" trimmed in gold-leaf, with two wide staircases and a swastika-inspired backlighted twenty-six-foot-high mosaic tile ceiling, served as a reception setting for Nazi officials, and another way for Hitler to enter the field.

Adjacent to the unfinished Congress Hall, Speer built a sixty-five-hundred-foot-long, 250-foot-wide parade avenue, the *grosser strasse* or "great street." Intended as the rally ground's central axis, it pointed toward Nuremberg Castle with its mystical memory of Charlemagne and the Holy Roman Empire—the "First Reich." Sixty thousand solid granite slabs quarried by concentration camp inmates were patterned with light and dark gray sections to coordinate precision marching, and thick enough to bear the weight of tanks. Incised grooves gave added support to the goose-stepping troops held in admiration by cheering crowds on adjacent tiered concrete risers.

On April 22, 1945, the US Third Infantry Division faced Hitler's empty rostrum and stands for an awards ceremony. From North Africa to Nuremberg's surrender, they had fought through the entire European campaign. A large American flag now covered the wooden swastika. Not present was Third Division Medal of Honor recipient Audie Murphy, the most decorated soldier of the war. Seventh Army commander, General Alexander Patch, awarded the Medal of Honor to five men in the storied division. Three days later dynamite blew into sticks the gilded swastika atop the Zeppelin tribune.

A portion of 1935 Nazi Party Congress Hall with granite awaiting installation. AUTHOR

From 1935, rally grounds show the high regard the regime had for itself. AUTHOR

Aftermath

Released from Spandau Prison after serving the full twenty-year sentence, the nearest to an admission of guilt by Albert Speer came when he wrote in his memoirs, "I ought to have known. . . ." After the October 1, 1946 sentencing of the war criminals, the ten convicted at Nuremberg were hanged in Spandau Prison on October 16. Hermann Göring cheated the hangman by ingesting a hidden potassium cyanide capsule the night before. The last prisoner, Rudolf Hess, committed suicide in 1987 in his cell with an electrical extension cord; the prison then closed and demolished. The same Palace of Justice wood-paneled Courtroom 600, where the trials took place, is open to visitors when not in session. A documentation center is on the top floor. Free admission.

Almost all the rally ground's structures and parade ground exist partially or completely. Through its portrayal of the regime's self-glorification, the ground's larger-than-life display dramatizes how the Hitler mystique ensnared its worshippers. A visit to the Documentation Center in one wing of the Congress Hall begins the experience. The dramatic unfinished shell leads to the nearly intact Zeppelin Field. The unchanged "great street" is used as a parking lot for public events. Tram 6 or 9 stops near the entrance. Free admission.

BERLIN—HEART OF THE REICH

By the spring of 1945, with the USAAF bombing in daylight and the RAF at night, incessant air attacks had nearly obliterated the Nazi capital. Encircling the city from early April, forty-one thousand Red Army artillery pieces further pummeled the city. Berlin's prewar 4.7 million residents had dwindled to an urban wasteland of 3.6 million refugees, most without shelter, water, electricity, food, or hope. The leader they glorified had brought them and the nation to ruin. Almost four generations later, only traces of the dictatorship remain in a city and country that again leads Europe in prosperity. But what remains is both a reminder from the past and a lesson to the future.

Anhelter Station
Built in 1880 as the largest and most lavishly decorated rail terminus in Berlin, trains once left every three to five minutes for all of Germany,

Hitler reviewing troops at the 1936 Nuremberg Nazi rally. AUTHOR

Current appearance of VIP section of Albert Speer–designed Zeppelin Tribune.
AUTHOR

and as far as Vienna, Rome, and Athens. Berliners often waited outside to greet Hitler and his followers with elaborate ceremonies, as inside from track #1 another of 116 transports took Jews east to Theresienstadt. The surviving entry façade became a memorial to the one-third of Berlin's 165,000 Jews deported from one of the three Berlin rail stations used in the Holocaust.

Air Raid Bunkers

When it became evident that Allied air attacks would only increase, some one thousand underground shelters were built throughout the city. One of the largest surviving bunkers became part of the Gesundbrunnen rail and subway (U-bahn) station. Still showing war damage, a central Berlin shelter became a postwar 120-room, thirty-two-thousand-square-foot, five-level exhibition space and art gallery, replete with a glassed-in penthouse covering the entire roof. Another bare-concrete, one-hundred-room above-ground bunker with fifteen-foot-thick internal walls and a twelve-foot-thick reinforced concrete roof hulks close to the former Anhelter Station. Tours in English are available to both the Gesund-brunnen and Anhelter bunkers.

Humboldt Park Flak Tower

After an August 25, 1940 RAF raid, an embarrassed Hitler who had repeatedly assured Berliners that no enemy bomb would ever drop on the city ordered the building of six massive flak towers. Of the three built, only parts of Humboldt Park's seven-story tower remain. It had an eighty-five-bed hospital, stores for one year, a climate-controlled room for museum art works, and a fifteen-thousand-person air-raid shelter. In view is the framework for the roof-mounted artillery in four twin mounts that fired ninety-six rounds per minute. U- or S-bahn to Gesundbrunnen station.

One of the remaining above-ground former Berlin bomb shelters. AUTHOR

Pre-war Anhalter Station, where adoring crowds awaited Hitler at the entrance and 55,000 Berlin Jews were sent to their deaths from the rear, and its present day ruins.

Kaiser Wilhelm I Memorial Church

On a square at the beginning of the *Kurfurstendamm* (KuDamm), Berlin's Fifth Avenue, rise what remains of the five-spired 1891–1895 Romanesque church named for the emperor who unified Germany in 1871 (the "Second Reich"). Raids leveled every nearby building and the church, leaving only the skeleton of one spire, rededicated in 1962 as a memorial to peace. A modernist new tower adjacent to the ruins has a photo exhibit showing the prewar appearance of the church and area. Near numerous S-U and bus stops. Free admission.

Buildings Near the Wilhelmstrasse

As the center of power for both Imperial Germany and the Nazi dictatorship, the elegant avenue housed numerous embassies and state agencies. Although most of the offices were destroyed in 1944 and early 1945, noteworthy remaining portions of former Nazi departments were used by the Communist GDR government, then converted again into offices of the *Bundestag*, the German parliament, and other ministries.

In Nuremberg, the bi-colored granite "great street," with incised grooves to aid in goose-step marching. AUTHOR

In the former East Berlin opposite the remains of the Berlin Wall, the 1935–1937 Hermann Göring–managed Ministry of Aviation, the ex–Reich Ministry of the Interior, and the former Joseph Goebbels Ministry of Propaganda survived the war, minus the partially-visible chipped-away imperial eagle and swastikas on the façade.

Planning for the failed July 20, 1944 coup against Hitler took place in the intact former Wehrmacht and Abwehr intelligence agency headquarters, known as the Bendlerblock, on the Landwehr Canal. Col. Claus von Stauffenberg, who planted the bomb near Hitler's chair at his East Prussia headquarters, was executed along with other conspirators, in the Bendlerblock courtyard. Although no organized opposition to Nazism existed, a modest courtyard memorial recognizes "the resistance that never was."

Wannsee—*The House on the Lake*

Berliners take pride in the necklace of eighty or so of the closest lakes that are only a fraction of over three thousand in the surrounding Brandenburg region. On the west edges of the city, Lake Wannsee's numerous coves offer havens for sailboats, vacation homes, even a lengthy sandy beach. But its charm has a notorious past. Prominently sited, a three-story stone villa with a wide terrace overlooks the lake. Throughout the war, the SS and other Nazi bureaus regularly frequented the many-windowed villa for meetings and meals.

Shortly before noon on January 20, 1942, a succession of black limousines turned- up an oval driveway to the Italianate mansion's portico, steps from a long sunny dining room with views of the lake. Typed cards at fifteen places outlined the meeting's purpose, from a letter sent by SD chief Reinhard Heydrich, who presided.

The attendees represented the broad intelligentsia of a regime not noted for its erudition. Among the brown- and black-uniformed and dark-suited participants were lawyers, judges, and five senior SS officers. Heydrich's letter set the meeting's goal: "to carry out all necessary

TOP AND BOTTOM: The confiscated Jewish home in Berlin's Wannsee suburb and the room where the "final solution" to murder all the Jews of Europe was made. AUTHOR

preparations in regard to organizational, practical, and material measures requisite (*sic*) for the total solution of the Jewish question in Europe." It stressed the "exceptional importance" of settling the Jewish issue as a structured, institutional process—the forced removal of Jews already well advanced in a non-systematized manner. The "common agreement" Heydrich expected came in only ninety minutes, as attendees amiably chatted across a narrow table. With the "final solution" decided, all were invited to a collegial lunch, first pausing to enjoy views of the lake from the terrace. One member, an SS *Obersturmbannführer*, to become notorious in accomplishing the unanimous decision, Lt. Col. Adolf Eichmann, prepared the post-meeting minutes. With a decision that required coordination throughout the entire government, he then organized the methodical planning for a genocide intended to murder the entirety of Europe's Jews and other "undesirables."

Heydrich's fate came quickly. Five months after the meeting, Czech agents ambushed and killed him outside Prague. In reprisal, all 192 men in the village of Lidice were killed, its two hundred women sent to Ravensbruck, where most died, with all the village's eighty-one children gassed in trucks. The village went up in flames. Escaping after the war Eichmann eventually reached Argentina, to be captured by the Israeli Mossad, brought to Israel and hanged in 1962. His last words to the hangman were, "I hope that all of you will follow me."

From Berlin, the unchanged Wannsee House is reached by S-1 or S-7 to Wannsee, then bus #114 to the house. Exhibits contain the original documents and invitation confirming the agreement. Open daily 10:00 a.m. to 6:00 p.m. Free entry.

May 8, 1945: Karlshorst, The Second German Surrender

At 2:41 a.m. on May 7, 1945, Germany unconditionally surrendered to the Western Allies in the preserved Reims, France schoolhouse serving as SHAEF headquarters. The Soviet command refused to accept the surrender's legitimacy, demanding that it be signed in Berlin, the seat of the enemy's government. Due to its devastation, no suitable location could be found in the city. Earlier, Soviet marshal Georgy Zhukov, commanding the final assault on Berlin, sited his headquarters in the officer's canteen of an engineering school in Karlshorst, seven miles northeast of Berlin. The alternate surrender would be signed there.

On the morning of May 8, deputies of the Western Allies arrived at Berlin's Templehof Airport, to be driven by Red Army forces through the city's destroyed center to Karlshorst. A US aircraft with the German delegates flew from Flensburg to Berlin, also escorted by a Soviet detail to the surrender site.

Led by Field Marshal Wilhelm Keitel, chief of the army high command (OKW), eight tight-faced members of the German delegation entered the building. Thickly gathered in the high-ceilinged dining room were staff members, translators, journalists, and assistants. Hours passed waiting for approval of the Russian-translated document. Keitel entered the room shortly before midnight followed by leaders of the Nazi military. Facing the assembly without speaking, he rigidly extended a gloved hand holding his field marshal's baton. Flags of the four victorious powers hung together above his place. Seated opposite Keitel, Marshal Zhukov began the proceedings. To his left and right were British air marshal Arthur Tedder, acting as General Eisenhower's deputy, and US Air Force general Carl Spaatz. Signed on May 9 at forty-three minutes after midnight, officials backdated the document to Wednesday, May 8 as Germany's official surrender, the date celebrated as VE Day.

On October 16, 1946, convicted at the Nuremberg Military Tribunal of crimes against humanity, Keitel and nine others of the Nazi leadership went to the gallows. The Karlshorst site, with the surrender room in its original appearance, remained as Soviet Fifth Army headquarters until 1967. A Soviet weapons and vehicle park is on the grounds. From Berlin, S3 to Karlshorst, then bus #296 to the entrance. Open 10:00 a.m. to 6:00 p.m. Tuesday–Sunday. Free entry.

Topography of Terror

Seen inside the Berlin Documentation Center, built near Hitler's Chancellery garden and destroyed subterranean bunker, a young teacher intently lectures German students of high school age. Behind him, six illuminated large-scale photos of boys, girls, men, and women look back. Their faces are bright and trusting in the expectation of study, careers,

TOP AND BOTTOM: The former Ministry of Aviation Building overlooks the remains of regime offices and parts of the Berlin Wall. AUTHOR

and family. The photos were taken before the unnatural acts that branded the Nazi regime for all history. They speak for the six million Jews taken from their homes and lives in the seventeen countries Germany invaded. They left little to tell the world their stories. The dictatorship destroyed every trace of their existence. History would be their voice. Black cinders cover the ground surrounding the museum in a bleak grip atop the ruins of government agencies that spread a plague of death through Europe. Protruding from the ground like rotting teeth, excavated remnants of fifteen connected buildings that were part of the regime face the largest remaining segment of the Berlin Wall. Inside the buildings, the SS, Gestapo, and the government operated as one during the twelve years of the Nazi revolution.

Memorial to the Murdered Jews of Europe (Holocaust Memorial)
Viewed from a distance the 2,711 charcoal gray monoliths by American architect Daniel Eisenman seem awkwardly placed in varying vertical and horizontal positions with no beginning or end, no entrance and no defined exit. The 4.7 acres extending over four prime city blocks confuse as much from near as from afar. The vertically placed columns or stelae vary from a few inches to fifteen feet tall, appearing as somber souls burdened with their destiny. Identically sized horizontal slabs suggest endless rows of crosses or tombstones desecrated by an unseen force. The pavement beneath undulates as does a wave with no start or finish. No name identifies the memorial's purpose or asserts a homily for its visitors' contemplations. As remote as it seems from the reality of artistic expression, its very isolation from the existing world accuses the evil that consumed Europe's most advanced nation. Its studied silence pledges *never again.*

TOP AND BOTTOM: In the heart of the German capital, the memorial to the murdered Jews of Europe. AUTHOR

Epilogue: Why We Fought

When GIs of the 6th and 4th Armored Divisions liberated the camps at Buchenwald and Ordrurf, they needed no explanation to understand why they fought in history's most destructive war. The reason showed on every emaciated face peering at them with hollow eyes, the stick-figures unable to bring tears to themselves, for their liberators, or for the millions who never saw this day of days.

NATIONAL ARCHIVES

NATIONAL ARCHIVES

When it ended on May 8, 1945, the GIs hugged and drank, danced, and dreamed of their own futures, for they too were survivors. Nearing home on the returning ships, they passed the lady in the harbor, the "mother of exiles," the symbol of freedom from tyranny and they understood its meaning anew, because so many of them were also immigrants or the sons of immigrants.

NAVAL HISTORY & HERITAGE COMMAND

As if emerging from a time-warp, they went back to the lives they left to save freedom in its darkest hour. They returned to families, to farms on the plains or factories in the cities, or to classes they quit, not knowing if it would be forever. Many would never speak of what they saw. Over the decades when thanked for their service, at most they would say, "I was only doing my job."

Oh, what a job. They saved civilization. Honor them!

Index